A Brief History of the Smile

For Mark

with admiration + best wishes

Angus

A Brief History of the Smile

ANGUS TRUMBLE

Angus Trumble

New Haven, Conn.

February 17, 2004.

BASIC
B
BOOKS

A Member of the Perseus Books Group
New York

Copyright © 2004 by Angus Trumble

Published by Basic Books
A Member of the Perseus Books Group

All rights reserved. Printed in the United States of America. No part of this book may be reproduced in any manner whatsoever without written permission except in the case of brief quotations embodied in critical articles and reviews. For information, address Basic Books, 387 Park Avenue South, New York, NY 10016.

Books published by Basic Books are available at special discounts for bulk purchases in the United States by corporations, institutions, and other organizations. For more information, please contact the Special Markets Department at the Perseus Books Group, 11 Cambridge Center, Cambridge MA 02142, or call (617) 252-5298, (800) 255-1514, or e-mail specialmarkets@perseusbooks.com.

Designed by Trish Wilkinson
Set in 12-point Goudy by the Perseus Books Group

A CIP catalog record for this book is available from the Library of Congress.
ISBN 0-465-08777-9

04 05 06 / 10 9 8 7 6 5 4 3 2 1

In memory of my father
Peter Campbell Trumble
1922–2000

He does smile his face into more lines than are in the
new map with the augmentation of the Indies.

WILLIAM SHAKESPEARE, *Twelfth Night*,
1598–1600, Act III, sc ii

What Mary is when she a little smiles
I cannot even tell or call to mind,
It is a miracle so new, so rare.

PERCY BYSSHE SHELLEY, adapted from
the *Vita Nuova* by Dante Alighieri

Pack up your troubles in your old kit-bag, and smile,
    smile, smile.
While you've a Lucifer to light your fag,
Smile, boys, that's the style.
What's the use of worrying?
It never was worthwhile, so
Pack up your troubles in your old kit-bag, and smile,
    smile, smile.

GEORGE ASAF (George Powell),
from *Pack Up Your Troubles*, 1915

Contents

List of Illustrations

Preface

L uis Buñuel wrote somewhere that solitude is marvelous, provided you can talk to somebody about it afterwards. How right he was, particularly where the solitary task of writing is concerned. This book would never have been completed without the help, encouragement, and support of many friends and colleagues, all of whom tended to smile when they learned what I was up to.

My thanks go first to Dr. Sydney C. Warnecke, former president of the Royal Australasian College of Dental Surgeons, and to Dr. Jonathan Rogers, convener of the College's Continuing Education Committee, for kindly inviting me to participate in the scientific program of the 14th Biennial Convocation of the Royal Australasian College of Dental Surgeons in Adelaide, South Australia (October 23–27, 1998). My colleagues Christopher Menz of the National Gallery of Victoria, Melbourne, and Betty Churcher, former director of the National Gallery of Australia, Canberra, paid me the compliment of suggesting my name in the first place.

I had further opportunities to revise and extend the original, tooth-oriented topic, first for a research seminar organized in 1999 by Dr. Robert Crocker of the Louis Laybourne Smith School of Architecture and Design at the University of South Australia in Adelaide, and subsequently for a paper I delivered in July 2000 at the eighth annual conference of the Australian Society for French Studies at Adelaide University. I am grateful to Dr. John West-Sooby for inviting me to participate in that meeting.

I am not the first person to have contemplated writing a book about the smile. It is a subject with which English, French, and German scholars have grappled in relation to Gothic sculpture, particularly statuary in the cathedrals of Naumberg, Magdeburg, and Lincoln, and some years ago an Australian colleague, Rex Butler, toyed with the idea of a more theoretical, cross-cultural treatment of the subject. In recent years some rewarding studies have appeared, for specialists and general readers, covering different aspects of the human face, crying, tears, and laughter. A major BBC television series has looked at the human face, ably and thoughtfully assisted by John Cleese. Marina Vaizey has compiled an exquisite pictorial essay on the smile in art, drawn entirely from the collections of the British Museum in London. There is even an ample literature specifically aimed at children. Particular smiles enshrined in the visual arts, such as that of Leonardo's famous *Mona Lisa* or Frans Hals's *The Laughing Cavalier* or Antonello da Messina's enigmatic *Portrait of a Man* in Cefalù have for the last 150 years or so lured countless scholars into print. I am indebted to their dogged groundwork, as the endnotes and bibliography amply demonstrate.

While a number of people helped me early on by asking good questions, I am even more indebted to the many others who were kind enough to provide the answers, as well as opinions and advice. At the risk of lining them up like so many scalps, to borrow the late R. C. K. Ensor's memorable phrase, the following colleagues and friends have provided me invaluable assistance of many different kinds: Ross and Fiona Adler; Professor Jaynie Anderson, Herald Professor of Fine Arts at the University of Melbourne; Mark Aronson, chief conservator at the Yale University Art Gallery; Professor Norbert S. Baer of the Conservation Center at the Institute of Fine Arts, New York University; Dr. Martin Ball; Alexander Bell of Sotheby's, London; Helen Bird; Paul Bonaventura of the Ruskin School of Drawing, University of Oxford; Susan Brady; Julia Delves Broughton of Christie's, London; Scott Brown; Alisa Bunbury; Pamela M. Clark of the Royal Archives at Windsor Castle; Dr. Jacqueline Clarke of the Classics Department at Adelaide University; Professor Emeritus Antonio Comin of the Flinders University of South Australia; David Ekserdjian; Barbara and Philip Fargher; Adam Free; Gregory Galligan; Geoff Gibbons; Dr. Diana Glenn of the Department of European Languages at the Flinders University of South Australia; Emilie Gordenker; Alex Green; Michael Gronow; Fiona Gruber; David Hansen, senior curator of art at the Tasmanian Museum and Art Gallery, Hobart; Margaret Hosking; Dr. Alison Inglis of the School of Fine Arts at the University of Melbourne; Jason Januszke; Dr. Adam Jenney; Jasmin Johnson; Barbara Kane; Dr. B. M. A. Keith; Peter King; Elizabeth Loane; Susanne Lorenz of the Staatliche Antikensammlungen, Munich; Dr. Ross Macdonald; the Reverend Dr. Andrew McGowan of the Episcopal Divinity School, Cambridge, Massachusetts; Natasha Maw; Dr. Joan Mertens, curator of Greek and Roman antiquities at the Metropolitan Museum of Art, New York; Tom Nicholson; David J. O'Callaghan; Dr. Margaret O'Hea of the Classics Department at Adelaide University; Lyn Pedler; the Reverend Dr. B. Meredith Porter; Dick Richards; Mark Richards of the Lewis Carroll Society; Professor Ronald T. Ridley; Dr. Peter Rofe; Dr. Rajah Selvarajah; Professor Giuseppe Simplicio of the Fondazione Culturale Mandralisca in Cefalù; Jeanette Sisk; Professor Judith Sloan; Hugh Spencer; Professor Peter Steele, S.J.; Robin Stolfi; Keinosuke Takada; Dr. Paul Thesinger; Sarah Thomas; Cynthia Troup; Nick Trumble; Dr. Jack Turner; Diane Waggoner; Wendy Walker; Ron Warren; Daryl Watson; Jin Whittington; Gareth Williams of the Victoria and

Albert Museum in London; Dr. Mark Williams; Nat Williams; the Hon. Sir John Young; Selma Zarhloul; and Paul Zbierski. I must also thank my dentist, Dr. Ian Bills, for sparing me pain.

The research for this book was conducted with the help and unfailing kindness of the staffs of the following libraries: (in Washington) the Library of Congress; (in New York) the Frick Art Reference Library, the New York Public Library, the Elmer Holmes Bobst Library, New York University, the libraries of that University's Institute of Fine Arts, and the Thomas J. Watson Library at the Metropolitan Museum of Art; (in New Haven, Connecticut) the Sterling Memorial Library, the Beinecke Rare Book and Manuscript Library, the Library of the Divinity School, and the Art Reference Library at the Yale Center for British Art, all at Yale University; (in London) the British Library; (in Rome) the Bibliotheca Hertziana; (in Canberra) the National Library of Australia and the Research Library at the National Gallery of Australia; (in Sydney) the State Library of New South Wales and the Research Library at the Art Gallery of New South Wales; (in Melbourne) the State Library of Victoria, the Baillieu Library at the University of Melbourne, the Leeper and Mollison Libraries at Trinity College; (in Adelaide) the State Library of South Australia, the Libraries of the University of South Australia and the Flinders University of South Australia, the Barr Smith Library at Adelaide University, and the Research Library at the Art Gallery of South Australia, for a time my supremely generous home base. Lately, a visiting research fellowship in the Department of History at Adelaide University, a brief period in residence at the School of Fine Arts at the University of Melbourne, and a Harold White Fellowship at the National Library of Australia in Canberra helped me over the line.

I must also thank the following art museums and organizations for permitting me to reproduce photographs of works of art in their collections: (in Athens): the Akropolis Museum; (in Cefalù, Sicily): Fondazione Culturale Mandralisca; (in London): the British Museum,

Kenwood House (through English Heritage), the National Gallery and the Wallace Collection; (in Manchester): Manchester Art Gallery; (in Marburg): Bildarchiv Foto Marburg; (in Munich): Staatliche Antikensammlungen; (in Nara, Japan): Yamato Bunkakan; (in New York): Mary Boone Gallery (on behalf of Barbara Kruger), the Metropolitan Museum of Art, and Salander–O'Reilly Galleries; (in Paris): Musée du Louvre (through the Réunion des musées nationaux and Art Resource) and the Donation J. H. Lartigue; (in Philadelphia): the Philadelphia Museum of Art; (in Phnom Penh): the National Museum of Cambodia; (in Toronto): the Art Gallery of Ontario; (in Verona): the Museo di Castelvecchio (through Archivi Alinari and Art Resource).

Material in the Royal Archives at Windsor Castle in the United Kingdom is quoted with the gracious permission of Her Majesty Queen Elizabeth II.

To Dr. Ian Jennings I owe a special debt of gratitude, as I do to my brothers and their families in Melbourne, to my wise uncle, John M. Borthwick, formerly of the firm of Barling of Mount Street, London, and, above all, to my mother, Helen Trumble, for her support and encouragement.

I am especially grateful to my editors, Jo Ann Miller, Linda Carbone, and Kay Mariea; to my Australian publisher, the late John Iremonger; to Claire Murdoch; and to my literary agents, Mary Cunnane and Peter McGuigan, for guiding me through unfamiliar territory with supreme tact and patience. They demonstrate the profound truth of that remark somebody made about how much easier it is to write a book than to recognize, foster, then edit one.

Angus Trumble
Yale Center for British Art, New Haven, Connecticut

There are only two styles of portrait painting, the serious and the smirk; and we always use the serious for professional people (except actors sometimes), and the smirk for private ladies and gentlemen who don't care so much about looking clever.

CHARLES DICKENS, *The Life and Adventures of Nicholas Nickleby*, 1839, Chapter X

Horace in his Odes confessed that for him one corner of the earth wore a special smile. I believe this to be true of all people who have roots.

MONICA M. HUTCHINGS, *The Special Smile*, 1951

INTRODUCTION
"The Serious and the Smirk"

The idea for this book came to me in 1998 after I was invited to address a conference of dentists and maxillofacial surgeons. Several good friends of mine happen to be dentists, but we do not often talk about teeth. I could not imagine why a large roomful of their colleagues would want to hear a lecture from me, a museum curator, about art.

They did not. Instead, I was asked to comment on the changing criteria by which European painters of the eighteenth and nineteenth centuries defined the beautiful face. This is a subject in which dental surgeons are interested today because the rapid technical advances in their profession now enable them to make more and more dramatic and, for people with hideous deformities, miraculous interventions. I was surprised to discover that some specialist dentists and cosmetic surgeons have quite a definite view of what today should constitute a beautiful face and what is ugly, undesirable, ripe for treatment. I was astonished to learn that the Golden Mean, that mathematical formula beloved of architects and theoreticians of esthetics in the West since antiquity, is also alive in the mind of the modern dentist and cosmetic surgeon. They use it to regulate the optimum distance between chin and lip, lip and nose, nose and eyebrow, and so on. I examined the dental literature and found it full of weird before-and-after photographs of patients—women, mostly, with sad eyes, drooping shoulders, and lank hair, the faces downcast, but full of character—who duly emerged from surgery with enormous white teeth and Amazonian grins.

I tried to think of works of art, any works of art, in which rows of human teeth were partly or wholly represented. Teeth, after all, are fiendishly difficult to draw, and the effects of foreshortening when viewing uneven rows between parted lips make this one of the hardest tests of the draughtsman. Some artists, such as the sixteenth-century Dutch artist Maarten van Heemskerck, drew teeth beautifully. But most artists have found it more trouble than it was worth, and apart from skulls, which are not uncommon as emblems of mortality in Renaissance and Baroque painting, there seemed to be comparatively few heads to choose from. There were severed heads with hideously gaping mouths, such as that of Holofernes, or the inert head of Goliath under the foot of David, or Géricault's macabre 1818 study of heads of cadavers in Stockholm. There were the satirical grotesques by the English printmakers James Gillray and George Cruickshank, for whom wide-open mouths and horrible teeth provided a convenient metaphor for obscenity, greed, or some other kind of endemic corruption in Regency England. There was the discrete subgenre of quack dentists and itinerant *cavadenti* or tooth-pullers that flourished in seventeenth-century European oil painting north and south of the Alps. A Tasmanian colleague reminded me of the less widespread religious subject of St. Apollonia, who was thought to have been tortured to death by having all her teeth extracted. And it was of particular interest to an audience of dentists that portraits of successive generations of distinctly lantern-jawed Habsburg kings and emperors enshrined that curious genetic inheritance that came with the thrones of Spain and Austria, namely a mandibular prognathism or Class III skeletal malocclusion. That genetic predisposition, with its disturbing visual consequences—a jaw that juts out like a battering ram, a thick, drooping lower lip, mildly everted lower eyelids, and so on—posed a tricky problem of decorum for seventeenth-century portrait painters like Diego Velázquez. Not so for Francisco Goya, who in 1800 made no attempt to flatter the unfortunate Infanta María Josefa of Spain.

In short, as far as I could see, most teeth and open mouths in art belonged to dirty old men, misers, drunks, whores, gypsies, people undergoing experiences of religious ecstasy, dwarves, lunatics, monsters, ghosts, the possessed, the damned, and—all together now—tax collectors, many of whom had gaps and holes where healthy teeth once were. Meanwhile, the worst teeth generally appeared in the passion narrative, jutting fang-like from the twisted mouths of Christ's torturers—to whom were applied a bewildering array of hairy warts, angry pimples, cysts, and other weeping sores. On the whole, the great traditions of portraiture, eastern and western, tended to conceal most skin ailments and keep the sitter's mouth firmly shut.

Just as exposed teeth in art seemed rare at first, only to multiply upon further investigation, so too I began to notice more and more smiling faces. I had thought that these were quite rare, notwithstanding the fame, even notoriety, of great iconic smilers such as

Leonardo's *Mona Lisa* or Frans Hals's *The Laughing Cavalier*. Yet as I looked into the matter, smiling faces began to crop up everywhere. My first glance at *Judith with the Head of Holofernes* by Lucas Cranach the Elder had been at the severed head and gaping mouth of Holofernes, upon which Cranach expended a good deal of effort. It was not until I came face to face with the picture in Glasgow that I became fully aware of the coolly nonchalant smile with which Cranach's fashion-plate Judith greets the startled visitor to this biblical crime scene. She is still holding in her gloved right hand the blood-stained sword with which she despatched the Assyrian drunk. Yet her little finger is delicately cocked. Not a hair on her head or feather in her hat is out of place. She is cool as a cucumber, and clearly means business—as if to say "Just you try it, buster."

A visit to the Frick Collection in New York offered up various smilers. Johannes Vermeer's laughing girl, unusually extroverted, entertains a charismatic visitor while cradling in her hands a glass of wine. Nearby the smile of William Hogarth's *Miss Mary Edwards* is framed by lace and jewels (she was rich) but seems also reflected in the soft muzzle of the good-natured dog at her knee. In the same room, George Romney's glamorous, doe-eyed, windswept *Lady Hamilton* poses, smiling, as "Nature." Meanwhile, in another room, Jacques-Louis David's decidedly plain, pink-cheeked *Comtesse Daru* smiles vacantly, as if she is tired of sitting still.

Likewise, to my surprise, an old sale catalogue chosen at random turned up a host of smiles. The infant Jesus beamed from the arms of the Virgin Mary in a late fifteenth-century German walnut sculpture. An early fourteenth-century French limestone head of an angel, bafflingly described in the relevant notes as "grimacing," quite obviously grinned from ear to ear. A crazy pair of Sicilian alabaster lions with big blunt teeth and long, wig-like manes turned their heads to chuckle for the camera, their leonine cheeks creased with laughter lines. There was even a primitive early fragment of English relief sculpture in oak, a fantastic, bald, bug-eyed beast-man poking out his tongue, sporting the lewdest of grins.

Books and exhibition catalogues turned up an ever-widening variety of smiler: Fuseli's pert but startling *Fairy Mab*, in several versions, and his leaping, fat-tummied *Puck* in Manchester, for example, or W. P. Frith's coquettish *Dolly Varden*, hand on hip, head thrown back, a character borrowed from Charles Dickens's eighteenth-century period novel *Barnaby Rudge*. Meanwhile, in one of his illustrations to William Clarke's *Three Courses and a Dessert*, George Cruickshank lifted the lid of the oyster shell to reveal its occupant, a smug, pear-shaped recliner, smiling most peacefully—a characterization that, to oyster-lovers, is wholly apt.

A little late-eighteenth-century picture of a Dutch boy sitting on a wall gutting and cleaning fish came up at auction. Why was he wearing a wry, mischievous smile? Even things as hum-drum as old buttons decorated with smiling faces caught my attention. I also noticed some beautiful, early English spoons that were decorated with top-knots or finials composed of tiny figures, grinning hairy men or "woodwoses," and oddly insouciant apostles in wide-brimmed hats.

A good number of biographers have approached famous men as diverse as Niccolò Machiavelli and Immanuel Kant through what they perceived to be a revealing aspect of their smile as represented in portraits or, in the case of Kant, on the 1796 frontispiece of his *Critique of Judgment*. Viroli's recent *Niccolò's Smile*, for example, opens by asking whether Santi di Tito's well-known portrait of Machiavelli captures an inscrutable sneer, a beatific smile, or an expression that "evinces nothing so much as a well-developed sense of the absurd." In her snobbish way, Margot Asquith recalled that the face of Benoît-Constant Coquelin, the great actor of the *Comédie Française*, "was as round as a Swiss Roll, and had the agricultural smile of a peasant; the cleverest make-up could not have made him look sinister." To some extent the smile has offered a convenient shorthand for far-reaching assessments of character, behavior, and temperament.

Moreover, some artists and traditions seemed more attuned to the smile than others, for example seventeenth- and eighteenth-century Dutch genre painting in general, and Jan Steen in particular. Even within the work of an artist as calm and apparently introverted as Johannes Vermeer, it struck me that a relatively large proportion of the *dramatis personae* are smiling (Fig. 0.1). By contrast, African and pre-Columbian sculpture, including statuary, masks, and other representations of faces, hardly ever allude to the act of smiling, even though the many discrete traditions on both sides of the Atlantic frequently employ vivid facial gymnastics—opened mouths, exposed teeth, bellowing, blowing, and biting—suggesting that sculptors might easily have represented a smiling face, but for some reason consistently chose not to do so.

So I decided to give my audience of dentists a talk about the smile, that would concentrate in some detail on Victorian Britain, an intellectual territory where I feel especially at home. Why did artists of the pre-Raphaelite circle such as Ford Madox Brown and William Holman Hunt seem so interested in teeth and open-mouthed smiling? Hunt's *The Awakening Conscience*, 1853–1854, caused a scandal when it was first exhibited because it faced up to the subject of sexual desire. Was it a coincidence that both the whiskery, lounging adulterer who sings at the piano and the fallen woman who, conscience-stricken, rises from his lap were each shown exposing the upper and lower rows of neatly delineated teeth? And what about all that grinning in Brown's 1852/1856 masterpiece *Work*, especially the strange smirk of Thomas Carlyle, who is portrayed with F. D. Maurice along the right margin as an interested passerby (Fig. 0.2)? Carlyle's book *Past and Present* (1843), in which he attacked the idea of laissez-faire economics and showed sympathy with the plight of the industrial poor, made a crucial impact upon political thought in the early years

FIGURE 0.1   Johannes Vermeer (1632–1675), *Woman Playing a Guitar, c.* 1672, oil on canvas, 20¾ × 18 in. London: Kenwood House, Iveagh Bequest. © English Heritage Photographic Library.

of Queen Victoria's reign. It prompted a new crop of socially conscientious novels in the later 1840s—by Mrs. Gaskell, for example—and influenced the young critic John Ruskin. Through Ruskin, Carlyle's influence reached artists such as Brown and, later, the pioneering socialist William Morris. Carlyle helped shape the vision of industrial labor that Brown chose as the subject of *Work.* Carlyle was no mere passerby. His smiling presence alludes to his fundamental role in this modern industrial allegory as an advocate of reform, as a friend to the working man.

The Victorian interest in teeth was evidently not confined to painters. The French scholar Hippolyte Taine drew from various

FIGURE 0.2   Ford Madox Brown (1821–1893), *Work* (detail showing Maurice and Carlyle), 1852 & 1856–1863, oil on canvas, 54 × 77½ in. Manchester: Manchester Art Gallery.

peculiar statistical data the bizarre conclusion that "meat-eating induced long teeth in English women." Anthony Trollope constantly mentioned the shape, color, and size of his characters' teeth, as his biographer has pointed out. In *Dombey and Son*, Dickens demonized the frightful Mr. Carker, Dombey's manager, simply by drawing attention to his teeth. From the first sentence in which he appears, it is "impossible to escape the observation" of his teeth, "for he showed them whenever he spoke." It is almost as if Mr. Carker's preternatural teeth are the real protagonist, not the character from whose mouth they protrude. Mr. Carker's teeth behave like eyes; they flash, penetrate, "suck forth secrets." "A cat, or a monkey, or a hyena, or a death's head, could not have shown the Captain more teeth at one time, than Mr. Carker showed . . . ." He grins like a shark. What might that mean?

Yet, while the Victorians apparently thought of opened, tooth-disclosing mouths as vaguely indecent, even at times violent, it seems they could also imagine them as the tantalizing personal adornments of the Oriental bather or odalisque, or the femme fatale. In 1891, for example, the *Boston Home Journal* published a detailed critique of the great actress Sarah Bernhardt in the provocative title role of Victorien Sardou and Émile Moreau's *Cléopâtre*, taking some trouble to emphasize the thrilling whiteness of her teeth, prominent in a long list of exotic features.

This fetishizing approach to teeth was related to the keen interest in the Oriental and the exotic and in strange phenomena such as the reception in England of Saartjie Baartman, the so-called "Hottentot Venus." Lots of nineteenth-century European descriptions of African faces laid particular emphasis upon the whiteness of native teeth, and in 1802 a French naturalist on board Nicolas Baudin's voyage to Van Diemen's Land observed that "it would be very difficult to find in Paris thirty-six mouths as well garnished with very white teeth" as those they admired on the faces of the gentle Aborigines they encountered in Tasmania.

I soon found that the subject of teeth and smiling had generated a huge scientific, psychological, and sociological literature, and that studies of subjects as varied as the behavior of traveling salesmen, men with high levels of testosterone, people in restaurants, and gold medal winners at the Olympic Games in Barcelona shed light not only on the representation of the smiling face in art, where I began, but on the complex manner in which all of us exchange, wear, and deploy the smile on our own. In the first example, thousands of itinerant fin-de-siècle commercial travelers were exhorted through pamphlets, handbooks, lectures, and daily catechisms to "carry the sunshine wherever they go" by nourishing big hearts and wearing big smiles—to be, in other words, "princes of laughter and mirth," the better to sell their wares. This was a highly organized commercial strategy that achieved startling results.

In the second, recent research suggests that American men whose bodies secrete high levels of testosterone are likely to smile much less than most other people, which seems to me a dreadful affliction. The third, a study in the late 1970s of 328 diners in three Seattle fast-food restaurants, found that women smiled and laughed much more than men and that men were far more likely to become distracted than women. As well, the older the diners, the less likely they were to smile under any circumstances, and solitary diners did not smile at all. These conclusions have recently been upheld by the authors of another study, who found that the smiling habits of men and women may also converge if they find themselves in a shared social or professional role and that the restaurant situation may well reflect the self-consciousness or contrasting expectations of men and women in relation to each other.

As for the twenty-two Olympic gold medalists in Barcelona, all of them later described the experience of ascending the uppermost podium as one of intense elation and happiness. Yet they were observed (by each other, and by outsiders) smiling only in those parts of the brief medal-giving ceremony when they communicated with other people—most obviously, of course, with the presiding dignitary or official presenting the gold medal, but also with the equally jubilant silver and bronze winners standing at either side. During the playing of national anthems, speeches, and other distractions, the gold medalists tended not to smile. Some of them were still physically breathless or even dazed, which is perfectly understandable. However, all observers agreed that these athletes nevertheless gave the impression of being supremely happy. The relationship between smiling and happiness in this instance was judged to be obscure. (Many questions arising from research of this kind have been investigated over many years by the distinguished psychologist Paul Ekman.)

It was also clear to me that various national and regional characteristics were thought to distinguish one sort of smile, or prompt, from another. According to one widely read guide for Americans in Paris, for example, the French do not apparently smile at strangers, or at all, without good reason, and are therefore likely to see the open smile of an outgoing American stranger on the street as a perplexing appeal to which they find it hard to respond with sincerity. A few might even think such "unsolicited" smiling mad or stupid or both. According to this source, the French smile as warmly as anyone else once the ice is broken, and the difference between "them" and "us" relates to the exact point of engagement.

A recent example of the cross-cultural vibrations that may from time to time arise from particular smiles is the case of a young Javanese mechanic called Amrozi, who was convicted of plotting with fourteen others to set off in Bali in October, 2002, a bomb that killed and injured many young people, including dozens of holiday-makers from western countries. After the Indonesian authorities arrested Amrozi, a press conference was arranged in Denpasar, ostensibly to demonstrate that the prisoner had not been tortured or in any other way mistreated. Such violations of human rights are not unknown in Indonesia, and given the international dimension of the crime, it was thought necessary to offer some public reassurance that the police were doing everything by the book.

What westerners saw on their television screens that night was mystifying. In front of a crowd of journalists, the prisoner, a pleasant,

youthful-looking man, exchanged handshakes, light banter, and winning smiles with the chief of police and a number of his junior officers, who appeared to return them with equal warmth. The effect was
chilling, and suggested a measure of collusion, or at the very least
some kind of shared joke in extremely poor taste. How could the
Indonesian authorities convey the impression that they and their
prisoner were old friends? What on earth were they smiling and
laughing about?

Amid the uproar that ensued, some anthropologists sought to explain that all was not as it seemed. The soothing phrase "cultural difference" was deployed. They do things differently in Indonesia.
There, according to Dr. Ariel Heryanto of the University of Melbourne in Australia, smiling does not necessarily "imply delight,
amusement, friendliness between the suspect and the officers, or an
antagonistic attitude towards the victims of the Bali bombing. They
'laughed,' but they did not 'laugh *at*' anything or anyone."

To some extent the anthropological literature provided some evidence that Indonesian smiles did indeed require careful elucidation.
As early as 1972, in a short book called *Smiles in Indonesia*, O. G.
Roeder, an expatriate Dutchman, suggested that although Indone-
sians in many day-to-day situations "seem to be born to smile," sometimes they also smile through tears. These and many of Roeder's
other remarks about the smile were based on close observation over
many years.

Another, rather unconvincing linguistic argument was added to
those relating to Indonesian or at least Javanese manners and customs, according to which the consonants *c*, *j*, *t*, or *p* may only be pronounced properly in the Bahasa (Indonesian) language if the lips are
drawn widely enough apart, so that, in effect, when one speaks Bahasa one has no choice but to smile. Indeed, the smiling press conference incident was largely ignored by Indonesian newspapers,
which noticed nothing particularly unusual about what transpired,

except, of course, the surprisingly strong reaction it provoked in some western countries.

Meanwhile, some degree of rational calculation was attributed to Amrozi's behavior and that of the men in uniform who surrounded him. By smiling a lot, the police sought to appear humane before the eyes of the world; by smiling back Amrozi did his best to cooperate or "behave," for obvious reasons. Yet the undeniable measure of informal bonhomie in evidence on that occasion, the relaxed atmosphere you might associate with the mess-room or the public bar, the way the prisoner lounged in his chair, legs akimbo, seemed essentially unstrategic and irrational, not staged. Indeed, perhaps the most logical explanation relating to "cultural difference" is that the policemen and the prisoner smiled "because they could not help it, because that is the way they were brought up since childhood." In other words, westerners tend to read more into the open smile worn by the Javanese, Balinese, or Sumatran than we should. From it we tend to form the impression of warmth and friendliness, of hospitality, gentleness, and generosity, largely because this is how we have come to interpret the open smile as it is customarily worn at home. In fact, according to this view, we ought to see the Indonesian smile as a kind of default position or mask of courtesy worn by convention in the interests of good manners.

The warm response of my audience at the conference of dentists encouraged me to pursue the subject at greater length. But what else was there to say? Surely the point about something as fleeting and as personal as a smile, whether you are wearing it yourself or observing it hover on the lips of others, whether spontaneous or tactical, is that it is self-explanatory. Smiling is perhaps the most immediately expressive muscular contraction of which our bodies are capable. The anatomy, neurology, and physiology of it are pretty well understood, and, deeply rooted in human instinct, the language and mechanics of the smile cannot have changed much over time.

Yet, it seemed to me, fundamental questions abound. Something like smiling is often observed in the animal kingdom, among creatures as diverse as dolphins and macaques and baboons and dogs, to say nothing of the Cheshire cat. For example, a humorous fourteenth-century Islamic miniature painting in Kuwait, an illustration of one of the fables in the *Sulwan al-Muta* of Ibn Zafar, represents a bear and a monkey in a landscape. The bear's open snout and jaw are carefully delineated with the upward arc of a happy grin, an obvious signal that he is playing with the monkey and not about to kill and eat him. But to what extent does an anthropomorphic image of a "smiling" animal such as this relate to the complex nuances we recognize among smiling people? Do we simply see in animals what we know in humans? When and how in infancy does human smiling become an eloquent beacon of recognition, attachment, and communication? When do we begin to smile to ourselves? To what extent does smiling harness facial features other than the mouth? Eyes, for example, are occasionally said to smile, Irish eyes in particular, presumably adding to the qualities of momentariness, fragility, and volatility that are frequently associated with smiling. This sort of question led me into ever more unfamiliar fields of inquiry, such as the history of cosmetics, humor, tattooing, moustaches and whiskers, tooth mutilation (a frightful practice that flourished in pre-Columbian Mexico), and various other methods of framing and decorating the human mouth.

So this book is about smiling in the broadest possible sense. Indeed, the very question as to what constitutes a smile—whether one may distinguish, for example, between a "real" smile and a fake—forms an important focus of discussion. For on this point there is much disagreement. I was startled by the philosopher Roger Scruton's claim in his book about sexual desire that the voluntary, as distinct from the genuinely self-revealing or involuntary, smile "is not a smile at all, but a kind of grimace which, while it may have its own species of sincerity . . . is not esteemed as an expression of the soul." Genuine smiling, he thinks, is a *response* not unlike blushing: "a kind of involuntary recognition of my accountability before you for what I am and feel." Yet if we accepted this principle, how would we decide which smile is a smile and which is a grimace? Surely there are situations in which the intentions of smilers and their involuntary reactions are hopelessly mixed up, making both varieties of smile equally "genuine." Nor can I agree with his view that to smile is necessarily "to smile *at* something or someone, and hence when we see someone smiling in the street we think of him as 'smiling to himself,' meaning that there is some hidden object of his present thought and feeling." This could never be said of Buddhas, for example, or the insane, and it strikes me as rather difficult to isolate the person or thing that makes you smile when, at the theater, you observe something complicated and amusing happen on stage.

The discussion that follows ranges from table manners to neurology, to the behavioral development of infants, to sex, to the history of art. I never meant to compile an exhaustive compendium of scientific and anthropological data with a mountainous scholarly apparatus. Instead, I wanted to write a more personal book in which I could explore in detail some varieties of smiling that seemed to me particularly noteworthy in our time: the polite smile, for example, as distinct from the lewd; the smile of the lover versus that of the deceiver.

The term "smile" can be applied to numerous phenomena relating to the movement of the lips and the contraction of various other muscles of the face, ranging from the involuntary reflex of the neonate to the mask of comedy, from the contemplative smile of the Buddha to the chilly rictus of the news anchor, and a vast assortment of other smiles in between. A smile may seem friendly to one person, obsequious to another, and frankly insane to somebody else. At the same time, smilers may not even be aware that they are displaying a smile; or they may have deployed it with subtle fore-thought, aiming to tease or mislead. Either way, knowing or oblivi-ous, the smile is a powerful form of communication.

Among the most intriguing aspects of this subject is the complex manner in which different peoples, cultures, and societies have as-sessed the personal appearance of individuals, whether smiling or not, according to completely different sets of criteria. In general, the remoter in time or place, the more surprising they are. However, we shall see that this rule does not always apply. The physical appear-ance of the great early presidents of the United States, for example, much conforms to the idea of republican virtue. Square jaws abound, and sobriety is the general pattern. Think of Houdon's great statue of Washington in the Capitol at Richmond. We know at his inaugura-tion in 1789, George Washington had only one tooth left in his mouth (one of the two lower left bicuspids). He wore carved hip-popotamus ivory false teeth sprung with wire, which must have been atrociously uncomfortable, presumably unattractive, and prone to snapping open. They were equipped with a hole to accommodate his one surviving tooth, and must have tasted disgusting. His solution to the taste problem was to soak his dentures in port overnight, which almost certainly did not help.

James Madison was so small that he was said to be scarcely visible at the Virginia Convention of 1776 although, according to Gaillard Hunt, "as he warmed with his argument his body swayed to and fro with a see-saw motion." We know very little of his smile. As a young man Thomas Jefferson had sound and regular teeth, but in later, pub-lic life, it seems they were not often displayed. The intellectual and moral focus in the life of John Quincy Adams, who occupied himself in retirement after 1830 by translating the Psalms into English verse, studying scripture, and so on, likewise conveys seriousness above all. Perhaps this is to be expected from a great New Englander. Much later, apart from his remarkable administration, President Abraham

Lincoln was remembered for his height (6 foot, four inches), physical strength, and good nature. A few anecdotes about the early days at Springfield emphasized young Abe Lincoln's capacity to spin yarns and make the boys whoop and roll off the log. Yet the iconography of the sixteenth president, clearly enshrined on the five-dollar bill, is overwhelmingly grave. This is hardly surprising.

A little later Ulysses S. Grant, who even more than Lincoln stood in the long shadow cast by the Civil War, made a tremendous impression in London in June 1877 at an evening reception held in his honor. According to his biographer James Penny Boyd, Grant had "a bearing as composed as when in 'Old Virginny' the drums beat to action and the boys went marching along." A viscountess who was present said, "He looks like a soldier." In other words, the idea of a *martial* president, "a first-class lion," excited much interest among English guests, as did the fact that he smoked cigars. The contrast between the popular soldier president, who was awarded the Freedom of the City of London, and the urbane, literary, not to say obsequious British prime minister, Benjamin Disraeli, must have been stark.

It is remarkable that, at least after 1893, President Grover Cleveland was able to smile at all. In that year, at the age of fifty-six, in the midst of an unprecedented economic crisis relating to federal reserves of gold and silver, President Cleveland discovered a growth on the left side of his upper jaw. A specimen of rough tissue in the roof of the mouth was taken and sent (anonymously) for pathological analysis. It was malignant. Upon further investigation, the cancer proved to have invaded the upper jawbone and spread from the bicuspid teeth (between the canine or eye tooth and the molars) to within a fraction of an inch of his soft palate. Cleveland was advised to have an operation immediately, in complete secrecy, on board a yacht steaming along the East River in New York. Seated in a chair propped against the mast, with a few close colleagues present, including Secretary of War Daniel Scott Lamont, the president was successfully anesthetized. The surgical team began by extracting the bicuspid teeth. Incisions were then made in the roof of the mouth to make way for the excision of the entire left upper jaw from between the first bicuspid tooth and the last molar. A large cheek retractor was used. The orbital plate—the floor of the bony enclosure that surrounds the eyeball—was left intact, and only a small portion of the soft palate was removed. Incredibly, there was no hemorrhaging, and only one blood vessel "was tied, and the wound was tightly packed with gauze."

After two days' voyage up Long Island Sound to Cape Cod, the president was up and about and was able to disembark unaided. Within three weeks he was back in Washington, equipped with an excellent prosthesis of vulcanized rubber, which filled the gap left by his excised jawbone. It was made by a New York dentist, Dr. Kasson C. Gibson. The president could speak normally. He lived on, with no recurrence of the cancer, for fifteen years. When news of the operation eventually leaked—Dr. Gibson was the boastful culprit—and its radical nature finally understood, many people simply disbelieved it.

In any case, public seriousness and strictly private levity (if any) seems to have been the pattern of presidential behavior right up to the time of President Theodore Roosevelt, who smiled a lot, particularly in public. Indeed, after his death in January 1919, erroneous reports suggesting that President Roosevelt had died as a result of an infected tooth circulated in the daily newspapers. This was untrue, as the *Journal of the National Dental Association* hotly protested in an editorial the following June. (In fact, Roosevelt died of coronary embolism.) Yet the tenor of the newspaper report is telling: "Those flashing white teeth won him millions of friends—yet one of those teeth killed him." Roosevelt, the man of action, somewhat self-styled, who told New York Republicans to "speak softly and carry a big stick," was frequently photographed and drawn grinning from ear to ear. In Europe his teeth were thought magnificent.

If nineteenth-century presidents were on the whole grave, could a similar distinction be made between public and private smiling in other vocational milieux? What about the pulpit, the bench, or the professorial chair? What smiling habits, if any, could be observed among the learned professions and, if any, usefully isolated? I was reminded of the old story about Sir William Orpen's portrait of Cosmo Gordon Lang, archbishop of Canterbury. Showing the picture to a group of visitors to Lambeth Palace in London, the archbishop said he did not much like it because an earlier visitor had told him that the picture made him look "proud, prelatical, and pompous." Quick as a flash, from the back of the group, the Very Reverend Herbert Hensley Henson, dean of Durham, "an old and candid friend," asked: "And may I ask Your Grace to which of these epithets Your Grace takes exception?" Afterwards the archbishop confided to Bishop Parker of Pretoria that his portrait was the way it was partly because he had not wanted to be handed down to posterity with an "amiable smile" on his face. However, Lang's biographer, J. G. Lockhart, thought he could detect "the ghost of a smile, almost as if the Archbishop's tongue was in his cheek and he was telling his friends that this was a portrait not of Cosmo Lang the man, but of Cosmo Lang playing the part of an Archbishop."

Nowadays bishops evidently smile a lot more than they used to—paradoxically, since there would not seem to be much for them to smile about—but judges in many jurisdictions remain, on the whole, grave. The risk of misleading a litigant, a defendant, or an applicant by smiling is obvious, although it has occasionally been discounted. In the 1860s, for example, Chief Justice Sir William Erle of England is reported as having said: "The Court is very much obliged to any learned gentleman who beguiles the tedium of a legal argument with a little honest hilarity." But he seems to have been something of a rarity. In places where the death penalty still exists, new judges are sometimes advised never to allow themselves to be photographed

smiling because inevitably that will be the photograph chosen to illustrate a newspaper article in which it is reported that this judge has
passed the sentence of death.

At the other extreme, the vast snow of advertising material that
for the last two hundred years and more has filled our newspapers,
covered the walls of our public buildings, adorned our public trans-
portation, and in every conceivable way attracted our attention does
seem to constitute a vast encyclopedia of the cheerful modern smile.
A small sample from the 1950s yields an almost unanimous company
of smilers—beaming fathers and mothers, carefree cigarette smokers,
contented motorists and golfers, healthy children with their socks
pulled up, movie stars. "'I love to see a man smoke a Cigarillo,' says
Mrs. Humphrey Bogart (Lauren Bacall)," beaming. "'Blatz is Mil-
waukee's *Finest* Beer'. . . says Milwaukee-born piano virtuoso Liber-
ace." "'Jeris rates cheers for greaseless good grooming and healthier
handsomer hair,' says Ronald Reagan." The woman in a halter-neck
evening gown cooking eggs and chops for men in tuxedos (Broil-
Quik) is, of course, smiling over her shoulder. "Good news for
women with dark oily skin," runs the Nadinola De Luxe Greaseless
Bleach Creme advertisement, accompanied by a sultry smile. The
man in the body-building ad grins proudly: "In 10 minutes of fun a
day I changed myself from this Bloodless, Pitiful, skinny shrimp to
this new, muscular, red-blooded, head-to-toe HE-MAN!" Never was
a grin more triumphant.

The smile in the poster for the McCarthyist 1950 RKO movie *I
Married a Communist* is sinister: "Trained in an art as old as time!
She served a mob of terror and violence whose one mission is to destroy! Trading her love . . . yielding kisses that invite, destroy . . .
then—KILL!" In fact, the only people *not* smiling are professional
boxers, brooding seductresses, one or two captains of industry, and
Edward G. Robinson. Even the elderly Winston Churchill, in a rare
departure from the iconography created for him late in life by Karsh

of Ottawa and other official photographers, is here to be seen with hat, smock, palette, brushes, and cigar, smirking most uncharacteristically: "Hallmark Christmas Cards now present the paintings of the Right Honourable Winston S. Churchill, O.M., C.H., M.P."

Novelists provided me with a particularly helpful source of inspiration. Albert Camus's *The Plague* (1947) is absolutely crammed with smiling faces. He tells us, for example, that the municipal clerk Joseph Grand, "who had all the attributes of insignificance," still had all of his lower but lacked his upper teeth, so his mouth when he smiled "looked like a small black hole let into his face." Indeed, it was not until I began to write a book about the smile that I realized how completely the writer of fiction depends upon smiling—more perhaps than any other facial calisthenic—to change conversational gears, to enliven the plot, or to give it a little nudge here and there. In a recent novel by Robert Littell, one character favors another "with one of his legendary gap-toothed smiles," something with which one somehow, for no apparent reason, seems instantly familiar. As with so many other aspects of English prose style, P. G. Wodehouse was the master. In one of his Blandings novels, *Service with a Smile* (1961), Lord Emsworth's awful secretary accepts a bribe. After sealing the pact: "Lavender Briggs' mouth twitched slightly on the left side, which was her way of smiling."

As the number of ways of approaching the subject of the smile multiplied, I thought it best to arrange the book thematically, so that each chapter might explore a different sort of smile, beginning with "Decorum" (the polite smile), and proceeding thence to "Lewdness" (rude grinning), "Desire" (the coy smile, lipstick), "Mirth" (smiling and humor), "Wisdom" (the smile of reason, the stoic smile, the saintly smile), and "Deceit" (the fake smile). Each offers a different porthole onto the subject. Some of these are panoramic and sweeping, like "Decorum," in which examples of polite smiling, mouth closed, act as a sobering reminder of the ancient distaste for the open display of teeth. Others focus more narrowly on particular representations of a smile, literary or artistic, rather like a cinematic close-up.

The hidden smile might also find a place here, partly or wholly obscured by the various kinds of purdah worn by millions of Muslim and Hindu women, to say nothing of other veiled peoples, the swaggering Touareg of North Africa, for example, although you do not need to see someone's face to know that they are smiling. Blind people are keenly aware of the change in timbre that may be detected in the voice of a smiling interlocutor. Many of us can tell when a person at the other end of the telephone is distracted by something funny but gamely tries to continue an otherwise serious conversation. Smiling changes the sound of the voice no less than the shape of the mouth.

Some chapters take as their point of departure a work of art that I have known and loved for a long time. How do we read a smile in art? What signals do portrait painters or sculptors give us when they offer up a smiling subject? How do they prevent something as naturally intriguing as a smile from becoming somehow inert or static when it is set down permanently in paint or stone? In the past, most artists approached the portrait as a quest for the best possible likeness; smiling or not, the painted image should resemble the living person as closely as possible. But within the art of portraiture, wherever it is practiced, artists have subtly modified facial expression so as to bring forward qualities they observe in the sitter's character or behavior. Perhaps they sense that the sitter is arrogant or kindly or cunning. The smile can be an important part of that characterization. We shall encounter numerous examples of the smiling face in art throughout this book, in many different media and contexts. Here let us look closely at a single famous painting, and consider what and how we see.

The Laughing Cavalier by Frans Hals (Fig. 0.3) is one of the most flamboyant of all baroque portraits. This unidentified twenty-six-year-old military officer or militiaman is represented half-length, in three-

FIGURE 0.3   Franz Hals (1580–1666), *The Laughing Cavalier,*
1624, oil on canvas, 33 × 26¾ in. By kind permission of
the Trustees of the Wallace Collection, London.

quarter view. He wears a big black hat set at a jaunty angle. He is clad
in gorgeous lace, a spectacular jacket embroidered with a marvelous
array of bumble bees, cupid's arrows, flaming cornucopias, lovers'
knots, the *caduceus* or wand of Mercury, and other motifs strongly suggestive of betrothal or matrimony. Hals has shown him with his hand
on his hip, a clever way of revealing the gleaming hilt of his sword and
of bringing forward his left sleeve and exposing between the slashed

portions of the fabric the frothing lace of the shirt beneath. His hair is curly, and his exceedingly long, wiry moustaches are trained upward. He engages the viewer with a charismatic sidelong glance which, combined with his full cheeks, his healthy complexion, and the undulating line of his lips, suggests a good-natured smile of urbanity. To me he is emphatically not laughing.

The title by which this painting is now universally known seems to have stuck in the nineteenth century. Earlier it was known merely as a portrait of a man, or of an officer. The earliest mention of laughter in connection with this picture was not until about 1880, and it has even been suggested that were his moustaches pointing down, not vivaciously upward, he might not even seem to be smiling at all. This I very much doubt, but it is beside the point. Why instead did the Victorians interpret the expression worn by our urbane friend as the outward manifestation of laughter? Is it really possible that this wry expression represented to them the furthest extremity of mirth, the equivalent of full-throated laughter? It seems unlikely. Some people who laughed sotto voce, as it were, in the interests of piety or decorum or self-control, may have recognized some similar air of restraint in the face of this seventeenth-century Dutchman. Such an outlook may have existed in sober Methodist or nonconformist congregations, but it would not have been shared by many picture-hungry Londoners who saw this masterpiece in the nineteenth century. They knew, through hundreds of genre pictures, what a jolly place seventeenth-century Holland was, with its bawdy taverns and rollicking belly laughs. Instead, I think *The Laughing Cavalier* stuck, as such titles do, because it was simply a good title, and the question whether the subject was actually laughing or not diminished into insignificance once you became aware of the charismatic presence of the man himself. For this portrayal of a self-confident, glamorous gentleman is especially captivating, and his faint smile particularly engaging, because of the way Hals makes him fix us with his eyes.

While the disposition of the lips and the muscles of the lower half of the face are crucial signs that someone is smiling, it is the eyes, and their capacity to fasten onto another person, that tell us that he is smiling at *you*.

One of the strangest art clichés that still circulates endlessly is the one about the eyes in a portrait "following you around the room." This non-illusion arises from somewhat muddled expectations about how a two-dimensional image might behave when seen from different angles in three-dimensional space. Provided the image is not a hologram, we can hardly expect it to take account of our position in the room. If the eyes engage us when we stand directly in front of the picture, they will also engage us from any other viewpoint, despite the distorting effects of foreshortening. I doubt if eyes "following you around the room" have anything at all to do with gothic fiction or those old movies in which real eyes spy through peepholes cut into the face of a portrait. Of course, they actually *do* follow you around. I suspect by its slightly supernatural, spiritualist note that we can safely blame the concept of eyes that seem mobile and, worse, intently watching *you*, on nineteenth-century French art critics, who got a kick out of that sort of thing. Nevertheless, it is the disposition of the eyes in a portrait, as between living people, that tells us that the smile of the subject is a direct avenue of meaningful communication, vividly reserved for you and me. There is no doubt that this sensation, this knowledge, has a profound impact on the viewer. It may be a blinding glimpse of the obvious, but it is worth noting in conclusion that the exchange of a smile—be it sincere or forced or spontaneous—makes us feel good. A smile may stimulate us in certain superficial ways, eliciting a ready smile in response, for example, but it also penetrates the deep recesses of our subconscious mind. What makes Hals's portrait great is that it convinces us that something similar is taking place, even though we know at the same time that the source of stimulation is nothing more than paint on canvas.

There are some people who raise their upper lip so high, or let the lower lip sag so much, that their teeth are almost entirely visible. This is entirely contrary to decorum, which forbids you to allow your teeth to be uncovered, since nature gave us lips to conceal them.

ST. JEAN-BAPTISTE DE LA SALLE,
The Rules of Christian Decorum and Civility, 1703

Francis Bacon somewhere remarks that politeness veils vice just as dress masks wrinkles.

JOHN DORAN, Habits and Men, 1855

⟨✣⟩

1

Decorum

If we think of the spontaneous smile of a little child as essentially truthful, we can be equally certain that, at times, the smile of the adult is a kind of mask. There are any number of situations in which we exchange smiles purely out of politeness, thus conforming to unwritten rules of good behavior, whatever they may be. Such smiles are not necessarily insincere. We offer them in good faith. The impulse is so strong that we may even respond to it invisibly when we answer the telephone. Yet we also distinguish between the smile by which we conclude a transaction at the bank—in all likelihood concealing the certain knowledge that that transaction benefits the bank far more than us—and the smile with which we greet a friend, husband, wife, or lover.

When in social situations we meet people for the first time, we notice if they do not smile, and may form the impression that they are unfriendly or cold. In some cases we will recognize that a painfully shy person finds this situation unbearably difficult, and does not smile for that reason. But if the person we have just met does smile, we tend to accept it as an expression of good manners, and refrain from reading that smile in any particular way. This may change within minutes, even seconds, by which time we may begin to observe mannerisms, facial appearance, or the tendency of specks of saliva to accumulate at the corner of the mouth. This may or may not make a difference to whether we like this person, find him or her attractive, or else conclude that we have little in common. In other words, no matter what follows or how quickly, the opening gambit tends to be conventional.

Professional encounters are more complicated. When we front up to a job interview, we will perform the rituals of greeting and smile gamely. In that situation experienced employers may make allowances for the many anxieties that our smile fails to conceal and, provided they are fair, will allow themselves to take notice only if our nerves continue to jangle long after the ice is broken. Others will adopt harsher tactics, which may better suit a more cutthroat industry in which the smile is a rarer commodity. Likewise, circumstances will nudge the polite smile in one direction or another in business meetings depending on whether or not negotiations are going our way. If the other side obviously has us over a barrel, nobody will be surprised if at the end of the meeting we do not beam with unalloyed pleasure. Smiles flow more readily from flight attendants greeting first- or business-class passengers than those herding the rest of us into economy, if not as we embark, then soon after takeoff.

For most of human history, in many cultures and societies, attitudes toward the smile have been strongly colored by social conventions, good and bad manners, arising from the concept of decorum. Indeed, modern minds have spent a good deal of energy seeking the origins of the smile not only among primates, but as a distinct mode of communication among prehistoric peoples. According to this view, the smile gradually acquired its meaning as a result of primitive social interactions, such as the encounter between two cavemen of roughly equal strength, locked in the stalemate of hand-to-hand combat—the result of some ferocious dispute over territory or food. In these circumstances, each combatant recognizes in the bared, clenched teeth, the squinting and frowning of his opponent, an intelligent signal that this useless contest need not continue. Such situations gave meaning to muscular twitches and spasms of the face, thus producing from the caveman's savage grimace the precursor of a prehistoric smile.

No doubt this is pure conjecture, but the idea vividly suggests two important points. First, the smile has always been associated with restraint, with the limitations upon behavior that are imposed upon men and women by the rational forces of civilization, as much as it has been taken as a sign of spontaneity, or a mirror in which one may see reflected the personal happiness, delight, or good humor of the wearer. Second, although the verb *to smile* is most often used intransitively, without an object, the act of smiling itself is inevitably social and communicative, part of the complex nonverbal language with which our bodies are equipped. A decorous smile, a smile of restraint, is therefore an important ingredient of good manners, just as the lewd grin has to do with the bad. It can be a kind of mask.

The vast literature devoted to etiquette and manners that blossomed in the nineteenth century offers up countless examples of manners that today strike us as alien, even bizarre. In his excellent book *What the Butler Saw*, E. S. Turner drew attention to the "servant problem," that is, the perceived shortage of good servants and the growing restlessness and intractability of below-stairs staff, which in the 1880s tormented upper- and upper-middle-class Englishwomen. One etiquette manual tried to help by suggesting that the formal (and necessary) boundary between servant and master or mistress might best be established by adopting a special voice:

> It is better in addressing them [your servants] to use a higher key of voice and not to suffer it to fall at the end of a sentence. The best-bred man whom we ever had the pleasure of meeting always employed in addressing servants such forms as these—"I will thank you for so-and-so" or "Such a thing, if you please"—with a gentle tone but very elevated key. The perfection of manners in this particular is to indicate by your language that the performance is a favour and by your tone that it is a matter of course.

Mistresses were advised to treat their servants humanely, to give them a whole holiday every third month, and a half holiday in each intervening month, to provide improving books, decent quarters, and so on. For their part, servants were encouraged to see their master and mistress as being entrusted to their care by God, and to be grateful for the benefits they obtained from this employment. One of these was religious instruction, for which servants could best demonstrate their gratitude by being loyal and resisting the temptation to move to a more advantageous post. Smiles between servant and master were on the whole avoided, since the servant faced the risk of being thought too familiar or insolent, and the master overly unctuous or insinuating, which might equally give offense below-stairs. More intimate relationships certainly developed between a trusted lady's maid and a decent mistress, for example, or a master and his valet, but these existed strictly in private. Some eighteenth-century lady's maids were even advised never to flatter their mistress, or to "praise the shape and quality of her teeth," because this would encourage vanity, quite apart from the fact that in doing so they would overstep the social boundary that separated them.

The domestic arrangements of large houses in earlier centuries were far more chaotic and reveal quite different codes of conduct and standards of decorum. The sixteenth-century chronicler Count Froben Christoph von Zimmern, for example, observed among boisterous, aristocratic guests at a Christmas feast the custom of hurling dog turds at each other across the dining table. This spectacle was surely no less disgusting in the sixteenth century than it strikes the modern imagination, but the fact that turd-throwing happened in a noble house appears to have made it by definition acceptable behavior. It goes without saying that the guests were drunk, loud, and roaring with laughter.

The words *decorum*, from the Latin, and its English synonym *propriety*, might seem old-fashioned at the beginning of the twenty-first century, mainly because we do not often hear them spoken, except occasionally in an ironic or even sarcastic sense. Yet a sense of decorum, emanating as it does from within, reflects in many different ways the strengths and weaknesses of our character and is no less crucial to the conduct of our societies than it was in nineteenth-century England or sixteenth-century Germany. I suspect we are more inclined these days to add the old concept of decorum to those ideas of self-regulation that are nowadays grouped under the popular, hold-all umbrella of *respect*. In any case, we wear our smile more often than we think as a dutiful, measured response to the standard of behavior that our own sense of decorum causes us to expect of ourselves.

Consider, for example, a textbook of manners, *The Rules of Christian Decorum and Civility*, written toward the end of the seventeenth century for his pupils by the French educator St. Jean-Baptiste de la Salle, the founder of the Christian Brothers. Here, in great detail, de la Salle described for poor boys—who, for reasons of class or upbringing, would not otherwise have known—exactly what constituted acceptable and unacceptable behavior among Christian gentlemen. Everything from how to get out of bed in the morning to conducting polite conversation was covered, as well as the care, use, and deportment of each part of the body.

Now Jean-Baptiste de la Salle was famous for the grace and elegance of his own manners, something that was understood as a reflection of his aristocratic upbringing. Yet the manual he devised for his pupils was obviously not meant to provide the same degree of refinement or polish, or indeed to reflect the manners and habits of the court of King Louis XIV at Versailles. Nevertheless his detailed recommendations manage to be both surprisingly familiar and, occasionally, quite alien. A passage on "The Mouth, Lips, Teeth and Tongue" is an especially rewarding source of information about the smile. The first point is that decorum requires above all else that the mouth be clean, so it should be washed out every morning—but obviously not in public or at the table. "Decorum does not allow you to keep anything in your mouth nor to hold anything between your lips or teeth." That includes pens and flowers. It is rude to keep your lips too firmly shut, to bite them, or to let them hang open. "It is intolerable to pout or make faces."

Lips should never be allowed to quiver, and should ordinarily be kept shut, unless you are speaking or eating. "There are some people who raise their upper lip so high, or let the lower lip sag so much, that their teeth are almost entirely visible. This is entirely contrary to decorum, which forbids you to allow your teeth to be uncovered, since nature gave us lips to conceal them." At the same time, however, teeth should be kept clean, with the aid of toothpicks and string. They should never be ground or clicked or clenched or spoken between or snapped with the thumbnail. When you speak, you should open your mouth properly. It is rude to advance your tongue to the edge of the lips and slide it from side to side. It is also rude to use the tongue or the lower lip to suck into the mouth a stray gobbet of food, or matter that has dribbled out of your nose. Nature made teeth for the purpose of enclosing the tongue, so never poke it out. Finally, it is important to spit out phlegm that may from time to time arrive in the mouth. Never swallow it. And never spit noisily, nor publicly, nor anywhere other than on the ground or into a handkerchief, if it can possibly be helped. Aim carefully, and try to conceal the fact that you have spat by stepping quickly on the spittle.

De la Salle was not out of step in thinking it acceptable, not to say natural, to spit in public. Right up to the end of the nineteenth century spitting caused little comment, and an exchange of letters in *The Times* newspaper of London in March 1900 drew attention to the issue. Having heard of a law in France designed to prevent the "odious habit of expectorating" in public, "A Sufferer" pled for something similar in London. "What women suffer cannot be easily expressed, for however careful they are they are bound to get their skirts contaminated." This apparently reasonable objection drew a sharp rebuke from Viscountess Harberton, the wife of an Anglo-Irish peer, writing from Elm Bank, Malvern. Lady Harberton could not see that "'Sufferer' has anything to complain of, as the habit of wearing dresses that trail along the ground is, in its way, equally disgusting and unnecessary. There are many other things on the ground that trailing the clothes into one would imagine to be repugnant to anyone possessed of the most rudimentary feelings of refinement, or even ordinary cleanliness." In fact, the modern objection to spitting, which led to laws prohibiting it in "covered places of public rest," grew out of research into the spread of disease, principally tuberculosis.

Jean-Baptiste de la Salle also had a great deal to say about conversation and laughter. He thought it was entirely consistent with the demands of decorum for boys to conduct an entertaining after-dinner conversation such as might be expected to generate laughter—laughter being good for the digestion, and the hiatus at the end of a hearty meal being good for very little else. However, funny stories should never be vulgar, irreverent, impure, or cruel or imply that the teller takes pleasure in anyone else's misfortune; instead, they should be uplifting and informative. Never laugh at your own jokes, at death, or at the Church. Never laugh so hard that you lose your breath, or make rude gestures, for, "says Ecclesiasticus, the fool raises his voice in laughter, but the wise man scarcely laughs to himself."

Not much of this mountain of advice acknowledges with any degree of practicality the actual behavior of adolescent boys. No doubt there were among De la Salle's pupils scruffy, bad-tempered, and disobedient ones, as in every school. But it does hold out the hope that children will somehow absorb high ideals and respond appropriately to noble sentiments, and that they may be prevailed upon not to behave like animals. The expectations of decorum—not just in a seventeenth-century French school but in any other context—may aim at a higher standard of behavior than is achievable by anyone other than the small minority who define it for the rest of us, at the same time preserving for itself some latitude. But these lessons, as well as the example of people we admire, inevitably take root. And having taken root, they equip us with the capacity to wear our smile like a mask.

People in many societies and eras have found it useful to wear real masks, substitute faces, synthetic smiles. Sometimes the elaborate cosmetics employed in some theatrical traditions, as in modern Chinese dramatic art, turn out to be vestigial references to the face-covering masks worn in earlier times. In the case of Japanese Noh theater, those masks endured and form a strict repertoire of enduring characters and types. But the practices not only of wearing masks but of concealing the whole head, and necessarily the smile, have also found their way into daily life. Islamic and Hindu purdah are perhaps the most obvious (to which I shall turn later on), but history offers many other examples. The wearing of masks or "vizards" that covered the upper part of the face became fashionable among English ladies in about 1660 at the time of the Restoration, but was by the early eighteenth century thought stale and, because it had become widespread, rather vulgar. The practice had also strayed into plays and stagecraft as a useful dramatic device, which further undermined its respectability. Instead, patches or beauty spots applied to the face were a beauty-enhancing alternative throughout the period, particularly at Court and, for the Duchess of Newcastle, served the useful function of covering angry pimples. (By convention, black patches were not worn when in mourning.)

The practice of mask-wearing is very ancient and has flourished all over the world, among carnival revelers, warriors, actors, dancers, priests, and other performers of sacred ritual. The actors in ancient Greek tragedy and comedy wore masks. These belonged to a small number of types, standard issue, it seems, in the late Classical and Hellenistic periods. In comedy Aristotle tells us that they were either supposed to be caricatures of particular people, or else as funny as possible. Careful comparisons have been made between a few rare texts in which particular plays and roles are, if not described, at least mentioned, other texts that discuss physiognomy in general, and surviving representations of masks in sculpture, frescoes, vase paintings, and little terracotta statuettes, of which there is a surprisingly large number. Although some care was taken to differentiate between the shape of the face and nose, the type of hair, and the disposition of the brows, comparatively few actors' masks carry an unequivocal smile.

According to a pseudo-Aristotelian treatise called the *Physiognomonika*, probably of the third century B.C., bad-tempered men had lots of wavy hair and an especially large beard (all adult men wore beards). People with straight noses were thought stupid; people who raised their brows, conceited; one eyebrow, crafty; and so on. Round faces suggested shamelessness, long ones vacancy. Earlier masks, belonging to what is called the "old comedy," in the period of Aristophanes, were probably less elaborately differentiated and may have been made to fit the actors themselves. Certain caricature masks are mentioned, and we know that the masks of young men with no beard were probably meant to indicate "luxurious effeminates." There is a certain amount of evidence about masks contained in the plays themselves—as, for example, when one actor playing the role of a hideous old woman must hurry off stage, change mask (but not costume), and hurry back on stage as an even more hideous one— but such evidence is only of limited value in reconstructing the actual appearance of the masks themselves. Elsewhere we know that some effort was made to differentiate the members of the chorus by casting them as "farmers, merchants, carpenters, craftsmen, foreigners," and so on. We have no way of knowing whether they wore masks appropriate to each category or if instead, as seems more likely (and less expensive), the farmer simply carried a hoe, the merchant a bag of grain, the carpenter a hammer. Costume presumably played a part. We are not even sure what the masks were made from, nor indeed exactly why they were worn. One suggestion is that they doubled as primitive megaphones.

The Greek world was awash with masks, which were used for many different purposes. Some masks were worn by priests and some by worshippers, certainly, but they were not always worn. They could be attached to posts, herms, and other upright supports, or else treated as freestanding objects, in connection with votive offerings, burial, and other forms of commemoration. A number of mask fragments, as well as fragments of mask molds, have been recovered from the Temple of Artemis Orthia at Sparta. They date from the seventh to sixth centuries B.C., and a good number of them are gap-toothed, open-mouthed, and grinning.

One of the most ancient of the Greek myths is that of the *Gorgoneion*, in which the hero Perseus kills the monster-queen Medusa, one of the Gorgon sisters, and uses the magical power of her severed head to turn his enemies to stone, rescue Andromeda, restore order to Greece, and carry out many other miraculous deeds. The gorgon head of Medusa became an enduring motif in Greek art from the eighth century B.C. and generally has big, bulging eyes, a wide, open mouth, and two rows of teeth, among which are usually two pairs of sharp fangs (upper and lower). She pokes out her tongue and often has snakes instead of hair. Later on she grows a beard. Monstrous and destructive, the head of Medusa became a formidable weapon when harnessed properly and a symbol of the majesty of justice. According to the myth, Perseus gave the severed head to the goddess Athena, who attached it to her armor, thus wielding its previously corrosive power for the protection of Athens.

As a recurring motif in Greek art the head of the gorgon Medusa is a mask, and a powerful one, but another, equally widespread convention, at least prior to the Classical moment of the mid-fifth century B.C., is the decorous "archaic smile" of Greek sculpture (Fig. 1.1). In the two centuries prior to this turning point in European civilization, archaic Greek sculptors very often represented men and women smiling, regardless of the circumstances—even soldiers in battle lying mortally wounded. The phenomenon is best illustrated by the many statues of young men, known as kouroi, a large number of which have been excavated all over the Greek mainland, Asia Minor, and on islands in the Aegean Sea. These statues were composed according to a strictly regulated set of conventions. A kouros was invariably a freestanding figure, the weight of the body evenly distributed on each leg, as if represented exactly half-way through the act of taking a short forward step; the big left foot (almost always the left) planted squarely in front of the right; the arms held rigid at either side of the body, fists clenched; the head held erect, the hair worn long. Very frequently the corners of the mouth were carved so that they turned sharply upward in a slightly pinched smile that gave to the face a degree of insouciant animation that today seems very distant from the rigid formality with which the rest of the body is held stiff.

Figure 1.1   Unknown Greek sculptor, *Kouros of Tenea*, c. 575–550 B.C., marble, 60 in. high. Munich: Staatliche Antikensammlungen.

Rigid is too harsh a word. The carving of many kouroi, particularly those dating from the early fifth century B.C., is often done with great subtlety, achieving very smooth, fluid transitions from the supple planes of the torso, for example, to the rounded forms of the shoulders and arms, or the junction of the thighs, hips, and abdomen. The flow of one part of the body into the next was normally achieved with great precision, although sculptors apparently did not wish to produce in the finished statue any illusion of motion. Certain regional variations have been identified, suggesting various fashions in different parts of Greece for more shapely, fleshy bodies, or slenderer, more angular limbs and narrow hips.

Invariably, however, kouroi are represented nude. Their posture is forever the same, and almost always they smile. Sometimes the expression is hardly noticeable, as in the powerful, early New York Kouros in the Metropolitan Museum of Art, in which two neat incisions at the corners of the mouth are sufficient to suggest the ghost of a smile. However, the majority of surviving kouroi carry heads that are carved so that the corners of the mouth turn emphatically upwards, often turning towards subtly modeled cheeks that reflect the muscular action that produces the smiling mouth.

For much of the last century, and the century before that, it was believed that kouroi represented Apollo, the god of music, of art and poetry. Such images of the god, it was thought, most probably served a religious function, to the extent that the religious and the secular could easily be distinguished in ancient Greek life. As well, kouroi probably served as votive statues, the permanent record of a prayer, an intention or a thank-offering to a god, or several gods. Another use to which these statues were put was funerary. They were placed over graves either as a memorial—that is, some kind of notional portrait image of the deceased, accompanied by an inscription—or as a marker, an image of some carefully chosen god-protector or supplicant deity, not necessarily a portrait of the deceased. Finally, there appears to have been some strikingly modern sense in which these statues were enjoyed for the frank, sometimes homoerotic, beauty that many adult Greek men similarly enjoyed observing in Olympian athletes and youths. The astonishing adaptability of the kouros and its extraordinarily steady development as a more and more naturalistic form, easily capable of many uses, make it one of the greatest

achievements of Greek civilization, and certainly a key to understanding the fundamental underpinnings of Greek art in this and,
indeed, later periods.

Some scholars have suggested that the archaic smile owes its existence to the effort of sculptors to represent all the muscles of the
body, including those of the face, in a state of extreme tension, and
that therefore what we see is not a true smile but nearer to a grimace
brought on by physical effort. Others suggest that the smile runs parallel with the Greek quality of *agalma*, the life-affirming capacity to
delight by means of sheer beauty, which was associated with the bodies of young athletes, both living and in stone. A third view, the correct one I think, is that the archaic smile came into being precisely
because of its capacity to animate a figure which in every other respect was held rigid—a figure whose function, after all, was to com-
memorate athletic prowess and youthful vigor, qualities that to
modern eyes may seem absent from the monumental stone bodies of
the statues, but certainly not from their faces, which are full of life.

On one simple level, the archaic smile owes its existence to the
influence of neighboring sculptural traditions. Whence and by what
means it flowed into Greece from the regions beyond Asia Minor,
the Black Sea, and elsewhere is open to much speculation. Yet the
fact that the smile is to this extent a motif imported from the Near
East does not really explain why the Greeks developed the need to
hold onto the archaic smile, and indeed develop it with particular
subtlety. Likewise we know that Egyptian statues served as a model
for early kouroi, but why the Greeks took the revolutionary step of
liberating their statues from the anchoring wall to which the backs
of so many Egyptian statues were fused remains a mystery. Why, too,
did the Greeks choose to depict the male figure nude, rather than
clothed in a kilt or tunic? It is almost certainly not because Greek
athletes competed nude; it is now well understood that as late as the
fifth century B.C. this practice was relatively novel.

The pronounced upward curve is what distinguishes the archaic from other smiles in sculpture. Perhaps this was an attempt among cautious but highly experimental sculptors to inscribe upon the face that subtle curve that was observed running from side to side in the horizontal alignment of real human lips. This they laid flat upon the front of the stone head of the kouros, thus rendering a kind of bird's-eye view of the mouth, a brave but awkward attempt to build a more elastic bridge than would otherwise join the two sides of a stone head. This might relieve not only its esthetic but also its purely physical weight. I do not agree with this view because if the archaic smile was created by accident, as it were, it is impossible to imagine that the convention would have persisted for as long and as consistently as it did. The archaic smile is nothing if not vivacious, and one notices it—even if some scholars, such as Brunilde Sismondo Ridgway, are today reluctant to describe the smile in terms other than "naïve excitement." Besides, this "accidental" view of the smile as a by-product of some effort to lighten the features of the head implies a degree of clumsiness in the sculptor, which is usually inconsistent with the high quality and discipline of the carving of other parts of the statue.

The literature of pre-Classical Greece offers us some intriguing evidence of attitudes towards smiling, for at a number of important moments in the great eponymous epic poem, Homer describes the wandering hero Odysseus as smiling. More often than not the smile of Odysseus is described as occurring within the hero's heart, unseen by those around him. This paradoxical imagery of the veiled smile, a smile that represents concealed plans, heroic self-control, and discipline, occurs more frequently than the smile with which Odysseus greets assault and battery. An example of that is when, disguised as a stranger, the hero returns to Ithaca and finds Penelope, his wife, besieged by the notorious palace-full of suitors. One of these, Ctesippus, provoked by the arrival of this unwelcome newcomer, fellow guest, and competitor, without any warning hurls an ox's hoof at

Odysseus. Managing to avoid the missile with a quick turn of his head, Odysseus smiles in his heart a "grim and bitter smile"; the ox's hoof bounces harmlessly off the wall.

Odysseus's smile is scornful, and privately experienced. Elsewhere, however, he uses his smile to lull the suitors into a false sense of security. It stands in stark contrast to the raucous laughter and disgusting, greedy chomping of bloody meat that goes on in the never-ending banquet to which the suitors help themselves, despite the angry warnings delivered by Odysseus's son Telemachus not to abuse his absent father's slaves and hospitality: "Among the suitors Pallas Athena roused unquenchable laughter, and turned their wits awry. And now they laughed with alien lips, and the flesh they ate was all bedabbled with blood, and their eyes were filled with tears and their spirits set on wailing."

It is highly unlikely that there will emerge any firm reason why the kouros—and his female counterpart the kore, who is invariably represented fully clothed (Fig. 1.2)—hitherto such flexible and popular types of statue, were gradually overhauled and superseded in the decades following the Classical moment of the mid-fifth century B.C. Later statues in bronze exhibited a far more sophisticated conception of the body as an exquisitely balanced system of asymmetrical rhythms, complementary and breathing. Yet it is difficult to imagine that these could have been achieved had it not been for the sculptural foundations laid by the kouros type, with its vigor, life, and potential for natural motion.

Nor is it conceivable that post-Classical societies of the West developed their longstanding prejudice against the open display of teeth as a result of any particular tendency of ancient Greek and Roman artists to conceal them. While archaic lips are mostly pursed, there are neat rows of teeth carefully drawn or incised on faces in certain Greek vase paintings, as for example on a calyx krater by the painter Euphronios in the Louvre, which carries a wonderful image

FIGURE 1.2 Unknown Greek sculptor, *Peplos Kore, c.* 540–530 B.C., marble. Athens: Akropolis Museum.

of the wrestling figures of Herakles and Antaios. There are many other examples. And the exquisitely well-preserved, bearded bronze statue of Zeus or Poseidon, which was recovered from the sea off Riace on the coast of Reggio Calabria in southern Italy, has two glorious rows of silver teeth visible between parted lips. The conventions of Greek metalwork most probably afforded many more opportunities to indulge in this kind of luxurious colorism than has hitherto been understood, mainly because most bronzes have disappeared, and Roman copies in marble form the vast bulk of the corpus of ancient sculpture.

While the archaic smile may be associated with the decorous function of the kouroi and korai it adorns, any particular meanings it may have had must remain more or less obscure. It is unlikely that any substantial documentation will come to light that adds to our knowledge of the archaic smile, which mostly comes from the surviving works of art themselves, some of them only headless fragments. But what about the decorous smile, the smile of reserve and restraint, that may be observed in more recent works of art, for example comparatively modern portraits? In many cases we know all about the artist, the subject, and the circumstances of their unique encounter. Does this better equip us to read the smile we see on the sitter's face, if indeed there is one?

A magnificent example of a supremely formal portrait painting is the Frenchman Jean-Auguste-Dominique Ingres's famous portrait of Pauline-Éleanore, the Princesse Albert de Broglie, 1853, in the Robert Lehman Collection at the Metropolitan Museum of Art in New York. In this very large canvas, Ingres observed, captured, and recorded a smile of exquisite faintness hovering over the young woman's lips. The painting and the smile have long fascinated me because of their sad beauty, their cool languor, and their air of inhibition. Hers is the decorous smile par excellence, the public smile, the smile of appropriateness and good manners, the smile that conceals (Fig. 1.3).

In 1851 the Princesse de Broglie was a wealthy woman. Her father-in-law, Prince Victor, was a senior minister in the recently defunct Orléanist government of France. Her husband, Prince Albert, a future prime minister of the Third Republic, was pious and unconventional. His mother was the daughter of Mme. de Staël and, like her, a committed Protestant. Out of favor with the new regime of

FIGURE 1.3   J. A. D. Ingres (1780–1867), *Portrait of Pauline-Éleanore de Galard de Brassac de Béarn, Princesse de Broglie,* 1853, oil on canvas, 47¾ × 35¾ in. New York: Metropolitan Museum of Art, Robert Lehman Collection.

Louis Napoléon (soon to become the Emperor Napoleon III), the young prince spent most of his time drafting and redrafting a mammoth, six-volume history of the primitive church. Pauline also wrote studies in religious history. Together they produced five sons. She died prematurely of consumption in 1860. The family house was not far from Ingres's studio on the Seine at 11 quai Voltaire, directly opposite the Louvre.

Ingres spent a good deal of energy avoiding portrait commissions, which he found troublesome and, artistically, not particularly rewarding. Moreover, 1853 was a particularly busy year because against his will he was bound to paint an enormous, difficult picture for the new emperor in which Napoleon I was to be represented, nude, driving a chariot up to heaven. It seems strange that an artist whose paintings of people exhibit such fluency and self-confidence should have found the genre of portraiture so draining. Ingres's astonishingly vivid portraits must count among the finest works of art produced in nineteenth-century Paris, offering the twenty-first century viewer a glimpse into the heart of that now-lost world of the prosperous metropolitan drawing-room, the arena in which much of the political life of France was for decades played out. Yet the process of painting portraits literally made him sick. Sometimes he hung onto his portraits for months, even years, while the queue of prospective sitters lengthened, and existing clients fumed with resentment. The problem was not technical, nor very often formal. Ingres was easily capable of rendering the subtlest textures so that, for example, the flesh of his subject seems to breathe with life. Rather, it was the curious, often painful balance of simplicity and splendor, of energy and stillness, of the casual with the formal that taxed him so much. It seems that there was no easy way to work his portraits out. He simply had to labor over them until he was finished.

The opulence and scale of Ingres's *Princesse de Broglie* are immediately arresting. It is big, well over a yard high, with a splendid frame. Light plays over the crisp blue satin of the princess's immense skirt and produces the sheen on the gold embroidery along the edge of her white shawl. Many other motifs encircle the young woman, among them those few fingers of a pair of hand-stitched kid gloves—not too stiff, not too floppy—that poke out from the things she has temporarily discarded on the chair: a wondrous shawl, an inlaid fan, a bag, and a muff. The chair itself is a seductive affair, plump and gorgeously upholstered in gold damask.

Dozens of seed pearls descend from the princess's earrings and seem almost to tremble in response to some slight movement of her head. Tiny sequins glint among the marabon feathers in her hair. The luster of the gold rings and the diamond clasp of her extravagant pearl bracelet, the shimmer of ribbons and lace, the gloss of the hair, even the low gleam of a gilded molding on the otherwise unadorned rear wall—all of these effects are so tangible as to transport you into the very room Ingres devised for his client. Yet gradually you begin to see beyond these sharp points of focus, and notice the cool languor with which the artist clothed his subject. Most of all, you wonder about her hooded gaze, the tilt of her head, and the melancholy of her smile.

The Princesse de Broglie's portrait was commissioned from Ingres by her husband, and it originally hung in their house. Indeed at her death in 1860, the heart-broken Prince Albert shut it behind a pair of heavy curtains. We shall never know what Ingres thought of his client's smile, whether he painted it as if it belonged to the public rather than to the private arena of the couple's married life. Yet I find it impossible to imagine that it did not suggest to him a moment of unspoken communication between husband and wife. The assurance with which Ingres traced the fluid lines of her arms and shoulders, and bathed her head with the soft light of a window, is no less remarkable than the sure and subtle manner in which he delineated her faint smile. And although it is complex, it is hardly enigmatic. Ingres would not have dreamed of allowing the Princesse de Broglie to cross the boundary that in the mid-nineteenth century still separated decorous reserve from the volatile realm of human spontaneity—at least not within the artificial world he created in her portrait.

Perhaps the most sustained and intriguing attempt to fathom the meaning of a faint smile of self-restraint is the 500-year quest to understand that small painting of a woman whom everyone in the English-speaking world knows as *Mona Lisa, c.* 1500–1503, an Italian Renaissance portrait by Leonardo da Vinci (Fig. 1.4). The famously enigmatic quality of the smile that is said to hover on the woman's lips has been so frequently remarked upon, so widely celebrated, especially in the last century, that it has become the single most famous representation of smiling in our culture. This has partially obscured the fact that the smile of the *Mona Lisa* was essentially the creation of nineteenth-century French critics who were determined to see the work as a miraculous achievement in the history of art, one of a handful of great masterpieces of Italian Renaissance painting in the Louvre, and the smile as the seat of the painting's mesmeric power. "This canvas attracts me, calls me, invades me, absorbs me," panted the historian Jules Michelet:

> I go to it in spite of myself, like the bird to the serpent . . . A strange isle of Alcina is in the eyes of *La Gioconda*, gracious and smiling phantom. You believe her attentive to light readings by Boccaccio. Beware! Vinci himself, the great master of illusion, was taken in by the snare; long years he remained there without power ever to emerge from this mobile labyrinth, fluid and changing, that he painted in the background of this dangerous picture.

To Michelet, writing in the mid-1830s, Leonardo's painting was great because it was dangerous; even the artist had been "ensnared," as it were, by his own enigmatic creation. Michelet's son-in-law, the critic Alfred Dumesnil, went even further, creating the impression of an almost diabolical power lurking behind the smile of the *Mona Lisa*. He thought he could detect a funereal pallor rising "from beneath the warmth of this slightly swollen flesh . . . A tragic and

FIGURE 1.4 Leonardo da Vinci (1452–1519), *Mona Lisa (La Gioconda)*, 1503–1506? Oil on poplar panel, 30¼ × 21 in. Paris: Musée du Louvre, inv. 779. Photo: R. G. Ojeda © Réunion des musées nationaux / Art Resource, New York.

somber sign wells up in this mirage of fantasy, the enchantment of the smile, the brilliant beauty. The smile is full of attraction, but it is the treacherous attraction of a sick soul that renders sickness. This so soft a look, but avid like the sea, devours."

These odd utterances by Michelet and Dumesnil clearly belong to the overheated intellectual climate of European Romanticism, whose influence was to some extent on the wane by the time J. A. D. Ingres was painting his portrait of the Princesse de Broglie. Yet the ideas to which they gave expression were tremendously influential and spread far beyond the charmed circle of a few progressive Parisian salons, to say nothing of radical French art journalism. They were not only familiar to the generation of Ingres and Delacroix; they inspired the subject matter of at least one major history painting that appeared at the Paris Salon in 1845, Aimée Pagès Brune's weird *Leonardo Painting the Mona Lisa*, a picture that was sold for the relatively large sum of 2,000 francs only two years later. Early in his career, Ingres himself had painted *The Death of Leonardo da Vinci*, 1818, which in accordance with historical tradition he set at Fontainebleau, the bearded artist expiring, rather improbably, deep in the arms of François I on a heavily draped four-poster feather bed.

Fortunately these peculiar ideas about the *Mona Lisa* were not allowed to pass uncontradicted. In a series of rambling lectures, first published in 1869 as *The Queen of the Air*, the English critic John Ruskin launched a surprising attack on Leonardo da Vinci, whom he thought an overrated painter, a capable draughtsman certainly, but essentially a crank, obsessed with odd inventions and flying machines. "Leonardo," complained Ruskin, "depraved his finer instincts by caricature, and remained to the end of his days the slave of an archaic smile."

Elsewhere, in his famous book *Modern Painters* (1843–60), Ruskin turned his attention to the precise manner in which the human mind formed its perception of beauty. Taking as an apparently random example the mouths of animals, Ruskin argued that the most beautiful of these are generally the ones that are most capable of expression—by which he meant expressiveness in general, certainly not biting, pecking, mauling, or tearing limb from limb. The ugliest mouths in the animal kingdom, he suggested, were either the ones least capable of expression, as in fish, or else the most effective instruments of destruction, as in alligators. Then, moving up the scale of beauty, "we arrive at birds' beaks . . . and thence we reach the finely developed lips of the carnivora"—which are beautiful at all times except when they snarl and bite. From these "we pass to the nobler because gentler and more sensible [mouths] of the horse, camel, and fawn, and so again up to man"—whose mouth exists "beyond and above its lower functions" of eating and breathing, as an organ of eloquent verbal expression. Kissing is definitely not mentioned. For Ruskin, as for all his contemporaries, beauty had a moral dimension, so that the majesty of a lion's mouth owed not so much to the fearsome gnashing of its teeth, nor to the wrathful wrinkling of its muzzle, but to "its strength and sensibility" in repose. Edwin Landseer's gigantic recumbent bronze lions that were installed in 1867 around the base of Nelson's column in Trafalgar Square, London, would appear to convey the same impression, even though each mouth is slightly open, partially revealing the formidable weaponry within.

Ruskin's dismissive assessment of Leonardo elicited in response the first article that ever appeared under the name of the brilliant young Oxford don Walter Pater, who before this had published his work anonymously. Like the French, Pater thought that Leonardo da Vinci was a defining genius of the Renaissance and that the *Mona Lisa* was his masterpiece. The *Mona Lisa* was by this time, of course, already famous: "We all know the face and hands of the figure, set in its marble chair, in that cirque of fantastic rocks, as in some faint light under sea," he began (launching a sustained and, it must be said, mystifying under-water analogy). As well, the expression of the face, he noted, was supposed to have been elicited from the sitter by means of performing clowns and flute players—so said Leonardo's sixteenth-century biographer, the Florentine artist Giorgio Vasari. (Aimée Pagès Brune had visualized a rather droopy ensemble of swan-waisted minstrels strumming gaily alongside Leonardo's easel.) That much at least was already understood. Yet the resulting portrait was surely more than the sum of its parts:

The presence that thus rose so strangely beside the waters, is expressive of what in the ways of a thousand years men had come to desire. Hers is the head upon which "all the ends of the world are come," (I Corinthians 10: 11) and the eyelids are a little weary. It is a beauty wrought out from within upon the flesh, the deposit, little cell by cell, of strange thoughts and fantastic reveries and exquisite passions. Set it for a moment beside one of those white Greek goddesses or beautiful women of antiquity, and how would they be troubled by this beauty, into which the soul with all its maladies has passed! All the thoughts and experience of the world have etched and molded there, in that which they have of power to refine and make expressive the outward form, the animalism of Greece, the lust of Rome, the reverie of the middle age with its spiritual ambition and imaginative loves, the return of the Pagan world, the sins of the Borgias. She is older than the rocks among which she sits; like the vampire, she has been dead many times, and learned the secrets of the grave; and has been a diver in deep seas, and keeps their fallen day about her; and trafficked for strange webs with Eastern merchants: and, as Leda, was the mother of Helen of Troy, and, as Saint Anne, the mother of Mary; and all this has been to her but as the sound of lyres and flutes, and lives only in the delicacy with which it has molded the changing lineaments, and tinged the eyelids and the hands. The fancy of a perpetual life, sweeping together ten thousand experiences, is an old one; and modern thought has conceived the idea of humanity as wrought upon by, and summing up in itself, all modes of thought and life. Certainly Lady Lisa might stand as the embodiment of the old fancy, the symbol of the modern idea.

Not until the close of the nineteenth century did a new generation, led by the American connoisseur Bernard Berenson, find it possible to object to the layers of "overmeaning" that had built up around the *Mona Lisa*, largely as a result of Walter Pater's flamboyant hymn of praise—though even Berenson thought she was full of "hostile superiority." The effect of lifting those layers from Leonardo's portrait—clearing the air somewhat for a new generation of visitors to the Louvre—was abruptly reversed by the publication of one of the most daring, inventive, and brilliant essays about the smile of the Mona Lisa yet to be written, that of Sigmund Freud.

In a landmark essay entitled *Leonardo da Vinci: A Study in Psychosexuality* (1910), Freud proposed that Leonardo was fascinated by the smile of the *Mona Lisa* because it awakened a dim memory in the artist of the smile of his natural mother, from whom he was known to have been removed as an infant. Leonardo's smiling women, argued Freud, were nothing less than representations of the artist's lost mother Caterina. By the time Leonardo re-encountered in Lisa that "blissful and ecstatic smile, as it had once encircled his mother's mouth . . . he had long been under the ban of an inhibition forbidding him ever again to desire such tenderness from a woman's lips." As a painter, however, he endeavored to reproduce his mother's smile with his brush, and with it "burnish all his pictures," none more powerfully than the *Mona Lisa*.

Thus Freud carried the smile of the *Mona Lisa* into his own, twentieth-century realm of psychoanalysis, using it as a point of access to the inner world of Leonardo's homosexuality, and propelled it onward into the present. Since 1910 numerous writers have revisited Freud's thesis, in several instances affirming that Leonardo was indeed homosexual, occasionally assuming that such a condition of life was pathological, and finding in it a plausible explanation for the artist's evident "empathy with women," a quality that seemed so vividly apparent in his subtle treatment of the *Mona Lisa*. Feminist critics have quite reasonably objected to this line of thought, asking why a man's empathy with women should necessarily be thought to indicate an abnormal psychology or sexual orientation.

It is hard not to concur with the view, so frequently expressed and for so long, that the *Mona Lisa* is indeed an exceptionally subtle and sympathetic image of femininity, at a time when very little effort was made by artists to endow female portraiture, particularly in Florence, with any degree of character. Earlier, fifteenth-century Florentine profile portraits tended to be inert mannequins used for the display of family wealth for the benefit of the subject's husband, and to show off to the male members of rival families. The *Mona Lisa* is very different from this earlier genre, and the striking manner in which Leonardo realized his subject in space and light seems to reflect not only an entirely different working method, but also radically different ideas about how a woman might inhabit a painting. At the same time, however, none of this would seem to have much to do with the strange process by which nineteenth-century male critics turned the *Mona Lisa* into a femme fatale, a sorceress, and a deep-sea diver.

It is easy to forget how the overheated imagination of nineteenth-century men such as these led them to fetishize lips and mouths. John Ruskin, for instance, recoiled from the idea that the petals of certain flowers might be described as "lips." Upon detailed investigation—literally, with tweezers and magnifying glass—he found that such petals of the genus *labiatae* as he could obtain did not appear to divide into two lips at all, "but into hood, apron and side-pockets." In the circumstances he thought the species ought to be called *vestales!* In the era of Freud the psychosexual connotations of remarks such as these—and one could point to endless examples—seem so obvious that they strike us as comical.

There is no evidence to suggest that the artist, the client, the sitter's family, or anyone else in the sixteenth century attached any special significance to the facial expression of the *Mona Lisa*, other than that the idiosyncratic painting technique was notably *sfumato*, literally smoky, a highly subtle and original manner with oil paint for which Leonardo was justly praised. Instead we now know that the *Mona Lisa* was most probably accepted and understood in its time as a betrothal or marriage portrait, of a very popular and widespread type, albeit remarkably well-executed and accompanied by a strange and fantastic landscape background unlike anything that had been seen in similar portraits. The subject was identified by Vasari as Lisa, the young wife of a prominent Florentine merchant named Francesco del Giocondo, hence *La Gioconda* or *La Joconde*, the names by which the *Mona Lisa* is known in Italian and French. Scholars are now inclined to agree that Leonardo's subject was Lisa Gherardesca (b. 1479), who married Francesco in 1495. In other words, it was not until nineteenth-century critics attempted to demonstrate the greatness of Renaissance painting by drawing attention to the timelessness with which Leonardo apparently rendered her physiognomy that the *Mona Lisa* actually assumed the shape of an enigma, able to plumb depths of experience in the viewer. The decorous smile that Ruskin had dismissed as "archaic" now reemerged as fleeting and mysterious.

For it is in the name of her husband, *Giocondo*, if Vasari identified him correctly—and what he says should always be treated with caution—that we may find the simplest and most wholly satisfying explanation for the smile of the *Mona Lisa*. Renaissance Italians were immensely fond of puns and other forms of word play. The name *Giocondo* is also an Italian adjective, descended from the Latin *iucundus, -a, -um*, that still means today what it meant in the late fifteenth century: *lieto* (happy or glad) or *gioioso* (joyful). I doubt if it would have surprised his contemporaries that Leonardo should choose to represent his subject, within the conventions of decorum that governed the marriage portrait, in precisely the attitude that her husband's felicitous name might suggest, simply in the state of being *gioconda*.

The street-lamp sputtered,
The street-lamp muttered,
The street-lamp said, "Regard that woman
Who hesitates toward you in the light of the door
Which opens on her like a grin."

T. S. ELIOT,
Rhapsody on a Windy Night, 1917

⁓⁓⁓

2

Lewdness

Not long ago a small Dutch painting of a grinning boy clutching a hen was sold at auction in London. That strange picture, in which the artist—an Utrecht painter named Jan Tilius—concentrated a great deal of attention on the deep creases in the lad's cheeks and the poor state of his teeth, belongs to a group of similar Netherlandish paintings of boys with hens that by the seventeenth century were widely understood as a rude joke. For the boy is not merely holding onto the hen; with his other hand he fumbles with her private parts to see if there is an egg on the way. The *hennetaster*, or chicken groper, in effect a discrete subgenre of Dutch and Flemish painting, was, it seems, riotously funny. Men fell about laughing at the crude double entendre of the Dutch words for bird or birds (*vogel, vogelen*), which doubled as *penis* and *to screw* or *to fuck*, while the common expression for bird-catcher, *vogelaar*, could also refer quite explicitly to a lover, a procurer, or pimp. Meanwhile, the word for hen (*kip*) stood in for the equivalent of *bird* or *chick* or *babe*.

A further source of meaning was the strong Netherlandish association between eggs and testicles. This was not merely a vague idea partly based on the general concept of fertility. A print by Cornelis Massys entitled *An Allegory of Adultery*, 1549, showed a woman stealing a basket of eggs from another woman's husband; the symbolism was specific, clear, and frank. As well, in at least one reliable source, a fifteenth-century carnival play, the male genitals are referred to as "the eleventh finger with eggs attached." Naturally, the connection between eggs and testicles gave another smutty meaning to the chicken groper.

The joke had several other dimensions. A dirty old man was sometimes substituted for the ribald youth, grinning lewdly and occasionally licking his lips. This more sinister type of chicken groper deliberately played to the gallery. He had warts, nasty wrinkles, stubble, and a few atrociously disfigured teeth protruding here and there from otherwise vacant gums. Dirty old men were in fact quite popular, and generally made their hideous appearance in a different but related genre, that of the "unequal couple," which originated in the fifteenth century. The more common variety of unequal lover, presumably in life as well as in art, was the grinning old lecher, his bony fingers exploring the attractive body of a much younger bride or girlfriend. The other, equally horrid, showed a wrinkled old hag drooling over a delectable young man. She was generally shown clutching a fat moneybag, a detail without which the situation was evidently considered implausible. These grotesque stereotypes had already solidified in contemporary literature. In his *Praise of Folly* of 1511, for example, the great humanist scholar Erasmus put the following words into the mouth of Dame Folly: "Nowadays any old dotard with one foot in the grave can marry a juicy young girl, even if she has no dowry—it is so common that men almost expect to be paid for it!" Clearly the "unequal couple" satisfied a particular demand for pictures both comic and lewd.

Meanwhile, the chicken groper, especially the dirty old variety, first appeared in the mid-sixteenth century and gained widespread currency through the circulation of prints. For a long time the earliest known example was by the mysterious "Master ISD," an artist active in Antwerp between about 1546 and 1580 whom we know only by his monogram. That print must have been made in about 1560. Later images by the printmaker Herman Muller, among others, served to disseminate the lecherous chicken groper further afield. However, the subject was well established by that date because a rather different, earnest-looking *hennetaster* is to be found busily groping hens in a slightly earlier work, *The Netherlandish Proverbs*, a magnificent oil painting executed in 1559 by Pieter Bruegel the Elder in which at least 115 common sayings and folk metaphors were given careful visual expression. At this date, the chicken groper could refer to somebody who "roosted with the chickens" or, in other words, simply went to bed early. It could also just as easily refer to a forlorn husband who is both literally and figuratively henpecked, or else to an equally boring husband who follows his wife around the house interfering with the housework, making a domestic nuisance of himself. It is not hard to see how fruitier minds could stretch the joke to accommodate the man who simply cannot leave women alone, making of himself a sexual nuisance. Whatever its origins, 100 years later the *hennetaster* was painted fairly often, particularly for some unknown reason at Utrecht, and the cleverer artists managed to improve the joke by giving to the hen a startled, even discomfited aspect at odds with the ribald expression on the face of the groper. That broad grin is indivisible from the various smutty associations of the subject.

The distinction between a broad, friendly smile and lewd grinning or leering in part comes down to a question of interpretation. The way we read another person's smile, and the emotions which it may be said to indicate, depends, after all, upon the mental faculties and instincts upon which we rely for guidance. That mental equipment is obviously unique to each individual, and therefore serves some people better than others. Naturally, it can improve or deteriorate with age, so that the naïve observations of youth may, with luck, give way to the wisdom of years. It may also vary in quality and reliability depending upon circumstances too various even to imagine. And sometimes we exhibit our full measure of humanity simply by getting it wrong. We are easily capable of misreading another person's smile, misinterpreting or misunderstanding it, and the consequences of that can be tragic or merely comical. The Netherlandish painters of "unequal couples," for example, go to some lengths to give the young bride a sweet smile of utter bewilderment that provides an absurd contrast with the panting old lip-smacker who reaches tremblingly for a pert breast or buttock. Everybody has a blind spot, and there is nothing quite so reassuring as the discovery that somebody else's is more ridiculous than your own.

Yet whether lewd or simply merry or good-humored, the smile that is worn by so many of the protagonists in sixteenth and seventeenth-century Netherlandish scenes of everyday life is ebulliently open. And it is particularly noteworthy that Dutch and Flemish painters of this period responded with such immediacy to broad grinning and belly laughs. Jan Steen portrayed himself as a jocular musician on several occasions, grinning and laughing uproariously (Fig. 2.1). Frans Hals gave his sitters and subjects all kinds of smiling countenance from that of *The Laughing Cavalier*, whom we met earlier, to his *The Lute Player* in the Louvre (Fig. 2.2).

This wonderful painting of a bright young musician with tousled hair and a splendid doublet of red and black captures the moment

FIGURE 2.1   Jan Steen (1626–1679), *Rhetoricians at a window*, c. 1663–1665, oil on canvas, 29 × 23¼ in. Philadelphia Museum of Art, The John G. Johnson Collection.

when in full swing he glances up sharply to the right, smiling merrily at an unseen protagonist, surely another player or maybe a singer standing beside him, much as we observe musicians today exchange a knowing glance, the consequence of some private source of amusement arising from the music, an unexpected change in tempo, a phrase negotiated in perfect unison. The handling of the reflected

Figure 2.2   Frans Hals (1580–1666), *The Lute Player*,
1625–1626, oil on canvas, 27¾ × 24 in. Paris: Musée
du Louvre, inv. RF 1984–32. Photo: Jean Schormans.
© Réunion des musées nationaux / Art Resource,
New York.

light over the planes of the lute player's forehead, cheeks, chin, and
the back of his wrist, even the gleam of light on the end of his stubby
nose, suggests the sheen of perspiration which, again, all stage performers know well.

With complete control, and with only a few carefully applied
strokes of the brush, Hals renders the upturned corner of the mouth
and the undulations at either side of the creases in his healthy-
looking cheeks. The glossy redness of the lips, the elasticity of the

whole face in this unconventional attitude, its youthfulness and immediacy make this, for me, one of the most memorable smiles in Dutch art. The lute player's expression, which suggests genuine joie de vivre, is far more open than the urbane half-smile worn by the moustachioed *Laughing Cavalier*, and an artist as fluent as Frans Hals could clearly capture such momentary expressions with dazzling effectiveness. It is worth noting that this superb facility was rarely demonstrated with such confidence in the European tradition prior to the seventeenth century. The broad smile is, in any circumstances, hard to portray; attempts to capture it frequently strike us as awkward or unsatisfactory.

The late fifteenth and early sixteenth-century Sicilian artist Antonello da Messina, who was taught to paint in Flanders, left several portraits behind in which he took pains to inscribe upon his sitter's face the unambiguous features of an open smile. One of them is today still in Cefalù, in the collection of the Fondazione Culturale Mandralisca (Fig. 2.3). Like the Paris *Lute Player*, the subject's identity is unknown. His costume, together with the fact that he had his portrait painted at all, suggests that he was a gentleman. The lips are drawn apart and the corners of the mouth turned upward. The nasolabial fold is carefully plotted, and forms a neat pair of parentheses at either side of the mouth. Most importantly, there are wrinkles or "laughter lines" at the corner of the eyes. The artist thus attempts to turn the smile into a function of the whole face, something that was seldom attempted in European portraiture. Yet in Antonello's painting there is considerable tension between the static quality of the image, somewhat formal in appearance and function, permanently frozen, and the fleeting quality of the open smile by which he sought to animate his sitter's entire face. That tension, which is absent from faint smilers such as Leonardo's *Mona Lisa*, is troublesome, and it characterizes many representations of the smile in art—in many media, running across many cultural boundaries. Why do artistic representations of brightly smiling faces so often

FIGURE 2.3   Antonello da Messina (*c.* 1430–1479), *Portrait of an Unknown Man* (also called *The Pirate of Lipari*), late 1460s, oil on panel. Cefalù, Sicily: Fondazione Culturale Mandralisca.

seem forced, anxious, unsatisfactory? Why do lewd ones seem so much more interesting?

The connection between the broad grinning we find in Netherlandish art and unambiguous jocularity, drinking, lewdness, and revelry is well documented, and partly recalls the ancient distinction between pornography and obscenity. Pornography is private, secret, for solitary delectation or for a closed circle of like-minded fantasists.

To some degree the fantasist blurs the boundary between his own sexual gratification and the performance he contemplates in private, with which he is thoroughly intertwined in his head. Certain pornographic smiles might plausibly reflect the pleasures of fellatio or any number of erotic stimuli, real or imagined. However, they are wound into that carefully generated fog with which the pornographer concocts his idea of sex. They are strictly rationed. With the approach of orgasm, the pornographer assumes a more Wagnerian mode, proffering gasps and contorted frowns and head-tossing accompanied by little cries and carefully chosen dialogue. Spicier minds might consider adding mild sadomasochistic gestures such as bottom-slapping or improbable undergarments to suggest further variations on what must be one of the most endlessly rehearsed narratives of any dramatic genre. In conformity with the requirements of Aristotle, all pornography has a beginning, a middle, and an end, provided the connoisseur is prepared to wait that long.

There is no doubt that the smile has a part to play in this treacly recipe for porn. Yet more steamy glances accompanied by vigorously pouting lips are frequently offered up as a silent invitation to let the pornographic festivities commence. This sort of gesture, with its "come hither" function, was presumably derived from the ancient stock in trade of street-walkers and prostitutes. By contrast, I have known people whose smile was quite startlingly attractive not only in the sense that it augmented the natural beauty of their face, but also in the sense that it made me conceive erotic fantasies about them.

Yet that kind of smile, effortless and untactical, is obviously quite different from the cold maneuverings that take place in the realm of porn, and it is clearly not what the lewd grinning and cackling in Dutch taverns was all about. Obscenity, by contrast, brings sex out into the open. It is about a whole audience laughing together at silly old fools with small penises, or overheated young men vainly attempting to bring under control rampant erections (to mention two examples from ancient Greek comedy). It is about what happens to wayward husbands when drunk, or about the pinching of bottoms, or the town harlot. It is about the ridiculous contrast between nudity on stage and a fully clothed audience collapsing into loud guffaws. It takes the fantasist's fevered pornographic imaginings, in which he is an enraptured secret participant, and turns them into an embarrassing joke with which the onlooker is engaged not erotically but uproariously. To some extent the shared energy of disinhibition is a warming oasis in the dark, drab wasteland of daily routine and, laughing, we will the warmth to continue—loudly, publicly, in taverns, theaters, and town squares. It leads to a good deal of energetic movement, sweaty brows, music, and vigorous dancing. It relies for its impact upon the separateness of our bodies from the body of the man who, in Roger Scruton's memorable analogy, slips on a banana skin. Observing "the way in which, for a moment, he is *all body*, I feel a strange embarrassment. I am pained and nonplussed; in my confusion I laugh, so distancing myself from the other's fate."

In his *Anatomie of Abuses*, the Elizabethan Puritan divine Philip Stubbes protested at dancing, which he described as "an introduction to whordome, a preparative to wantonnesse, a provocative to uncleannesse, and an introite to all kinde of leaudnesse rather than a pleasant exercise to the mind, or a holsime practice of the body." Attacks on dancing in the sixteenth and seventeenth centuries extended from detailed theological protestation, invoking the memory of the idolaters who danced around the Golden Calf (*Exodus*, 32), to practical legislation. Dancing in the streets of Antwerp was still prohibited as late as the 1580s. Strict Calvinists also prohibited dancing in any form, and in some places fined offenders and put them in prison for three days with nothing to eat but bread and water.

Vigorous dancing was associated with drunkenness, and the uncontrolled hopping and jumping and hobbling about to music was further associated with madness or even devil worship. These prejudices were deeply rooted and troubled many serious minds. Dancing was thought to lead inevitably towards gluttony and sexual stimulation and fights. The churches, both Catholic and Protestant, watched in dismay as, after church, village people withdrew to a tavern or a neighbor's house, had too much to eat and drink, then began to dance. Even at more decorous gatherings in which more formal dancing was tolerated—aiming at what Cicero called "*otium cum dignitate*," leisure with dignity—dancing was suspect. Extreme merriment, it was thought, could all too easily conceal improper or indecent jokes "under a veil of seemliness and dignity," the better to corrupt the young and innocent.

It is of considerable interest in connection with the buffoonery of seventeenth-century Dutch genre painting—the belly laughs and wide open-mouthed grinning, the generous wine- and ale-quaffing, the smoke-puffing, the chaos of upended furniture and domestic disorder—that Jan Steen, an artist who specialized in subject matter of this kind, could acquire the reputation in subsequent generations of having been himself a hugely funny man. An eighteenth-century biographer, for example, described Steen's "farcical life," and told how his famous teacher, Jan van Goyen, loved him for his wit and banter. Alcohol is never far away. Steen's father was a brewer, and in his early years as a painter, Jan Steen supported himself by running a brewery in Delft. He was hopeless, according to this early source, because he was his own brewery's best customer. Early owners of Steen's paintings included delivery men and other creditors at the brewery. He was jovial and fat.

These tropes are also to be found among later accounts of other seventeenth-century painters who favored jocular subject matter. Adriaen Brouwer was a prankster. Adriaen van Ostade loved hanging around peasant fairs. Pieter Bruegel told marvelous jokes. Very often the ridiculous nature of certain subjects has vanished. Just as the chicken groper requires some degree of reconstruction before we can appreciate the lewd joke—even if relatively few of us can bring ourselves to laugh at it any more—so, too, a swath of seventeenth-century Dutch genre subjects turn out to have been hilarious, for example paintings of mystified doctors visiting young women whose only problem is that they pine for absent lovers, or quack tooth-pullers getting stuck into poor, screaming yokels.

Boisterous scenes of musicians and tavern-dwellers were not confined to seventeenth-century Netherlandish painting. Another example, *A Girl Playing a Tambourine* by the Spanish-Neapolitan painter Jusepe de Ribera, known as Lo Spagnoletto, was sold at auction not long ago in London. It was evidently one of five allegorical paintings in which each of the five senses was represented by a different genre subject. In this case, the girl with the tambourine stands for the sense of hearing, but seems in many respects to conform precisely to the standard of behavior deplored by Stubbes and others, to say nothing of mendicant preachers of earlier centuries. She grins, somewhat lopsidedly, from ear to ear, and, like Hals's *Lute Player*, wears on her face an earthy film of sweat. The shiny pinkness of her nose, the disorder and shortness of her hair, the gaping collar of her blouse, and the dirt on her hands, in which she holds a very large but surprisingly modern-looking tambourine—all of these are low-life details that were in Naples, no less than Holland, associated with the rowdy licentiousness and chaos of the tavern. Ribera also took particular care to represent both rows of teeth, deeply discolored. That dark color may to some extent be ascribed to the natural process of "sinking," in which certain organic pigments bound in oil gradually darken over the course of several hundred years. The original spectacle of the teeth was presumably even more surprising when the painting left the artist's studio, because they were most probably painted green or brown.

The lewd grinning we see going on in this and other seventeenth-century genre paintings, north and south of the Alps, is merely a far more conspicuous expression within a rapidly expanding art market, the forerunner of our own, of something that is very ancient and finds expression much earlier in the European tradition, even if one must search quite hard to find it.

In the early to mid-nineteenth century pioneering antiquarians and other enthusiasts, many of them Church of England clergymen, sought to document, preserve, and restore the ancient stone buildings of the British Isles. This effort led to a great upsurge of interest in antiquarianism in general, as well as in the history of primitive Britain. It also led to the Gothic Revival in art and architecture, which was brought to its climax by Augustus Welby Northmore Pugin. One of the most troublesome discoveries that was made, generally by methodical draughtsmen carefully surveying the crumbling stonework of neglected country churches, was a particular kind of ornament, a recurring naked female figure, which at first they simply ignored because they thought it was not merely unpalatable but repulsive and unpublishable. In Ireland local people called her *sheela-na-gig* or, more commonly, the sheela.

Many forms of primitive, pre-Christian, totem-like, magical beasts or monsters found their way into the rich cargo of ornament on corbels, quoins, bosses, lintels, capitals, and other features of Romanesque church architecture of the eleventh and twelfth centuries. They grinned or grimaced, slavered, scowled, poked out their tongue or dragged their lips apart with both hands. Frequently they burrowed their way into the ornaments that surrounded more conventional Christian narratives. But the sheela was different from the rest. Deeply primitive or naïve in execution, the sheela either gestured with both hands to her exposed genitals, or else held her legs wide apart, thus exposing her vulva as prominently as possible. Sometimes her legs were shown propped right back, almost behind her ears, her knees forming the lateral points of a schematic diamond or lozenge-shaped motif, easily accommodated in frieze recesses or spandrel compartments. Occasionally the sheela was shown dragging her labia apart with both hands, as in a grinning example that was carved on a corbel in the church at Kilpeck in Herefordshire. This image so baffled the artist and antiquarian G. R. Lewis that he simply drew her with her hands on her hips and hoped that this would do. Other nineteenth-century observers attempted to convince themselves that what they saw in the defiant sheela was in fact a male fool or demon tearing his heart out of a cavity in his chest. Some progress was made by travelers to Ireland who took the trouble to consult local people and were astonished to discover that in some places there still existed a strange custom according to which from time to time certain powerful women of the village, women associated with supernatural powers, were prevailed upon by men to lift their skirts and display their genitals for good luck, or to guard against misfortune, if that was for some reason anticipated. Under these circumstances the frank symbolism of the sheela swam into vivid focus for those few who cared to look into the matter.

In fact, witches were thought to be common in Ireland, right up to the end of the nineteenth century. According to the collector of folklore Thomas Doherty, who investigated the customs of peasants in County Donegal and published his findings in March 1897 in the *Transactions of the Folk-Lore Society*, red-haired women were especially suspect. Meeting a woman with red hair was an omen of ill fortune. Any animal (except an ass) which was looked at by a witch was said to be "blinked" and therefore under the influence of the evil eye. Meanwhile, some witches were believed to be able to turn themselves into hares, the better to gain access to other people's dairies to steal milk and butter.

Doherty was also informed that if a pregnant woman encountered a hare, any hare, the child would be born with a *hare-shagh* or harelip. Today we know that this is a congenital condition. Approximately one out of every 1,000 babies is born with a harelip, but presumably this figure was higher in places like Donegal where the genetic predisposition was evidently greater. A harelip results from the failure of the two sides of the upper lip to fuse properly during the first month of prenatal life. This deformity may, in its most extreme form, result in a fissure that divides the whole upper lip. It may also occur on its own or in connection with the more serious problem of cleft palate, which results in a fissure in the roof of the mouth. Today the deformity is normally corrected by a straightforward surgical operation. Surgery for harelip was also practiced on children in the nineteenth century, though with an alarming rate of mortality: in Heidelberg in the 1880s 10 percent of 337 children died following surgery for harelip, and in other places the mortality rate was far worse, up to a third. If they were not deliberately misleading him, Doherty's informants in Innishowen, County Donegal, blamed the incidence of harelip on the nefarious activities of witches from whom the sheela apparently offered some protection to their distant ancestors.

Numerous examples of this mysterious exhibitionist have been documented. She has at times been explained as the descendant of an ancient pagan fertility symbol, or as a magical device not unlike the head of Medusa—the image of a witch used to guard against witchcraft—in any case she seems to have originated among the earliest Gaelic carvings of the Dark Ages. The largest concentration of sheelas is to be found carved in the stonework of churches in Ireland, but there are large numbers in England and Wales, and a few in remote parts of Scotland. In many cases sheelas are so weathered that they are scarcely recognizable, but for their distinctive posture and the deep incision by which the vulva is represented. She is frequently shown with her mouth wide open, showing two rows of big teeth, and in many cases she wears a defiant grin. A few sheelas were made especially prominent by being incorporated into the carved mullion of a window or gate so that the sharp point of the arch coincided with the exact position of the vagina, as for example at the medieval church of Kilsarkan in County Kerry or in the refectory of the ruined nunnery on Iona. But more usually the sheela lurks in some discreet spot, such as the underside of the sarcophagus slab of Bishop Arthur Wellesley in Kildare Cathedral.

There are several groups of related "exhibitionist" carvings in France, a few in Brittany, some in Normandy, and a cluster in the valley of the Dordogne. These women are sometimes veiled, some-times straddling a pair of pillars, sometimes dangling among the carved ornaments on a stone capital or indeed helping to prop it up with both hands. The French examples are particularly interesting, because they have long been explained away as acrobats, on account of their weird posture. And close inspection reveals that while the position of the hands is very similar to that of the sheela, a small round anus takes the place of the vertical furrow of the vulva. It seems these grinning contortionists are displaying their bottom, not their genitals.

No doubt the strange, powerfully confronting sheela partly relates to the ancient myth of the *vagina dentata*, which has flourished in many parts of the world, among Maoris in New Zealand, in India, pre-Columbian America, and Africa. According to this ancient, universal superstition, the vaginas of certain powerful women, witches, or sor-ceresses are formidably armed with teeth. Any man who is unfortu-nate enough to gain entry may have his penis (and sometimes his testicles) severed or grotesquely bitten off. In some cases the girl or woman does this involuntarily and is therefore an unwitting source of danger to men; others wield their hidden armory with malevolent cal-culation. Freud's characterization of the woman's genitals as the "homestead whence once we were evicted" offered to twentieth-century psychologists a promising avenue of enquiry by which to make sense of this primitive myth and the primitive fear it represents. To them the *vagina dentata* myth seemed to be an eloquent expression of man's deep-seated fear of woman, his fear of the unknown.

The resolution of the myth, its second half, usually relates to the extraction, snapping off, or knocking out of those perilous teeth, thereby destroying the threat to the man by disarming or neutralizing the woman. This in turn is held to be one of the ancient folkloric origins of the frightful practice of clitoridectomy, the surgical excision of the clitoris, which of course permanently destroys a woman's ability to experience orgasm. This and the related practice of infibulation are still practiced today in the Horn of Africa, where it has long been believed that a man who had sex with an "uncircumcised" woman ran the risk of being punctured by her "dart" or clitoris.

Why is the sheela grinning? Among the thousands of cross-cultural meanings that have been identified by the compilers of one old dictionary of gestures and attached to the movements of mouth, the licking or smacking of lips, for example, various forms of blowing or noise-making, even belching, appear to be far more readily associated with lewd behavior than the smile or the grin. The Psalms tell us that to shoot out the lip is to show contempt. The Romans thought that licking your lips or burping was debauched. How then do we form the impression that the sheela's smile is necessarily lewd, not, say, defiant, triumphant, or, indeed, malevolent?

Today lewd smiling is enshrined in popular entertainment and music no less than it was in vaudeville, music halls, or long before in Dutch taverns, though it has to some extent been reined in by new conventions of behavior, which no longer tolerate the "unequal couple," nor indeed the sheela. Yet we think we recognize a lewd smirk when we see one, as for example when with pride somebody regales us with a rude joke and awaits a response he hopes will be uproarious. This is his signal that for the time being we may for his benefit stretch or even set aside the rules we normally agree to adopt as civilized people. It may suit us to follow that cue by laughing at the joke, or we may sense that he has gone too far. Professional comedians know only too well the peril of straining these elastic boundaries of taste beyond their breaking point. The fiction of Dashiell Hammett, one feels, is full of lewd smilers, some of whom are made to conform to cruel racial stereotypes, which today we rightly shun. Translated to the screen, Hammett's oily spiv was tactfully transformed into a vehicle for Sidney Greenstreet, the rotund Englishman, whose smile is coldly calculating, but hardly lewd. The world of popular music, however, is largely unencumbered by such limitations, and when some writhing microphone fondler fixes us with a leathery smile, whether we can actually see him on stage or, rather more clearly, close-up on video, we sense that he earns his millions by doing more than simply cheering us up. Bon Scott, lead singer of ACDC, was noted for the particular lewdness of his stage smile, to which crowds responded with brio. Johnny Rotten of the Sex Pistols was also particularly gifted in this respect, as was Divine. All died too soon, but not before they offered their audiences, like that woman in T. S. Eliot's poem, a lurid glimpse through the door that "opens on her like a grin." Given the opportunity most of us will gladly take a peek.

What heavenly smiles! O Lady mine,
Through my very heart they shine;
And if my brow gives back their light,
Do thou look gladly on the sight;
As the clear Moon with modest pride
   Beholds her own bright beams
Reflected from the mountain's side
   And from the headlong streams.
–WILLIAM WORDSWORTH, from *Poems*, 1845

It is very rude to take close-ups and, except
when enraged, we don't:
lovers, approaching to kiss,
instinctively shut their eyes before their faces
can be reduced to
anatomical data.
–W. H. AUDEN, from "I Am Not a Camera," 1971

3

Desire

E very smile—whether staged for the camera, involuntary or spontaneous, deceitful or licentious, friendly or wicked, rude or polite—begins with an instantaneous chemical reaction in the human
brain. This is what all smiles have in common—perhaps the only
thing. When the consequences of that chemical reaction are carried

to their conclusion, activating through certain nerves the muscles of the face, they may give to the wearer the power of wordless communication with other people. Alternatively, the chain reaction may simply end as a set of muscular contractions hidden from everybody else, even from the consciousness of the wearer. It is surely among the most mysterious and enthralling aspects of the human smile that it is thus capable of revealing—should we so choose—our involuntary thoughts and desires, as much as it offers us a mask with which to present another version of ourselves to the outside world.

The inner life of the smile commences with various stimuli that arise in the cortex—or gray matter—of the brain. Such stimuli might result from the pleasure of unexpectedly receiving a large sum of money, lingering on a happy memory, or hearing a joke. The relationship of such external promptings with the millions of stimuli that make up thoughts and emotions is not well understood. However, such impulses are known to act upon receptors so as to carry forward an impulse from one of the nerve cells or neurones to the next, thus delineating a fiber or pathway. These neurones lead from the gray matter, not far below the inside of the top and front of the skull, down and inwards where they collect to form part of the internal capsule of white matter at the center of the brain. From there the neurones head backward, entering the brainstem, terminating at the primitive root of the brain in what is called the *pons*—and in that part of the *pons* which is called the VIIth nerve nucleus. By now, the neurones have also crossed from one side of the brain to the other, the same side as the set of muscles they will eventually activate. They cross in both directions, from left to right and right to left, depending on the region of the face concerned.

Cranial nerve number VII—CN VII for short—the nerve that emanates from the VIIth nerve nucleus, controls all of the facial muscles associated with smiling, and its paths are therefore worth plotting in some detail. Emerging from the front and side of the *pons*, CN VII commences its journey along the side of the skull (inside the temple) to the inner ear, where it passes through a small cavity and out onto the face, not too far from the place where the mandible or jawbone hinges against the base of the skull. At this point the nerve is situated in front of the ear, between two layers of the parotid, the largest of the saliva-producing glands, whence it separates into five branches reaching out to the various muscles of the face. The uppermost branch, the temporal, heads north, so to speak, and connects with the muscles of the forehead, the temple, and the brows. The zygomatic branch, named after the cheekbone it traverses, controls the muscles around the eyes and nose. The buccal and mandibular branches perform the extremely complex task of controlling the muscles of the mouth, cheek, and chin, while the cervical branch of CN VII goes down into the neck where it acts upon the muscles that depress the mouth and chin, mainly the *platysma*.

In its awesome way, a single nerve, CN VII, thus stimulates a sequence of muscular contractions and relaxations, and it is certain of these motions in combination that form the smile. Obviously these motions vary from person to person, depending on the size and shape of each of the relevant bones and muscles, so as to give each one a unique appearance and manner of smiling. The movements must also vary according to the type of external stimulus processed by the gray matter of each person, producing all sorts of smiles, from the polite no-thank-you-I've-had-enough-Brussels-sprouts smile to the smile deliberately worn by Ozzy Osbourne just to annoy people like Tipper Gore. Even a particular joke will stimulate a wide variety of smiles from one of genuine hilarity all the way down to the generous smile by which you attempt to disguise the fact that you have heard it a hundred times before, or that you do not find it remotely funny, or that you do not get it.

The origins of those initial stimuli that activate the CN VII are tremendously complex. The frontal lobes of the brain are concerned with the emotions, among other areas of higher thought, and to the extent that they exert a measure of control over the actions of the body, they appear to control the opposite sides, the left frontal lobe controlling the right side of the body, and vice versa. Children born with encephaly, that is no cortex or gray matter, will in their brief lives smile, but purely as a reflex. As well, the stimuli that normally occur in the cortex can also occur deeper in the sub-cortex, but above the VIIth Nerve Nucleus. This is presumably why some patients with cortical damage may not be able to smile when asked to, but will involuntarily smile at a joke. Conversely, a patient with Parkinson's disease, which affects the making of connections between neurones in the brainstem, may be able to turn up the corners of the mouth when asked to smile but, fully understanding or "getting" the same funny joke, may simply lack the ability to smile as an automatic response. Therefore, while the motor functions of smiling are largely the same whether voluntary or spontaneous, the chemical reactions from which they receive their cue are, it seems, various, erratic, and imperfectly understood.

The muscles over which CN VII exerts control consist of all the superficial sphincters and dilators of the orifices of the head, that is the ears, eyes, nostrils, and mouth. The wrinkles that we observe in the mirror, multiplying daily, generally occur at right angles to the contracting and relaxing muscle fibers nearest the surface, immediately underneath the skin. The forehead is lined, for example, due to the worried contractions of the *frontalis*, the muscle of the scalp, which raises the eyebrows and furrows the brow. The *oricularis oculi* surrounds each eye, causing it to open and shut, to varying degrees of width and tightness. In all sorts of ways the *oricularis oculi* protects the eyes—from light, by contracting into a frown; from dust and wind, by contracting slightly differently into a squint and by regulating the flow of lubricating tears; from drying out, by maintaining a regular blink. Its work is assisted by the neighboring muscles called *corrugator supercilii*, which correspond roughly with the position of the eyebrows and pull the brows together at times of anxiety or stress, thereby gathering the vertical wrinkles between. Unlike many other muscles that start and finish on the firm bedrock of bone, the numerous muscles of the face, including *oricularis oculi*, simply begin and end with each other, forming a volatile mesh of tissue capable of an almost infinite variety of motion and manipulation upon which we depend for subtle shades of expression. The ancient belief that the eyes are the window of the soul owes less to the distinctive appearance or fascination of the eyeball itself, than to the vast expressive range of all the muscles that surround it.

The nose is rather less mobile than the region around each of the eyes. Even so, three principal muscles govern it by pulling this way and that. The *procerus*, which contracts across the bridge, hitching up the skin at each side of the nose like a drawstring, shores up the frown and is generally prompted by bright sunlight or intense concentration. It may also be activated by an unpleasant odor or a feeling of disgust. Meanwhile, the *nasalis* (also known as *compressor naris*) and the *depressor septi* are there to dilate the nostrils. These muscles vary in flexibility and range of motion, yet they make possible the kind of nostril-flaring that I am assured is occasionally associated with sexual arousal.

If the upper part of the head is capable of an astounding range of movements stimulated by the various branches and twigs, as they are called, of CN VII, the lower half is at least twice as complex. The mouth is surrounded by numerous groups of muscles the action of which is regulated by a remarkable interdependence that is held in perfect balance by the impulses received from any combination of the five branches of the nerve, or all of them at once. Moreover, these muscles largely float above the neighboring bone structure of the skull and are therefore among the most independent and mobile. The *modiolus*, a small mass of nine fibrous muscles, lies to each side of the mouth and may be said to integrate its various activities, making sure for example that when we chew or bite, our lips and the inside of the cheek are protected from injury. As anyone who has bitten down hard on the soft lining of their cheek will attest, the system is not foolproof and accidents do happen.

Beyond the subtle modulations of movement made possible by the *modiolus*, more radical adjustments to the shape and function of the lower part of the face are made by the *risorius*. Tethered to the upper facial, cheek, or *zygomatic* bone and reaching down to each side of the lower lip, the *risorius* provides the principal mechanism for pulling back the corners of the mouth when we smile or laugh or for some other reason drag or stretch the lips back in the direction of the ears, as it were. Finally, running right around the mouth, giving tension and animation to the lips, enabling us to compress them against the teeth or lift them away, as for a kiss, is the *orbicularis oris*. That amazing muscle, combined with the action of the *modiolus*, has such a capacity for fine adjustment and flexibility that it is possible for us to speak, whistle tunes, play the flute or the oboe—think of the difference!—blow bubbles, kiss, chew, swallow, or drink from a straw, a glass, a teacup, or a bottle. Further muscles connecting the upper part of the mouth to the *maxilla* (lip) and *zygomatic* (cheek) bones enable us to lift, roll, or curl our upper lip, the better to sneer disdainfully (on those occasions when such a thing seems called for), while the *zygomaticus* muscles, major and minor, further uplift the corners of the mouth and lengthen the upper lip in what might be described as a broad or open smile, exposing the teeth. The so-called *depressor* muscles, below each side of the mouth, as well as the muscles called *mentalis* and *platysma*, enable us to do the opposite, namely to drag down the corners of the mouth, thus apparently demonstrating displeasure, disappointment, irritation, or sadness. The same muscles may also be activated, or the *mentalis* made to tremble involuntarily, when weeping. Everybody has observed this phenomenon.

Other muscles governed by CN VII add to the emotional expressiveness of the head. For example it is not entirely clear to me why I possess on my scalp the so-called *superior auricular* muscle, which lets me wiggle my ears, yet I have discovered by looking in the mirror that whenever I smile I use it involuntarily to hoist my ears at the same time. The movement is slight, but it is there. Moreover, running between the corners of the mouth and each side of the nose is the nasolabial fold, which when activated by smiling or laughter forms a visible boundary between the compressed muscles of the cheek, which in that situation necessarily protrude, there being no other direction in which they may go, and the region of the upper lip. The nasolabial fold constitutes an important element of the whole visual effect of the smile. It is one of a number of prompts, together with the crescent-shaped alignment of the lips (when the mouth is closed) or the wider arc of the lower lip (when the mouth is open), that apparently indicates to an interlocutor or passerby that the smiler is a happy person.

Indeed, the nasolabial fold is possibly more fundamental to the distinctive or recognizable anatomy of smiling than the characteristic, gently upward-curving line with which a child draws a smiling mouth, that familiar crescent shape that seems to have solidified as the shorthand symbol of the smile in many parts of the world since prehistory. One study of 1,000 Americans conducted in the 1990s found that the majority of people (67 percent) turned up the corners of their mouth when they smiled, their parted lips forming that apparently characteristic crescent shape. This was said to be the result of a dominant *zygomaticus major* muscle. Yet a large proportion (approximately 30 percent) exhibited a tendency when smiling first to raise the upper lip and expose the canine teeth, so that the corners of the mouth did not in fact appear to be lifted at all, merely drawn apart. For them the generalized shorthand of a saucer-shaped smile is completely misplaced, except to describe the shape of the lower lip alone. Even then the lower lip more or less retains that sort of curvature all the time, even when inert. The remaining 2 or 3 percent exhibited the somewhat alarming tendency when smiling to expose all maxillary (upper) and mandibular (lower) teeth at once, by a simultaneous contraction of almost all the muscles surrounding the mouth. That ferocious effect seems even farther removed from what might be described as the "classical," crescent-shaped smile. Yet in all cases the nasolabial fold—those curving lines that divide the cheeks from the flat plane of the upper lip and connect the edges of the smiling mouth to the outer corner of the nostrils—appeared to be the cornerstone of the smiling mechanism.

Of course, the smile is more than a chemical reaction, a series of muscular contractions, or a mechanism. It is a highly sophisticated concept, an expression of the emotions, a mode of communication, a beacon of desire, a ritual—an occasion, in other words, of intense psychological, anthropological, and social interest, the product of acute observation, cognition, and interpretation. In the West, the smile is also embedded in the Romantic tradition of poetry. There, it is constantly deployed as an expression of love and celebrated for its capacity to radiate beauty from the face of the wearer. The poets thus endowed it with the power to attract and fascinate, to stimulate desire. Indeed, most adults would have some idea of what Wordsworth meant when he described the smile of his beloved as shining "through his very heart," as indeed they would know something of the distress of having the same familiar smile of love withheld or cut off.

The game of love is perhaps the most obvious context in which the smile receives the tribute of art, poetry, and music. But the meaning of a lover's smile is obscure. It is inflected, indeed often transformed, when combined with a glance or some other gesture. Nor are those gestures, and their immediate or cumulative effects, readily understood. Presumably that is one reason why the flirtatious smile wields such power.

So a lot has come to depend upon lipstick and other cosmetic treatments with which to enhance and rally the smile, as if for combat. "Speak softly, and carry a lipstick," said one style guru recently, and one senses that this advice (from a Frenchwoman to other women) is neither wholly playful nor facetious. There are many western women who say they feel "undressed" without applying makeup. For many the cue for lipstick is when you cross the boundary between the domestic and public spheres. According to one historian of cosmetics, writing in 1970: "The swift limning of a mouth with lipstick is usually the last thing a woman does before she steps out of the house and into the street, not with the intention of transforming herself into somebody more attractive or more colorful, but in order to make herself complete." It would be otiose to point out how completely attitudes have changed in the last thirty years, but it is worth noting too that the ground floor of today's department store is no less than yesterday's crammed with row upon row of expensive lipstick, just as our fashion magazines continue to be full of glossy photographs of unctuously lipsticked mouths, a fact to which twentieth-century artists frequently drew attention. In 1927, the French photographer Jacques-Henri Lartigue took a series of photographs of actresses, cabaret singers, prostitutes, and transvestites in which heavily applied lipstick forming cupid's bow lips, dazzling teeth, and cigarettes were harnessed and intertwined as motifs more of glamor than of vice (Fig. 3.1).

Some women say that although they do not wear any other kind of makeup they still put on lipstick. In times of economic hardship, sales of lipstick actually increase. Toward the beginning of the current recession, in 2001, American women spent more than $836 million on lipstick, 6 percent more than the year before. According to Leonard Lauder, chairman of Estée Lauder, "When things get tough, women buy lipstick." Perhaps.

No doubt the custom of tinting the lips originated among the magic, apotropaic, and religious practices from which certain warpaint customs, tattooing, and scarification in tribal societies are also descended. The warrior or priest might transform his facial appearance into a "devil mask" to invoke against enchantment, for example, just

FIGURE 3.1   Jacques-Henri Lartigue (1894–1986), *Sim Viva* (from the series *Femmes aux cigarettes*), 1927. Photo © Ministère de la culture, France / A.A.J.H.L.

as the porcupine raises its quills or the cat makes its fur stand on end to frighten or ward off. On his return from an expedition to Greenland, the seventeenth-century theologian and diplomat Isaac de La Peyrère reported that the Eskimos were wild savages, "sullen and untameable," and, or maybe because, they "painted their faces blue and yellow."

There is plentiful evidence of the widespread use in antiquity of many kinds of lip-coloring. Natural ochres, berries, seaweed, and other vegetable dyes were used in Mesopotamia, Egypt, and the Near East to obtain a wide variety of colors and effects. Papyri survive in which women are shown holding a mirror in one hand and applying color to the lips with the other. We know the Egyptians used henna and carmine (which is derived from cochineal-producing insects). The Greeks and Romans experimented with all these, as well as iron oxides and fucus. Medieval and Renaissance recipes gradually became more complicated. Queen Elizabeth used cochineal bound with gum Arabic, egg white, and the juice of figs, but many variations of dye, stain, paint, or balm were also available, and easily prepared either at home or by the apothecary.

Modern lipstick is not so different. It is composed largely of various kinds of pigment, usually about 2 percent of bromo acid and approximately 10 percent of lakes (organic pigments), which disperse effectively and retain a high degree of intense color. These are bound with different oils, including sesame, olive, castor and other vegetable oils, lanolin, petrolatum, mineral oils (for glossiness), cacao butter, carnauba and candelilla waxes, lard, and beeswax. Other chemicals are generally added as pearlizing or wetting agents, and nowadays there is sometimes sunscreen as well as perfume and occasionally menthol. The recipe is generally governed by the need to balance rigidity (which is achieved by using enough wax to solidify the oils) and smoothly consistent application, which is best achieved by making sure the stick is not too hard. It is necessary to maintain a relatively high melting point, to prevent the lipstick from sweating or sagging in its case, and the thinner the film of color applied to the lips, the better it adheres.

The red parts of each of our lips, the so-called vermilion, are red because they are highly vascular and tend to gush when nicked or cut. People who have split their lip in a sporting accident will know how much blood can flow from it. The numerous vessels which supply such a lot of blood to the lips are very tortuous, so that they can accommodate the mobility and elasticity of the mouth. This makes any kind of surgery on the lips and mouth, such as the procedure to correct harelip in newborn babies, extremely delicate, more so because of the exact way in which our eyes fasten on even the slightest irregularities. (To this subject I shall return.) The problem for the surgeon is particularly acute at the border of the vermilion of the upper lip, which forms the natural undulating line we sometimes refer to as the cupid's bow because of its shape. The philtrum, the area that sometimes forms a depression between two slight ridges that run vertically between the center of the upper lip and the division between our nostrils, often forms a visual fulcrum for the cupid's bow and for some people it can be rather short so that their nose moves slightly when they speak. This, I have found, can be an endearing quality. In any event, minute accuracy is needed when repairing or joining a broken section of the vermilion border, because our eyes will pick up the slightest discontinuity.

Given the delicate nature of our lips, which lack the horny layer that protects the rest of our body, it is somehow surprising that we are prepared to expose them to such an exotic brew of coloring agents, oils, and fats, but I suppose this is nothing compared with the infinitely greater variety of oddments that we gladly allow to pass between them. Some people are allergic to lipstick, and others develop from it a condition called cheilitis, which is a kind of dermatitis of the lips. The symptoms may be as insignificant as chapping or cracking, but in some rare cases there may also be swelling or blisters. These conditions are usually blamed on certain indelible dyes that are occasionally used in some lipstick lines, and generally a change in color or brand is sufficient to cure the problem. But some women have also developed some gastrointestinal problems resulting from consuming, as is inevitable, tiny quantities of lipstick.

A great deal of energy has always been expended in formulating and then debating large moral questions arising from the use of cosmetics. Following the Protestant Reformation, Puritan sentiment was unflinchingly hostile, and treatises such as the Reverend Dr. Thomas Hall's *Comarum Akosmia: The Loathsomenesse of Long Haire . . . With the concurrent judgment of Divines both old and new agaynst it, with an appendix agaynst painting, spots, naked breasts, etc.* (1654) are not uncommon, leaving those readers who are inclined to continue beyond the title page in little doubt as to the contents or the general outlook of the author. (Incidentally, by "spots," Hall here meant "beauty spots" or patches, rather an early occurrence of this largely late seventeenth- and eighteenth-century beauty requisite.) In line with Puritan attitudes toward other forms of wickedness and frivolity, Dr. Hall's position on artificially colored lips was uncompromising. Face-painting was the work of the devil. Women who adorned their lips with paint were, in fact, engaged upon a terrible plot "to ensnare others, and to kindle a fire and flame of lust in the hearts of those who cast their eyes upon them." Nor was Hall's position thought particularly extreme. In fact he was fondly remembered by a follower writing in 1675 as "a pearl in an oyster shell."

Yet by the eighteenth century the French consumed approximately two million pots of rouge each year, of which a certain proportion was applied to lips as well as cheeks. The reason we can be sure of this figure is that an attempt was made to impose a tax on each pot at a rate of 25 *sols*, in this case to finance pensions for the widows of poor army officers. Comparable amounts of rose and patchouli scent were consumed by women of rank. Indeed, the use of cosmetics was to some extent enshrined in portraiture and, perhaps more visibly, in rococo imagery of shepherdesses and Classical deities whose cheeks, particularly when represented by François Boucher, blush not with modesty but with rouge.

When in 1716 Lady Mary Wortley Montagu passed through Hanover, she was struck by the fashions then prevailing at Court:

All the women have literally rosy cheeks, snowy foreheads and bosoms, jet eyebrows and scarlet lips to which they generally add coal black hair. These perfections never leave them until the hour of their deaths, and have a very fine effect by candlelight; but I could wish they were handsome with a little more variety. They resemble one another as much as Mrs. Salmon's Court [waxworks], and are in as much danger of melting away from too near approaching the fire, which they do for that reason carefully avoid, though it is now such excessive cold weather that I believe they suffer greatly by that piece of self-denial.

These German "jet eyebrows" were probably not shaved, but darkened with a comb made of lead, or else gall water, green vitriol, and gum arabic. However, in eighteenth-century England eyebrows *were* shaved off and replaced with arching strips of mouse-skin, dyed various colors and attached with glue. Dean Swift poked fun at "Her eyebrows from a mouse's hide/ Stuck on with art on either side," but the practice was widespread.

From time to time fashion propelled some men toward powder, pancake, and rouge. In 1754, the *Connoisseur* found it necessary to remark about numerous men of rank that the ruddiness of their countenance or complexion owed more to the application of rouge than to fitness or good health. Gentlemen, it claimed, were inclined to spend an entire morning "dressing their hair, and arching their eyebrows." Even so, the foppish "Macaronis," who founded the Macaroni Club in 1764, flourished in the 1770s and represent a startling amplification of the masculine interest in cosmetics. The *Town and Country Magazine* thought they made "a most ridiculous figure with hats an inch in the brim, that do not cover but lie upon the head, with about two pounds of fictitious hair formed into what is called a club hanging down their shoulders . . . Such a figure, essenced and perfumed with a bunch of lace sticking under its chin, puzzles the common passenger to determine the thing's sex." Ostentatious and flamboyant, the Macaroni liked to wear form-hugging trousers, colorful waistcoats, lots of braid frills, and superfluous accessories such as quizzing glasses, tassled canes, and charming nosegays. But it is the wearing of make-up that attracted most hostility: "Soft, silky coxcombs full of nice punctilio," as George Coleman put it. "All paste, pomatum, essence and pulvilio." The old American song *Yankee Doodle* in fact refers to the dandyish taste of the Macaroni, whose arrogance, languor, and various affectations were nicely captured for a new generation of enthusiasts by the popular Edwardian novelist Baroness Orczy in her 1905 creation *Sir Percy Blakeney* (also known as *The Scarlet Pimpernel*).

The most elaborate schemes and methods of cosmetic enhancement have evolved in Japan. There, bemused westerners, such as Lesley Downer, the author of a popular account of this private realm, may be astonished by the sight of a geisha, glossily coiffured, gorgeously bedecked in layers of kimono, her face "masked in dead-white powder prepared from ground nightingale droppings," the underlip "stained peony red." Downer recalls her first encounter with such a "tiny, fairy-like" geisha. "I gasped when she opened her small mouth. In the chalky-white face with the blood-red lips, her teeth were painted black. It was macabre, like looking into a black hole."

Tooth-blackening is not unique to Japan. The custom is still practiced among some tribes of the Upper Amazon basin, for example the Achual, and it is also mentioned in the *Kama Sutra* among the sixty-four cosmetic arts to which the perfect woman is expected to devote herself, in those brief periods when her attention is not entirely focused on the immediate needs and pleasures of her husband. It is relatively high on the list, at number nine: "coloring the teeth, garments, hair, nails and bodies," three notches down from tattoo-ing. Yet, nowhere did the custom of painting the teeth black send down such deep roots as it did in Japan. *Ohaguro* or *kane*, the ancient Japanese custom of tooth-blackening, evolved over centuries and, like so many other Japanese manners and customs, has meant vari-ous things at various times, some of them quite contradictory.

According to one school of thought, *ohaguro* originated in the Bud-dhist idea that white teeth reveal the animal nature of men and women and that the civilized person should conceal them, if by no other means than beneath a coating of black dye. A more pragmatic, historical explanation is that *ohaguro* was first adopted in the house-holds of samurai warriors as a measure to protect their wives and daughters from being kidnapped or raped by their enemies. In other words, the teeth were originally painted black to look rotten and, therefore, repellent. The dye was for centuries produced by scraping oxides from nails and other scraps of iron soaked in tea, *sake*, and other ingredients. Many sources agree that the practice was also thought to protect against tooth decay, and even to encourage the de-velopment of healthy teeth. This belief may well be an example of that universal tendency in the nursery, schoolroom, and dispensary to affirm that something really unpleasant is actually good for you. No wonder tongue-scraping was a prominent part of the daily toilette; the bitter taste and black stains of iron oxide must have crept into every corner of the mouth and spoiled, or at the very least radically altered, all but the strongest flavors, making a misery of eating and drinking.

In fact, for centuries right up to the nineteenth century the Japa-nese disregarded serious levels of toxicity in their cosmetics: *oshiroi*, the powder used to whiten the face, was imported from China as early as the seventh century. It consisted of *keifun*, mercury chloride, and *empaku*, white lead, and was carefully applied to the face by suc-cessive generations of aristocrats for 1,000 years; by the seventeenth century the practice had spread throughout all regions of Japan and all classes of people. The long-term effect of rubbing in these toxic chemicals does not bear thinking about, and it is hardly surprising that by comparison nightingale droppings offered a welcome alternative when, in the 1870s, the poisonous properties of lead and mercury were finally understood.

In the earliest times, the custom of tooth-blackening gradually came to symbolize the high status of those of the nobility and samurai class who practiced it; black teeth were, in effect, socially exclusive and therefore smart. Smartness duly transformed the practice into a mark of beauty. Well before the twelfth century, tooth-blackening marked a girl's coming of age. So did *okimayu*, the practice of shaving off her eyebrows and substituting painted ones; *konezumi*, a mixture of lampblack, rouge, gold leaf, and sesame oil was occasionally used, but there were plenty of other recipes and a variety of brushes and spatulas with which to apply the gooey makeup. At first these "adult" cosmetic procedures were adopted by girls of thirteen, but eventually, by the nineteenth century, the acceptable age climbed to seventeen.

Having become identified with mature women, *ohaguro* was also adopted by certain noblemen and high-ranking samurai, as well as some *geisha* and high-class prostitutes. Accounts of several twelfth-century campaigns by the armies of Yoshitsune and Noriyori mention certain courtiers who had adopted the "effeminate" custom of tooth-blackening and were thus easily identifiable by their opponents in battle. One warrior, upon removing the helmet of a slain nobleman, found his opponent to be a boy of sixteen, his face powdered, his teeth elegantly blackened.

Later, the practice of *ohaguro* was again mainly confined to women, but to women of all classes. By the eighteenth century it seems to have become almost universal, before reverting in the nineteenth century to married women only. Similarly the shaving of eyebrows was only done by brides, or by mothers following the arrival of their first-born child. By then, convenient extrapolations had been formulated according to which "the permanence of the color black" embodied in *ohaguro* "symbolised the fidelity of a married woman whose loyalty to her husband remained as constant and deep as this pigment." Symbolic exegeses of this kind, with their tendency to discover large truths in small things, typically follow in the wake of cosmetic treatments, not the other way around.

In Edo (Tokyo), only the prostitutes of the famous pleasure district of the Yoshiwara adopted the custom of *ohaguro*. At first, Yoshiwara prostitutes who wore makeup were regarded as inferior to "natural" beauties who, it was thought, had no need of it. According to one seventeenth-century account, a visitor to the Yoshiwara gasped with admiration at the sight of some of the working women, remarking to a broker: "My god, even the powdered and rouged faces of empresses and concubines of China couldn't be more beautiful." The broker replied: "Don't you know that they use cosmetics to hide their inferior faces? Besides these women, there are incomparably beautiful courtesans called *osho*, who are true natural beauties, who know nothing of cosmetics. Their faces are more beautiful than flowers and the moon!" One hundred years later, a nostalgic samurai, Hara Budayu (d. 1776 or 1792), mourned the passing of the good old days, when

> prostitutes considered it unattractive to make up their faces with rouge and powder, and even those high-class courtesans who put on light makeup for trips to the *ageya* were scorned as "common." The high-ranking courtesan's hair was casually and simply combed, and tied in a *Hyogo* knot, and only this characteristic hairstyle and the light rouge on their toenails and the beautiful slippers that hid their toes set courtesans apart from ordinary townswomen. But now, their fashion is to plaster their hair with grease. They display seven or eight decorated hairpins, and wear two or three huge

combs that look like cleats of wooden clogs. It is difficult to distinguish them from the toy peddler, or large *Benkei* dolls at festivals.

The practice of *ohaguro* is an excellent example of an inherent contradiction in Japanese etiquette, for to visiting westerners one of the most conspicuous outward manifestations of modesty, particularly among women, is the gesture of covering the mouth to conceal a smile or even a titter. Indeed, the mouth is carefully hidden for a variety of other reasons, when picking the teeth, for example—not a habit confined to Japanese manners. According to another authority, the mouth is hidden "to avoid polluting the atmosphere with one's breath," a phrase somewhat over-laden with that brand of deference that in Japan strays toward self-abasement.

What then does it mean to foster an elaborate cosmetic enhancement such as *ohaguro* when the very features it is there to adorn, the teeth, are customarily hidden from view? Why did Japanese women apply delicate rouge to their toenails, only to conceal them inside gorgeous slippers? Why did they shave off their eyebrows, only to reapply them in paint composed of anything from black soil or lampblack to the soot produced by burning ears of Indian rice? These ambiguities are not unknown to the West, although nowadays the international cosmetics business, which likes to use words such as "enhance," "soften," "define" or "accentuate," would in all likelihood prefer not to think of women plucking out one by one the hairs of their eyebrows, or shaving them off, only to draw them on again with a pencil. They would wish to see the process as a way of making real features look more beautiful, not as a way of substituting synthetic ones.

In *ukiyo-e*, or Japanese woodblock prints, particularly the subgenre that is devoted to *bijin* or "beauties," the curious balancing act between exposing and concealing blackened teeth is generally handled by reducing the size of the mouth to the tiniest scale. In a series of prints by Tsukioka Yoshitoshi entitled *Bijin Shichiyōka* (*Beauties and the Seven Flowers*), each elaborately dressed and coiffured single-figure subject is paired with a different botanical companion. In one, *Yanigihara Aiko* (that most beautiful of all sights in Japan, the *Cherry Tree*, when the blossoms arrive in the first two weeks in March) (Fig. 3.2), a beautiful woman reaches up and breaks off a bough laden with gorgeous buds and blossoms. Her makeup is ghostly white, apparently caked on thickly according to the manner prevailing in the third quarter of the nineteenth century, her mouth is exceedingly small, and the lips are slightly parted to reveal a neat row of tiny, jet-black teeth. No attempt is made to hide or conceal them, other than to reduce their scale almost to the point of invisibility compared with the pair of broad eyebrows (each one twice as wide as the mouth), to say nothing of the nose and ears (all three times as long as the mouth is wide). Of course, Japanese mouths are no larger or smaller than any other sort of human mouth, but the conventions of *bijin* persuade us that elegant mouths are minuscule.

The Japanese draw from a deep well of ambiguity and indirectness. It penetrates the bedrock of their language in which the simple word and idea "yes" is shunned in favor of such fantastic convolutions as "one might think that it would not be incorrect to say so." Indeed, westerners who do business in Japan are occasionally given the sage advice never "to take a smile for yes" and never "to take yes for an answer." One European visitor, a scholar of linguistics, was baffled to find that communication by sign language was almost impossible in Japan, that all his attempts at wordless communication were greeted with a smile or a "blank stare," or else by looking away. It was explained to him that his interlocutors smiled or looked with a blank stare because he was a westerner, a person to whom deference was owed. Those who smiled did so for one of two reasons: to show respect, in spite of their inability to understand what he was

Figure 3.2 Tsukioka Yoshitoshi (1839–1892), *Yanigihara Aiko (The Cherry Tree)*, 1878, woodblock print from the series *Bijin Shichiyōka (Beauties and the Seven Flowers)*, 13¼ × 9¹⁄₁₆ in. Philadelphia Museum of Art, Gift of Sidney A. Tannenbaum.

frantically gesturing about; or because they were embarrassed at not understanding or at not being able to respond helpfully as the situation required.

As well, in Japan turning the eyes away is a mark of respect, as if the person finds you so awesome that he must turn away to avoid being blinded by your radiance (another example of what non-Japanese might think of as an almost embarrassingly deferential concept). To avert the eyes, to turn them downwards, or even to turn the entire head away are typical gestures by which the Japanese handle each delicate encounter with somebody to whom they are persuaded by conventions ancient and modern that deference is due.

The most obvious form of modesty or physical concealment is the Muslim custom of purdah, which means *curtain*. From the eighteenth century Europeans in general, and many artists in particular, were fascinated by the idea of the veil, and the life of the harem. The pictures they painted for a burgeoning, metropolitan picture-buying public only partly satisfied a growing demand for glimpses of a hidden world of luxury and opulence that was known only through travelers' tales. Statuesque bathers (called odalisques) and other nude subjects proliferated in large numbers, together with scenes of the bazaar, latticed interiors, and enclosed gardens. In many instances the erotic dimension of this species of Orientalist image, particularly in colder climates, was frank and unambiguous, and the demand for pictures of this kind was obviously driven by a strong desire to lift the veil, to see behind screens, to peer into secret places.

In its strictest form, purdah not only conceals from view the entire face and body of a woman, but also, through various kinds of seclusion, removes her from many kinds of day-to-day social interaction that we take for granted in the West. In recent times, largely owing to the Taliban rulers of Afghanistan, we have come to see purdah as cruelly repressive, but this is only one side of the story—a story often told by the western media with depressing one-dimensionality. The practice exists in many forms and many places. It has advocates as well as detractors. It is not only practiced in many parts of the Muslim world, but by many Hindus as well. It is exceedingly widespread. Bedouin women wear a *burqa*, or face-masking veil, which entirely conceals their faces but for slits or perforations through which they may see out (without being seen to do so). Images of similar costumes were seen very frequently during the recent war in Afghanistan.

In parts of Baluchistan, however, which is situated between Iran and Pakistan, not far from the mouth of the Persian Gulf, the local style of burqa reveals a good deal of the wearer's face, hiding only the upper lip, the eyebrows and the bridge of the nose. The eyes are exposed, as are the cheeks and the chin. In Malaysia and in Indonesia, the largest Muslim nation, the most common form of veil is a large headscarf, which covers the head and neck but leaves a convenient porthole for the whole face. There are many other variations.

In some places, such as the Punjab, purdah has obvious socio-economic implications because only relatively prosperous families can afford to segregate women in their own part of the house, and many poor families must obviously adapt to more practical realities, quite apart from the hard manual labor that makes wearing the burqa or an equivalent head covering or veil very inconvenient. This class distinction is quite ancient and existed among wealthy households in the Muslim world. Yet in many Bengali and Pakistani villages the practice of wearing the burqa is today upheld with greater determination by poorer families than by the rich; the same applies in Egypt, where on the whole women in purdah are more likely to be poor. Wealthier women continue to eschew it.

In fact, purdah has its roots in pre-Islamic antiquity and was practiced widely around the Mediterranean, though not, it seems, among the Egyptians or the Jews. According to tradition, the wives of Mohammed wore the burqa as a sign of their high status, and to set them apart from the large crowds who congregated around him. There are various prescriptions set out in the Koran (c. 610–620 A.D.) but most of these provide no more than a basic set of principles relating to the overall status of women, many of them genuinely enlightened. The most explicit passage relating to the concept of modesty comes in Sura 24 (*Light*), verses 30–31, where the main concern

is to define the degrees of kinship and affinity within which concealment (or purdah) among women need not occur. The only explicit
reference to physical veiling applies to the bosom, and not to the
face, though it is not hard to see how concealment of the face might
eventually follow from the stipulation that women "should lower
their gaze and guard their modesty."

No matter where we see it, the westerner is today obliged to see
purdah from the point of view of an outsider. We do not look into
the face of a woman who wears the burqa, we do not see her smile,
and we are not aware that she may wear lipstick like many western
women (as in Iran), simply because we are by convention prevented
from looking. We dislike the fact that an entire set of customs, upheld by millions, automatically prevents us from peering into the
face of another person. For obvious reasons we resent the idea that a
young woman may not see or be seen by anyone she chooses outside
the domestic sphere, while a young man may do as he pleases. But
we are also troubled by the thought that those who uphold the practice of purdah may see us as unwelcome, threatening intruders who
cast about for people, things, and places, not fearing to look at what
they think we should not.

The vulgar often laugh, but never smile; whereas well-bred people often smile, but seldom laugh.

THE EARL OF CHESTERFIELD, February 17, 1754

The intrepid Saxon race likes to mock at everything which inspires man with a feeling of fear. Illness, death, the hangman, the gibbet, the terrors of the natural and supernatural world, become to him a subject for buffoonery in conversation and on the stage. "The English laugh, as if in defiance, and ridicule everything," one of them said to me, "excepting money losses."

ALPHONSE ESQUIROS, *The English at Home*, 1861

─────────────────── ⊱✶⊰ ───────────────────

4

Mirth

Dr. Samuel Johnson once complained that during the long years spent laboring over his great *Dictionary* (1755) and despite having dedicated his "Plan" to him, Lord Chesterfield, the man he hoped might be his patron, never offered "one Act of assistance, one word of encouragement, or one smile of favor." The rebuke was especially stinging since Chesterfield's opinions about the desirability of smiling as opposed to the offensiveness of laughter were widely known. "How low and unbecoming a thing laughter is," he wrote to his son on March 9, 1748, "not to mention the disagreeable noise that it makes, and the shocking distortion of the face that it occasions. . . . I am neither of a melancholy nor a cynical disposition, and am as willing and as apt to be pleased as anybody; but I am sure that, since I have had the full use of my reason, nobody has ever heard me laugh." He went on: "Having mentioned laughing, I must particularly warn you against it; and I could heartily wish that you may often be seen to smile, but never heard to laugh, while you live. Frequent and loud laughter is the characteristic of folly and ill manners: it is the manner in which the mob express their silly joy at silly things, and they call it being merry. In my mind there is nothing so illiberal and so ill-bred as audible laughter." In turn, Dr. Johnson did not think much of the mountains of advice Chesterfield offered in his much-publicized volumes of *Letters*. In his characteristically forthright way, he thought they taught "the morals of a whore and the manners of a dancing-master" and did not hesitate to say so. (To be fair, Lord Chesterfield took the abuse with good humor and proudly showed Johnson's written fulminations to his friends.)

What is the relationship between smiling and laughter? Chesterfield's sharp distinction between the two was in line with the consensus of opinion among seventeenth- and eighteenth-century physiognomists such as the Swiss theologian and poet Johann Caspar Lavater, a friend of Goethe and of the Romantic artist Henry Fuseli, also a Swiss. An abridgement or digest of Lavater—and in turn of his seventeenth-century predecessor, the French academician Charles Le Brun—which was compiled for children in 1815 by George Brewer reflected the views of the previous centuries:

> Laughter is produced by joy mixed with surprise, the eyebrows rise towards the middle of the eye, and bend downwards towards the side of the nose. The eyes are almost shut, and sometimes appear wet or shed tears, which make no alteration in the face. The mouth, half open,

shews the teeth; the corners of the mouth drawn back, cause a wrin-
kle in the cheeks, which appear so swelled as in some measure to hide
the eyes; the nostrils are open and all the face is of a red color. Laughter is at all times ungraceful, therefore you will observe, that vulgar
people are most addicted to it: well-bred persons manage this passion
better; they seldom do anything more than smile.

Brewer's text combined observations made much earlier by Le
Brun—whose famous 1668 lecture on expression ran to sixty-three
editions—with the adverse judgments of the Chesterfield tradition.
The arching brows, eyes almost shut, teeth exposed, swollen cheeks,
tears, and redness all come from Le Brun, who by placing laughter
immediately after joy in his sequence of expressions clearly stopped
short of condemning it.

Yet the story was not quite so clear-cut in a slightly earlier passage
in which Brewer described the facial expression called "joy with
tranquility." Here, "very little alteration is remarked in the face of
those who feel within themselves the sweetness of *Joy*. The forehead
is serene; the eyebrows without motion, elevated in the middle; the
eye pretty open, and with a laughing air; the eyeball lively and shining; the corners of the mouth turn up a little; the complexion lively;
the cheek and lips red." What are we to make, then, of a largely pejorative view of fully blown, red-faced laughter, and a calm and evidently more desirable state in which redness is tolerated in the
cheeks and lips, and the eye alone exhibits a "laughing air"?

Lavater was one of the most important scholars who popularized
the scientific study of the muscular composition and mechanical
functions of the human face, drawing on a tradition of speculation
that extended as far back as Aristotle. The publication of Lavater's
four-volume book, *Physiognomical Fragments* (1775–1778), was pro-
foundly influential throughout Europe; indeed it made him famous.
He wanted to investigate the relationship between the anatomy of

the head and the emotional significance of the face, the better to understand the capacity of both to be read cogently and, of course, usefully. Like Le Brun, Lavater believed that the human face was a deep well of information from which important meaning with deep moral implications could be extracted.

Lavater's ideas attracted the interest of many artists and art critics, most obviously because they were directly relevant to the methods by which faces were drawn and painted from life, and frequently improved upon. The flow of ideas may well have traveled in the opposite direction as well. Lavater particularly admired the work of the Englishman William Hogarth, whose great series of satirical prints such as *The Rake's Progress* (1735) seemed to embody the moralizing flavor of his own work. Indeed Hogarth's theoretical treatise called *The Analysis of Beauty* (1753) was strongly influenced by Charles Le Brun and has much to say about physiognomic meaning.

Hogarth was in no doubt that the face was, in his words, "the index of the mind." "How often is it said," he asked,

> that such a one looks like a good-nature'd man, that he hath an honest open countenance, or looks like a cunning rogue; a man of sense, or a fool, &c? And how are our eyes riveted to the aspects of kings and heroes, murderers and saints; and as we contemplate their deeds, seldom fail making application to their looks. It is reasonable to believe that aspect to be a true and legible representation of the mind, which gives every one the same idea at first sight; and is afterwards confirm'd in fact: for instance, all concur in the same opinion, at first sight, of a down-right idiot.

But by what mechanism did that particular conjunction of physical features convey the notion of "idiot"? The infinite variety of the human face, Hogarth thought, depended on the pattern and distribution of lines and creases, hardly a surprising conclusion coming from a draughtsman, printmaker, and caricaturist. Infants, whose faces consist mostly of simple forms and relatively few lines, have as a result "an uninformed and unmeaning stare, an open mouth, and simple grin," such as are generally retained by idiots in later life.

Moreover, the lines of the face can by their shape and distribution produce confusing effects like a "pretty frown" or a "disagreeable smile." The lines that "form a pleasing smile about the corners of the mouth have gentle windings . . . but lose their full beauty in the full laugh." The expression of "excessive laughter, oftener than any other, gives a sensible face a silly or disagreeable look, as it is apt to form regular plain lines about the mouth, like a parenthesis, which sometimes appears like crying." As an example, Hogarth remembered once seeing a wan country beggar who wore on his face "a grin of pain and misery," an expression apparently calculated to win sympathy but which looked more like a "joyous laugh."

Finally, Hogarth concluded, nature has unfortunately given to the human face many lines and shapes that indicate "deficiencies and blemishes of the mind," while providing none at all that point to its perfections "beyond the appearance of common sense and placidity." So while some faces positively scream "idiot" or "murderer," others tend not to reveal a person's qualities of wisdom, wit, humanity, generosity, mercy, or courage. For these instead one must rely upon deportment, words, and actions—in other words, behavior.

By the time Lavater published his book, the study of physiognomy and phrenology had already generated a large and cumbersome literature, upon which William Hogarth and many others had drawn freely. What distinguished the contribution of Lavater and a few of his contemporaries was that they succeeded in propelling this highly speculative subject into the biological sciences. There it remained, doing more harm than good, for well over 100 years. Indeed scientific minds in the nineteenth century continued to ask questions about character and morals that were to be found in the old literature of physiognomy.

A remarkable series of experiments was conducted, photographed, and later published in Paris by a doctor, Guillaume-Benjamin Duchenne de Boulogne, under the title *Mechanism of Human Physiognomy, or Electro-physiological Analysis of the Expression of the Passions* (1862). Duchenne used electrical currents passing between electrodes to trigger in human subjects a very wide variety of facial expressions ranging from hysteria to coquettishness, from surprise to excruciating agony, documenting each effect in the photographs. By this method Duchenne attempted to analyze the capacity of human anatomy to convey emotion.

What anatomists had hitherto known simply as the muscle that pulls upward the corner of the mouth, *zygomaticus major*, thus became Duchenne's "muscle of joy." *Orbicularis oculi*, the muscle that raises the cheek and crinkles the skin around the outer corner of the eye, was the "muscle of benevolence," and so on. The action of the *modiolus, risorius, platysma,* and *depressor* muscles were likewise tested, documented, and photographed, always with the aim of bridging the gap between the mechanics of the face and its capacity for eloquence. Lavater, Hogarth, and Duchenne were not particularly interested in how faces ought to look; their inquiries were mainly concerned with the interpretation of every possible attitude and expression in the human face. One gets the impression that they were more interested in fiends and idiots than what the optimum facial expression of a mirthful soul might look like.

Today we tend to ignore the eighteenth-century distinction between smiling and laughter made by Lord Chesterfield and others. We may recognize many situations in which the smile is a silent prelude to the more intense physical and sound-producing experience of laughter. These are many and various and we often sense that they form a continuum. We also recognize the obvious similarities between a face that is smiling and the disposition of the same face when laughing. Photographs further underline the point, since they remove sound and motion from the formula and freeze the laughing face in its most smile-like aspect, mouth open.

Curiously, in the English language there is no etymological link between the words for smiling and laughter. To speakers of the Romance languages this is especially mystifying because there and, indeed, elsewhere, the relationship is directly spelled out. The Latin verb *subrideo, -ere* or *surrideo, -ere*, to smile, is merely a qualified form of the verb *rideo, -ere*, to laugh, and clearly indicates by means of that crucial prefix that smiling is preliminary to laughter or that it is suppressed laughter or that the two states at least stand in some such close relationship, which everybody knows. The Italian words *sorriso* and *sorridere*, the French *souris* and *sourire*, the Spanish *sonrisa* and *sonreír (se)* necessarily follow suit. German has also retained an obvious link between the verb *lächeln*, to smile, and *lachen*, to laugh, that was for some unknown reason never adopted by the English language in its earliest forms.

Like the most ancient English words, the verb *to smile*, which according to the *Oxford English Dictionary* means "to give to the features or face a look expressive of pleasure or amusement, or of amused disdain, scorn, etc.," has close relations in Middle English (*smīlen*), Old and Middle High German (*smîlan, smîlenter* and *smielen*). There are related words in Danish, as well as in Swedish and Norwegian. The *OED* thinks that these last were adopted from Middle Low German, which may well have provided the immediate ancestor of the English word.

In the beginning a wide variety of spellings was used at different times and in different places, for example *smyle, smale, smyl, smylle, smyll, smill, smoyle* and *smoile*, though the weirder ones do tend to occur in Scotland. At the same time, the noun *smile*, meaning the act of smiling that we read on a person's face as a result of a movement of their countenance—the *OED* defines it as more or less involuntary and "expressive of pleasure, amusement, affection, etc., or of amused contempt, disdain, incredulity, or similar emotion"—likewise descends from the

Middle High German *smile*, the Swedish and Norwegian *smil*, or an identical word in Danish.

Now, the verb *to smile* acquired some additional meanings early in its life. It spawned the noun *smiler* almost at once; this, meaning a person who smiles a lot, or too much, is to be found in Chaucer's *The Knight's Tale*. At the beginning of the fifteenth century, *to smyle* could also mean to smile *at* someone or something. As well, to *smile on* or *upon* someone or something meant to look upon it with favor, approval, or encouragement; this meaning is still current, though gradually passing out of use. It is unlikely that today's presidents, prime ministers, or chief executive officers would tell their staff that they were prepared to smile on such and such a measure, though it seems likely that the usage would not have seemed especially contrived or pompous fifty years ago.

By the sixteenth century, *to smile* could mean to bring or convert or transform something into a specified condition, whatever that may be. A good example is Maria's memorable remark about the ridiculous Malvolio in Shakespeare's *Twelfth Night*, who "does smile his face into more lines than are in the new map with the augmentation of the Indies." As well, in the sixteenth century, *to smile* could simply mean to have or present an agreeable aspect, again, whatever that may mean (that is, not necessarily involving a particular movement of the lips or mouth), or else to dismiss or get rid of something, that is *to smile it away*. In the seventeenth century, the story becomes even more interesting in that *to smile* could mean to answer or respond or repeat by smiling, or else to exhibit, indicate, or express by smiling. The seventeenth century bequeathed to us the adjective *smileful*; it was not until the eighteenth century that *smileless* (*smyless*), meaning wan, came into being. No wonder that by the eighteenth and nineteenth centuries we find that *smile* had, as if by slight of hand, been turned back into a verb that applied exclusively to the particular action that produces a smile, namely *to smile a smile*. The word had come full circle. Further contortions were attempted, such as *smiling-ness* (by Lord Byron, no less) and the grotesque *smilefulness*, but fortunately neither took root, though their source, the gerund *smiling*, and the adverb derived from it, *smilingly*, are both exceedingly old.

None of these *smile* words is nearly as ancient as *smirk* and *smirking*, which were well established in Old English (where the form is *smerian*), and its predecessors. *Smirk* appears to be unrelated to comparable words in any cognate language. The similarity with the Sanskrit word for smiling (*smáyate*, he laughs) seems altogether too remote to be taken seriously, although a tenuous but scholarly argument has been mounted in support of a firm link via Greek (*meidios*, *meidian*, laugh), to Old Slavonic (*smìjo sê*, *smijati sê*, laugh), and thence to German (*schmieren*, smile). And it is true that stranger migrations of words than this have been documented. In any case, despite their lack of resemblance to *smirk*, the earliest forms of that word, *smearcian* and *smercian*, are, for reasons that we had better not dwell on here, nevertheless true Old English ancestors, and they make their first appearance as early as the ninth century A.D. It is not possible to find a more indigenous English word. (Later Scottish dialect borrowed *smirk*, adapting it for a roguish half-smile and, quite specifically, a flirtatious smile, whence, in the late nineteenth century in the northeast, it ended up meaning a kiss. Scots also has the marvelous word *smirl*, reduced from *smirtle*, which means a sneer, a smile of mockery, or a snigger—all three, and presumably anything in between.)

With the arrival of the newer, imported *smile* words, the far older expression *smirk* was nudged sideways, and its meaning changed from smiling in general to that particular kind of affected, self-satisfied, or silly smile that we associate with the modern word *smirk*—a sad fate, undeserved. Something similar happened to the word *leer*, whose form in Old English (*hléor*, *hlíor*, and so forth) is found as early as the eleventh century, and for centuries simply referred to the face or countenance, and hence the look or appearance of the face. Only much later did this useful word acquire the sense of a side glance, "a look or roll of the eye expressive of slyness, malignity, immodest desire, etc."

Another ancient word has a history similar to *smirk*, though its original meaning was different. *Grin* first appeared in Old English about 1000 A.D., and originally meant to draw back the lips and show the teeth in pain or anger, *or* a smile. It was certainly related to the Old and Middle High German words *grennan*, to mutter or grunt, and *grennen*, to wail or to grin. Meanwhile the Old Norse *grenja* meant to howl and the Old Swedish *gränia* meant almost the same thing, to roar. Not surprisingly all these words found frequent application among Vikings and other fearsome seafaring peoples from whom the English language has descended. The interesting thing about the Old English *grin* is that it applied equally to men and animals and, not unlike that later arrival *smile*, gave rise to numerous related words and phrases such as *grinagog*, one who grins incessantly.

There is one further usage that is genuinely baffling from a social or anthropological point of view. Consider the following brief report about a strange contest in Yorkshire that was published in London in *The Times* newspaper on June 11, 1804:

> A grinning-match lately took place at Bridlington, for a quantity of tobacco. There were three competitors for the prize, all of whom were speedily seized with the most painful symptoms, in consequence of their violent contortions, and two of them died in a few days; the third lies dangerously ill.

Grinning matches or grotesque face-making contests were well established more than one hundred years earlier, when Joseph Addison devoted an entire issue of the *Spectator* to them, and there is no reason to doubt that their origins are ancient, although virtually no record of their earlier existence has survived, except a few rare engravings that appear to allude to something similar (Fig. 4.1). Addison's attention

FIGURE 4.1 Unknown engraver, late sixteenth–early seventeenth century, *Head of a Jester, c.* 1600, engraving on paper, 15¾ × 11 in. Art Gallery of Ontario, Toronto; Gift of the Trier–Fodor Foundation, 1985.

had been drawn to an advertisement in the *Post-Boy* (September 11, 1711, and again on September 15) for a day of horse and ass racing at Coleshill Heath in Warwickshire. On the same day, said the ad, a Gold Ring was "to be Grinn'd for by Men." This valuable prize, wrote Addison,

has raised such an Ambition among the Common People of Out-grinning one another, that many very discerning Persons are afraid it should spoil most of the Faces in the Country; and that a *Warwick-shire* Man will be known by his Grinn, as Roman Catholics imagine a *Kentish* Man is by his Tail. The Gold Ring which is made the Prize of Deformity, is just the Reverse of the Golden Apple that was formerly made the Prize of Beauty, and should carry for its Posie the old motto inverted.

Detur tetriori

Or, to accommodate it to the capacity of the combatants,

The frightfull'st Grinner,

Be the winner.

In the mean while I would advise a *Dutch* painter to be present at this great Controversy of Faces, in order to make a collection of the most remarkable Grinns that shall there be exhibited.

It is not clear from the rest of Addison's account (see Appendix, pp. 167–169), which goes on to describe various hideous contestants, whether grinning matches always took place at race meetings, or whether this event was exceptional. Later in the eighteenth century, the grinning match was apparently performed by two or more people, each with their head thrust through a horse's collar. Nor is it clear how such contests were arranged, conducted, or brought to any conclusion; Addison mentioned that a Whig justice of the peace, the donor of another prize on a different occasion, disqualified an entrant, a Jacobite, for refusing to swear an oath. Yet the winner appears to have been chosen by acclamation, presumably drunken.

Nevertheless, grinning matches made their way into the figure of speech *to grin through a horse's collar*, meaning to grin lewdly. By the third quarter of the nineteenth century, the *horse's collar* stood for unacceptable or indecent humor; it was said that when one encountered the poorest sort of jokes, the horse's collar was not far off. A report in the Bow Street column of *The Times* on September 20, 1833, a generation after Bridlington, mentions the strange case of a young shopkeeper, a Mr. Cave, who was dragged before the chief magistrate of Bow Street for causing a crowd to assemble outside a penny show-room in High Holborn for the purpose of picking pockets—so alleged his accuser, a Mr. Symonds. It seemed that Mr. Cave had stopped outside Mr. Symonds's premises and, tickled by something in the window, possibly a waxwork, "burst into a loud fit of laughter, which naturally attracted the attention of passers-by, and as laughing is said to be contagious, the persons assembled soon joined in the merriment, and a general horse-laugh was raised, without any visible motive to induce it." The chief magistrate, Sir Frederick Roe, ascertained that Mr. Cave was not intoxicated, heard his indignant protest at being accused of picking pockets, admonished him for being foolish, and fined him five shillings.

Today, a form of grinning match has survived in Cumbria in the north of England, where a weird activity called *girning* or *gurning* (the word is derived from Scottish dialect) still takes place in pubs and other public places, namely the making of grotesque faces by people with no teeth. The commonest form of hideous face is made by jutting the mandible forward and forcing it up and over the maxilla; not having any teeth makes this a relatively straightforward proposition. At the same time the muscles of the cheeks and lips, and sometimes even the nose itself, are gathered or sucked in behind the protruding mandible. These effects are grotesquely disfiguring, and especially thrilling to small children.

Lewd smiling, smirking, and grinning enjoy a longstanding and continuous association with the penumbral zones of society in which certain of the vices have at one time or another been permitted to flourish. In fact, it is clear from even the most cursory glance at any dictionary that of the many senses in which the English words *smile*, *smirk*, and *grin* have descended to us from earlier usage and word forms—to say nothing of their equivalents in other languages—a surprising number have nothing at all to do with happiness, pleasure, good cheer, empathetic communication, or affection. On the contrary, many clearly relate to craftiness, mockery, greed, cynicism, malevolence, gloating, and plain lewdness. The relevant page of any number of literary concordances will attest to this. For example, the works of Jean-Jacques Rousseau contain numerous references to the smile and to smiling dramatis personae, but a relatively high proportion of them smile "*malignement*" (malignly); "*dédaigneusement*" (disdainfully); or "*malicieusement*" (maliciously). One is to be seen "*souriant toujours, ne riant jamais*" (always smiling but never laughing), as if the absence of laughter somehow makes the smile the lesser half of some incomplete thing. There are references to smiles that are "*amer*" (bitter), "*sardonique*" (sardonic), and even "*insultant et moquer*" (insulting, to mock). There is one reference only, in the *Confessions*, to "*un sourire angelique.*" To some of these senses I shall return at greater length.

In various contexts, particularly in nineteenth-century underworld slang in English on both sides of the Atlantic, *smile* meant drink (alcoholic), both as a noun and as a verb. Most commonly *to smile* meant to drink whisky or bourbon. A *smiler* was by extension the same as a *bumper*, a kind of glass; the *OED* defines the same word as a kind of shandy-gaff, that is, a drink made from mixing beer and ginger beer. The much older, seventeenth-century English expression *to smile like a brewer's horse* is more or less self-explanatory, though it has also been explained, for the benefit of more gentrified readers, that "a brewer's horse thrives on its food and the circumambient odor of hops." In certain English regional dialects, meanwhile, *to smile* meant to ferment, and a *smile* or *smail* meant the foaming "head" on beer, especially in Yorkshire. In the same part of England, a *smiler* is the largest and heaviest hammer in the blacksmith's shop, while in Lincolnshire the same word is used for a red-hot poker, both expressions possibly derived from the traditional effects of a bad hangover. Also in Yorkshire *to smirk* meant not merely to smile a kind of suppressed half-smile, but to beat or slap. The same verb was used in Kent to describe a vigorous method of getting creases out of linen. In Norfolk *smile* was used to describe a kind of trap for hares, or else a gap in a fence dug and used by rabbits, though these expressions may have evolved from the Anglo-Saxon *smygela*, the word for a burrow or a place to creep into. In Middle English wine that "shall *smyle*" is wine that has been well made or kept; the *smyler* in Chaucer's *The Knight's Tale* is a dissembler "with the knyf under the cloke."

It is not hard to see how the gentle crescent shape that is generally drawn by children to describe the upturned corners of the smiling mouth has inevitably contributed to the filtration of smile words into ever-widening idioms. These range over great varieties of subject matter. For example, in the United States *smile* has occasionally been used for the suety midriff exposed between shirt and trouser, a definition that acquired an erotic charge when, in due course, it came to refer to the more suggestive, flesh-disclosing gap between stocking and garter-belt (American, prior to World War II). As a neologism noted in 1993 by the *OED*, *smiling* means a process connected with electrophoresis, the migration of colloidal or gluey, as distinct from crystalline, particles suspended in a liquid under the influence of an electric current. The terms *smile* and *smirk* are also used in that branch of economics that concerns techniques of financial estimation and forecasting. In this instance, the term was suggested by the shape of a line on a graph. The French use *souris* to describe the "small, sweet, rounded [flavorsome and quite delicious] piece of meat at the knuckle end of a leg of lamb or mutton." An unhappier and, fortunately, now completely vanished slang usage of *smiler* for boiled beef was adopted between about 1860 and 1914 by the boys of Cotton College, near Stoke-on-Trent, apparently prompted by the atrocious quality of a particular dish that was thought to be reminiscent of a poor, weary old horse whose name was *Smiler*.

One of the most interesting senses of *smile* that belongs, as it were, to the pejorative, rather than the affirmative family of definitions, came to Britain from the United States in the 1890s. *I should smile* is a kind of vulgarism that, judging from the brief but detailed essays that accompanied it into various dictionaries, was for many years evidently regarded as an ephemeral product of humorous small-talk. Yet it endured as a sardonic way of signaling acquiescence with, and ridiculing, the preceding statement. Eric Partridge illustrated the term with some lines in a play by one Charles H. Hoyt, *A Bunch of Keys; or, The Hotel* of 1883. In Act III, the following exchange takes place at the front desk:

> SNAG: Do you require a room?
> P. F.: You bet.
> SNAG: Single room?
> P. F.: Well, I should smile.

What would P. F. need a double room for? The sense here is evidently jocular. *I should smile* crossed the Atlantic, and was occasionally heard in Britain between the two World Wars. However, it appears to have undergone a fascinating transformation into the related expression *I should worry*, meaning "I'm certainly not worrying about that!" In a curious twist, it was thought that this expression had migrated from the United States, which is certainly true, but that it had been borrowed or adapted from the Yiddish. Certainly the possibility of using *I should smile* or *I should worry* ironically suggests that this assumption was partly correct. The Yiddish for *smile* is *shmeichel* or *shmeichlen*, but apart from the phonetic similarity there is no direct evidence of any link. Meanwhile, H. L. Mencken noticed that something odd had happened to *I should worry* after it had settled into regular use in Britain. It gradually turned into the entirely unironic *I should not worry*, occasionally tacking on the subjunctive coda *if I were you*. I am quite sure that this later form was, in turn, the springboard for a unique Australianism, *no worries!*, that

breezy and, at times, irritating injunction much favored by shop-
keepers and tradesmen who, wishing to banish all doubts from the
mind of the customer, merely cause them to multiply.

The idea that smiling and laughter form a continuum, or a kind of
bridge from one mental state to the next, can be deceptive, for some
behavioral scientists have long argued that although smiling and
laughter often seem to converge in human behavior, that convergence actually conceals completely different phyletic or evolutionary origins. According to one team of scientists at the University of
Washington in Seattle, "smiling and laughter were originally two
different displays in nonhuman primates" that have merged in humans, "smiling having its origins in the silent bared-teeth submissive
grimace of primates and laughter evolving from the relaxed open-
mouth display of play." Consequently, among children laughter is far
more readily associated with the rough and tumble of play, while discrete smiling, stopping short of laughter, appears to be more often
held in reserve for that cluster of behaviors that are held to be more
directly communicative, face-to-face.

As we have seen, some languages treat the word for smile merely
as a qualified form of the word laughter. Unlike Greek, which had
separate words for smile and laugh, Medieval Latin had some difficulty creating out of the word *rideo*, I laugh, a satisfactory definition
of *subrideo*, which for centuries did not mean *I smile* so much as suppressed or secret laughter, sniggering, or "laughing up one's sleeve."
As the French historian Jacques Le Goff has pointed out, it was only
after a long period of gestation that, in about the twelfth century
A.D., *subrideo* came to mean *I smile*, a state wholly distinct from the
physical and sound-producing experience of laughter. We shall see
in the next chapter that echoes of this change reverberate in nearly
contemporaneous sculpture.

Laughter is mostly involuntary, and produces noise. The types of
sound we make when we laugh have only recently been studied in

any detail, largely thanks to the improved analytical possibilities of accurate sound-recording equipment. Clearly, the way we produce the sounds of laughter is far more complicated than the stock formulas of "ha-ha," "ho-ho," or "tee-hee." Seal-bark, sustained machine-gun, high-pitched, nasal, bell-like or musical, baboon-screech, gutteral, or grunting laughter are commonplace, and may be heard in any public bar, particularly later in the evening, as well as laughter that clearly continues to grip the utterer long after his breath is spent and the sound dries up, only to resume upon taking a deep breath. The way we start off, bursting suddenly or spontaneously into loud guffaws or instead taking a long run-up, shifting from mild titters through an accelerating peal to the hearty crescendo of what the show-business newspaper *Variety* calls "yocks," further complicates the picture. So does the manner in which some people crow or add nonverbal groans or nonverbal protestations, as if to acknowledge their helpless exposure to some foreign, irresistible force welling up inside. The amplitude, volume, duration, rapidity and rhythms, the intensity of laughter "peaks," and their relationship with the utterer's corresponding patterns of speech have been analyzed in some detail and confirm what many people observe every day, namely, that the longer we laugh the louder we become. Also, the number and intensity of laughs we produce in each bout of laughter correspond with the number of syllables we group together in a spoken sentence or utterance, and the rate at which we project them. The way we laugh is somehow tied to the way we speak.

Laughter produces unique breathing patterns that have been described in one psychophysiological study as "an abrupt, strong expiration" followed by "a series of expiratory–inspiratory microcycles superimposed upon the larger expiratory movements." In other words, the hyphens that separate the "*ha*" elements of "*ha-ha-ha*" and, in effect, prevent laughter from sounding like "*haaaaaaa*," stand for little convulsions in our breathing pattern, rather like serrations, over which we have very little control. An accompanying phenomenon is the tremor that, above and beyond the odd way we breathe when laughing, makes our shoulders heave and our tummy muscles hurt and in various other ways "quake" with laughter, sometimes convulsively so. One traveler to Africa in the 1960s observed Pygmies fall on the ground and kick their legs in the air, wholly possessed by paroxysms of breathless laughter, though he does not say if he himself was the butt of the joke. (Other ethnographers say they can easily draw on a map a line dividing Papuan hilarity, with wild bodily expression, from Melanesian dourness, which largely reflects some tribes' belief that laughter is essentially derogatory.)

In these respects laughter is an entirely different proposition from the smile and has long been thought to have beneficial or therapeutic effects as a kind of valve to release nervous tension—or, of course, by Freud, as the discharge of "a sum of psychic energy." Charles Darwin was aware of this basic idea and, in the following passage, cited in support of it his colleague the philosopher Herbert Spencer, who coined the familiar phrase "survival of the fittest":

> If the mind is strongly excited by pleasurable feelings, and any little unexpected event or thought occurs, then, as Mr. Herbert Spencer remarks, "a large amount of nervous energy, instead of being allowed to expend itself in producing an equivalent amount of the new thoughts and emotion which were nascent, is suddenly checked in its flow. . . . The excess must discharge itself in some other direction, and there results an efflux through the motor nerves to various classes of the muscles, producing the half-convulsive actions we term laughter."

Modern science has not entirely dispensed with this notion. Some acoustic studies of laughter continue to differentiate between types of laughter produced by tickling, jokes, ordinary conversation, and what is described as *release of tension*. During the recent war in Iraq, an e-mail message was circulated to all BBC television presenters reminding them to look grave throughout the coverage. As one seasoned journalist remarked at the time, instructions of this nature ran the serious risk of prompting a sudden burst of manic laughter—a release of tension.

As a general principle, however, the idea that laughter constitutes a pressure valve bears little or no relation to the way our nervous system actually works, but there are still plenty of doctors and therapists who regard laughter as a useful remedy for depression, or even as a kind of placebo. Certainly the appreciation of humor, as distinct from laughter, is now thought to have generally positive effects upon the immune and central nervous systems. The right frontal lobe of the brain seems to be essential to this process. Medical scientists have observed that patients with injuries to that part of the brain are most likely to find it difficult or impossible to react to basic attempts to stimulate their sense of humor. Common sense and our own experience of laughter, together with the languor that follows a sustained burst of it, must tell us that, beyond the appreciation of humor, the physical experience of laughter constitutes at least some kind of catharsis, good or bad, mostly good. That catharsis can come as an intimate experience shared among friends or as something we experience as a large group, most commonly nowadays as an audience in the theater, where, clearly expecting to laugh, we willingly respond to simple cues and laugh like mad, sometimes even when upon reflection we cannot recall exactly why we laughed at all.

Concrete medical evidence for the health-giving properties of laughter is thin indeed, even though the media take up such claims with gusto. For example, an Associated Press story dated Chicago, February 14, 2001, reported the findings of a Japanese study in which it was claimed that one group of people experiencing allergic reactions to dust mites lost their skin welts more rapidly after being shown a Charlie Chaplin film than another group who were made to watch a weather report. This study, which drew on the populist work of Norman Cousins in the 1970s, purported to present evidence that inducing laughter in patients "may play some role in alleviating allergic diseases."

India has the long tradition of laughing holy men or *sadhus*, and in recent times a series of widely publicized, not to say lucrative, "laughing clubs," founded by Dr. Madan Kataria, has sprung up across the subcontinent. These take the form of spontaneous, outdoor groups practicing a yoga-like thing Dr. Kataria calls "laughter therapy." These exercises, in effect breathing exercises, he claims, assist "the systems of the body" by reducing stress, and because the position generally adopted for each session involves raising the arms above the head, it seems likely that some beneficial physical exercise may also result.

Dr. Kataria's activities take advantage of the contagiousness of laughter, which, as we saw in the case of Mr. Cave in High Holborn, is well documented, and indeed familiar to everyone. When we witness people overtaken by paroxysms of laughter, it is difficult not to anticipate by several steps the source of amusement by beginning to laugh ourselves, partly with them, maybe even partly *at* them—particularly when they are doubled up or in some other way deprived of self-control—even though we have no idea what they are laughing about. We laugh far more often when we are in company than when we are by ourselves, and we often respond to a group of laughing people by joining in, even if that laughter is at our own expense. A good sport laughs anyway.

The psychologist and neuroscientist Robert Provine, of the University of Maryland, recounted a remarkable episode that occurred in 1962 in a girls' boarding school in the village of Kashasha, not too far from Lake Victoria in what was then called Tanganyika (modern Tanzania). Between January 30 and March 18 what began as an isolated incident spread throughout the school and forced it to close.

At first, three girls were stricken by attacks of uncontrollable laughter, sometimes lasting for a few minutes but soon recurring for much longer periods, sometimes hours on end. The symptoms spread rapidly so that in the end no fewer than ninety-five of the 159 girls living at the school were afflicted. The laughter was accompanied by extreme agitation, tears, and general hysteria, and in several cases the sufferer was trapped in this state for periods of up to sixteen days. While normal routine was completely disrupted, there were no serious physical consequences of these attacks apart from the obvious: distress, exhaustion, and, possibly, embarrassment. Nobody suffered from permanent ill effects. Nobody died.

To the authorities' dismay, after the Kashasha girls were sent home, the symptoms began to spread among their families and throughout whole communities, and thence to other schools as well. A plucky attempt in May to resume normal school life at Kashasha resulted in a disastrous resurgence of the condition among fifty-seven girls, leaving the staff no choice but to close once more. In the end, over a period of two years, fourteen boarding schools and entire villages and towns were afflicted around the eastern shore of Lake Victoria. The worst incident occurred in a place called Nshamba, where these attacks of uncontrollable laughter spread to more than 200 people in a population of 10,000. As Provine pointed out, this example of eerily synchronized mass hysteria may be explained as the result of a trigger mechanism in the brain that easily replicates a powerful behavioral prompt, making the sufferer unwilling, or even powerless, to stop it. Though deeply disruptive, in this case the condition is not thought to have been pathological in the sense that a neurological disorder such as Tourette's Syndrome harnesses that same trigger mechanism in the otherwise respectable little old lady and makes her mutter obscenities, or indeed shout them from the rooftops. Anyone who has observed that bizarre symptom at first hand is not likely to forget it.

Laughter is evidently infectious, but it can also be stimulated in other ways. Laughing gas, nitrous oxide, N_2O, was discovered at the turn of the eighteenth and nineteenth centuries by the "pneumatic chemist" Thomas Beddoes of Bristol, in partnership with the engineer James Watt and his apprentice Humphry Davy. The original idea was that this gas, a weak anaesthetic, might benefit sufferers of consumption, which it did not. Soon, however, its amusing side-effects, light-headedness and stupor, led to its consumption as a form of carnival entertainment. By the 1830s laughing gas parties had become popular in the United States. Today the practice is illegal in many places, including California, where, according to the penal code, "any person who possesses nitrous oxide or any substance containing nitrous oxide, with the intent to breathe, inhale, or ingest for the purpose of causing a condition of intoxication, elation, euphoria, dizziness, stupefaction, or dulling of the senses or for the purpose of, in any manner, changing, distorting, or disturbing the audio, visual, or mental processes, or who knowingly and with the intent to do so is under the influence of nitrous oxide or any material containing nitrous oxide is guilty of a misdemeanor." Samuel Taylor Coleridge experimented with laughing gas as a recreation, as did Robert Southey and Josiah Wedgwood, but the heyday of laughing gas came later, after the 1840s, when its mild anaesthetic properties over very brief periods were exploited by dentists to ease the pain of tooth extraction.

Just as we can wear a false or insincere smile and seem credible, so too we can produce synthetic laughter. Actors must turn it on, and sometimes expose themselves by trying too hard, going on too long, or producing a sound that is forced or over-loud. In conversation a dry laugh may indicate that our interlocutor is finding the exchange heavy or dull or in some other way unsatisfactory. Ghastly social situations in which we may from time to time find ourselves trapped may elicit nervous laughter where tears of exasperation would seem more apt—as, for example, at a party when we find ourselves having to endure the endless soliloquy of a fully paid-up, card-carrying bore. At other times short bursts of laughter may serve to fill a difficult silence, such as the one that generally follows a gaffe, a dropped brick, a sharp marital altercation to which one is reluctantly privy, or some other situation in which conversational first aid is desperately needed and professional assistance is not yet at hand.

As one critic has pointed out, in the fiction of Stendhal, characters do not laugh, so much as laugh *at* each other—haughtily directing their laughter at somebody else, a group of washerwomen, for example, to affirm or even demonstrate their own superiority, to enjoy some tactical triumph, to pose a threat, to exhibit aggression or scorn. The technique serves to put down the person who is laughed at, but equally it condemns the laughing aggressor; the laughter is cold and calculating, strategic, as is the smile that accompanies or, at times, replaces it.

I once knew a dog, a very beautiful cocker spaniel–golden retriever cross called Sandy, who without a shadow of a doubt was endowed with the ability to smile. Sandy was in any event a happy dog, but when she was particularly friendly or cheerful, and in a receptive mood, she would lower her head, pull back her ears, wag not just her tail but the entire hindquarters and scrunch up her muzzle, eyes half closed, in what nobody doubted was an affectionate smile of unalloyed mirth. It was occasionally accompanied by a little noise, not exactly a whimper nor the curious downward-swooping sigh that generally came with one of her full-throated yawns. And the smile was generally followed by enthusiastic licking. Charles Darwin had noticed something similar, and collected anecdotes about other grinning dogs, for example Sir Walter Scott's Scotch greyhound Maida. "The upper lip during the act of grinning is retracted, as in snarling," he wrote, "so that the canines are exposed, and the ears are drawn backwards; but the general appearance of the animal clearly shows that anger is not felt. [The Scottish surgeon and anatomist] Sir

C[harles]. Bell remarks, 'Dogs, in their expression of fondness, have a slight eversion of the lips, and grin and sniff amidst their gambols, in a way that resembles laughter.' Some persons speak of the grin as a smile, but if it had been really a smile, we should see a similar, though more pronounced, movement of the lips and ears, when dogs utter their bark of joy; but this is not the case, although a bark of joy often follows a grin."

The biologist Konrad Lorenz was likewise convinced that *his* dog, whose "slightly opened jaws which reveal the tongue, and the tilted angle of the mouth which stretches almost from ear to ear" not only grinned, but gave the strongest possible impression of laughter, generally coming as an invitation to play. Nor did Thomas Mann doubt that his dog laughed as, for example, when he tapped his snout and the dog, whose name was Bashan, responded by snapping at his hand as if it were a fly. The game made them both laugh. "Yes, Bashan has to laugh too;" Mann wrote, "and as I laugh I marvel at the sight, to me the oddest and most touching thing in the world. It is moving to see how under my teasing his thin animal cheeks and the corners of his mouth will twitch, and over his dark animal mask will pass an expression like a human smile."

Scientists who know all about animal behavior will sometimes insist that laughter is the prerogative of humans alone, but no doubt many more people will have formed a different impression based on the behavior of domestic animals, in our time and in the distant past, as the great English tradition of animal portraiture attests. Other genres offer many more examples of smiling animals. William Hogarth's beautiful portrait of the children of the wealthy apothecary Daniel Graham (Fig. 4.2) is remarkable for many reasons, not least because the painter captured the smiles of each child, animated in their different ways, with such freshness and individuality. The baby, Thomas, on the left, who is according to custom dressed as a little girl, did not survive infancy—indeed, he was dead by the time Hogarth

FIGURE 4.2   William Hogarth (1697–1764), *The Graham Children*, 1742, oil on canvas, 63¼ × 61¼ in. © National Gallery, London.

finished this portrait. The daughters, Henrietta (who looks out at us) and Anna Maria, stand in the center, and the eldest son, Richard, sits on the right, turning the handle of a bird-organ. Smiling, he looks up at the caged songbird suspended overhead unaware that over his shoulder, clinging to the back of the chair, a bewhiskered cat stares at the same bird, grinning with gleeful expectation.

No doubt we humans are inclined to read the merry smile in the muzzle of the dog, or a craftier grin playing over the face of a hungry and not yet entirely frustrated tabby cat, in the light of our own experience. We take heart from the fact that the animal in question is unlikely to deceive us. I always felt that the smile of Sandy the dog was real and felt. Yet it is an equally human characteristic again and again to see ourselves reflected in the strange habits of the animal kingdom, such is our vanity.

Among the scores of instantly recognizable, mass-produced images circulating in the western media, one has particular relevance to the complicated relationship between smiling and mirth in humans. It is the "smiley" face, a yellow disc with two black dots for eyes and a wide, crescent-shaped mouth. In the "classical" version, short lines or apostrophe-shaped lugs, suggesting the dimpled corners of a broadly smiling mouth, are placed at each tapering end of the single black line of the lips (Fig. 4.3). This gesture is reminiscent of the technique by which Chinese calligraphers terminate a line, thus endowing it with what they call "the bone of the brush." Like other potent examples of modern design, the extreme simplicity of the original idea, its adaptability and boldness, practically guaranteed success. For a time, in the 1970s and 1980s, the smiley face was an

FIGURE 4.3   Harvey Ball, *Signature smiley.*®

enormously popular fad. It stood alone on buttons, stickers, and pins (of which an estimated 50 million were at one time in circulation). It was printed on T-shirts, ballpoint pens, stationery, sew-on buttons, pieces of jewelry, cookie jars, coffee mugs, and any number of other products. Schoolteachers used it to reward pupils for doing good work. At different times it has been associated with the curious 1980s Acid House phenomenon in London; with Václav Havel's Czech political resistance movement called Civic Forum, which in 1989 brought about the so-called "Velvet Revolution"; with the evangelical literature put out by fundamentalist Christian churches; and with people who like to display bumper stickers on their car.

Some people alluded to the mass-produced smiley face by adding a quickly drawn pictograph to their signature in handwritten correspondence, along with the more conventional hugs and kisses. Now that e-mail and other forms of typewritten communication between computers have lured so many of us away from handwritten letters and cards, the colon and the closing parenthesis have been co-opted from the keyboard to achieve the same effect, although the smiling face thus delineated is turned on its side. A related hieroglyph uses the semi-colon to indicate a cheeky wink (in the right eye).

The smiley face was borrowed, copied, and recycled so frequently, in an effort to brighten so many different sorts of message—deploying and exchanging it as a kind of currency of good cheer—that its origins are surprisingly difficult to locate. Numerous prototypes circulated in advertisements and other ephemera prior to the early 1960s when an orthodox smiley emerged. In the 1930s, for example, Sunkist oranges employed a version, which, not surprisingly, took the form of a beaming valencia. The fruit and its sunny associations obviously dictated the round form and bright color, while the facial features followed naturally. A glance through registered trademarks in many jurisdictions yields hundreds of smiling faces adorning sweets and light bulbs and any number of other rounded things that might legitimately claim to have prophesied the classical smiley of the 1970s and 1980s. A particularly suggestive one was trademarked in the late 1940s by a large drug company for use on pills, and similar motifs are registered in connection with vacuum-cleaning equipment, kindergarten furniture, industrial cleaning services, legal services, food dyes, sound-recording equipment, frying pans, lotteries, cookies, and sushi.

A more fully developed prototype of the modern smiley face was devised in 1961 for a community-spirited advertising campaign by the Los Angeles public relations and advertising agency Carson Roberts. Another, almost certainly unrelated "proto-smiley" was printed in 1962 on sweatshirts given away by WMCA Radio in New York. In late 1963, Harvey R. Ball, a graphic artist who lived in Worcester, Massachusetts, designed what one might call the canonical smiley face. It was conceived as a morale-boosting exercise for the worried staff of a newly acquired Ohio subsidiary of the East-Coast State Mutual Insurance Company. Ball's first idea was simply to produce a sunny, yellow button or pin with the simple, crescent-shaped line of a smiling mouth running across the middle, without any other facial features. The eyes were added, and the yellow disc thus turned into a face, when it was pointed out that otherwise one could easily subvert the exercise by wearing the badge upside down. In the circumstances this seemed distinctly possible.

According to a different account, the smiley emblem was invented later, in 1967, by David Stern, an advertising executive, who planned a campaign to encourage people to open accounts at a small bank in Seattle called University Federal Savings and Loan. The campaign motto was adapted from a song in *Bye, Bye, Birdie*, the hit musical by Charles Strouse and Lee Adams which opened in April 1960, and ran: "Open a savings account, and put on a happy face."

Evidently a good number of people followed this advice, though the question remains whether, as an insistently yellow, coin-sized

blem of enormously wide circulation and graphic strength, the
ley could conceivably have reflected the smiling and laughing
pits of real people. In the mid-1970s, a Bay Area church devised a
n to redeem the neighborhood from "drugged-out hippies," and
gaged a button factory in San Francisco to produce a batch of
eerful smiley pins, accompanied by the brisk motto "Have a nice
y, and stay off drugs." Today we may regard this as a forlorn ven-
e, anticipating by at least a decade Nancy Reagan's impractical
85 "Just Say No" anti-drug crusade. And presumably the smiley
de no difference at all to the Bay Area hippies; ironically, it had
years been imprinted upon tablets of LSD. But the fact that the
ley should have been sent into the world on a godly mission to
deem and enlighten demonstrates how successfully it had crept
into the visual language of the moment. Should we be worried that,
like so many other mass-produced commercial tags and mottoes,
once phenomenally successful but now moribund, the cheerful smiley has also had its day? I doubt it.

Jésus a pleuré, Voltaire a souri; c'est de cette larme divine et de ce sourire humain qu'est faite la douceur de la civilisation actuelle.

Jesus wept; Voltaire smiled. Of that divine tear and that human smile the sweetness of our current civilisation is composed.

VICTOR HUGO, Centenary Oration
on Voltaire, May 30, 1878

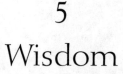

5

Wisdom

Some people recall an art exhibition they saw years ago as a life-changing experience. Even allowing for hyperbole, the effect is real and is what most exhibition curators hope they may replicate for the next crop of visitors. One does not expect many people to experience it, nor very often, but when they do, it makes curators feel that the whole enterprise is worthwhile. I came closest to feeling that feeling myself a few years ago in Washington, D.C., where in a magnificent exhibition of ancient Cambodian sculpture at the National Gallery of Art I came face to face with the serenely smiling head of King Jayavarman VII of Cambodia (Fig. 5.1).

Exhibitions of sculpture are technically difficult, logistically fearsome, and mind-numbingly expensive. They cause upheaval in carpenters' workshops; they strain the muscles and sinews of art handlers,

FIGURE 5.1   Unknown Cambodian (Khmer) sculptor (Angkor period, style of the Bayon), *Head of
Jayavarman VII*, late twelfth–early thirteenth century,
sandstone, 16 × 11 × 12¼ in. Phnom Penh: National Museum of Cambodia.

and indeed expose them to some danger; they are extremely awkward
to light properly. But the effect can be startling. In this case, tons of
life-size sandstone statuary, fragments, and reliefs, together with a crop
of wooden statues and bronzes, were brought together from three
American art museums, the Musée Guimet in Paris, the Staatliche
Museen in Berlin, and that pathetic ruin, the heartbreaking National
Museum of Cambodia in Phnom Penh, whose remarkable collection

was vandalized in the 1970s by Pol Pot, looted, and, until not long ago, left to molder in bat dung. Many of the sculptures were originally carved between the ninth and twelfth centuries A.D. for sites in and around the great temple of Angkor Wat. What visitors saw when they entered the temporary exhibition galleries in the National Gallery's East Wing was not only visually spectacular, but something of a miracle of survival. Although it prompted sad thoughts about the dreadful fate of a once-glorious civilization, its esthetic impact was tremendous.

Cambodians, it seems, were born to carve stone. The techniques and tools they used were relatively simple, but the effects they achieved were fantastically sophisticated, from the writhing floriate ornamentation of certain door lintels—in which obsessive detail never drowns the muscular, serpentine rhythms of the whole, nor disturbs the discipline of complex interlocking planes and registers—to the undulating volumes of smooth-bellied giants, guardians, elephants, and other deities with their thick ankles and big feet. The instinct for swelling volumes, the way in which limbs are intertwined in three dimensions as if it were no more than an exercise in simple masonry, the deep love of animals, and most importantly an alertness to the balanced forms of the human head—these things evidently place the ancient Cambodians among the first rank of sculptors anywhere in the world, and in any period.

King Jayavarman VII (1181–1218?), who greatly expanded the territorial boundaries of Cambodia, adopted Mahāyāna Buddhism as the state religion, with its belief in the existence of many levels or stages of life preceding buddhahood, the so-called *bodhisattvas*. The king had numerous portrait statues of himself carved at sites throughout his expanded kingdom, the better to solidify his personal rule. The experts can easily distinguish between these beautiful late twelfth–early thirteenth-century portrait statues and the schematic forms chosen to represent the Buddha in his many incarnations, but to the layman, by any measure, the portraits of Jayavarman VII closely resemble nearly contemporaneous buddhas. One obvious clue that is easy to detect is in the hairstyle. The king wears his hair in a simple chignon-like knot, while buddhas have the more elaborate, conical *uṣṇīṣa* consisting of orderly rows of tight curls; in some examples the young king's fine moustache is carefully traced, a thin line along the undulating upper lip. In any case, by contrast with his reputation as a great warrior, the king had himself portrayed sitting in the humble attitude of a worshipper, eyes closed, deep in meditation, the head slightly lowered. The king's posthumous name of *Mahāparamasaugatapada*, which means "he who has gone where the great followers of the supreme Buddha reside," attests, at least, to his posthumous reputation as a holy king. But there is some evidence in the form of inscriptions on surviving stelai that he was known to be pious during his lifetime: "The king suffered from the ills of his subjects," reads one, "for it is the suffering of the people that causes the suffering of kings and not their own."

The idea of a holy king wearing what the Indian art journal *Marg* once called this "strange smile of benign comprehension" runs parallel with the widespread currency of holy smiling among buddhas and *bodhisattvas*. In such smiles the observer may perceive various radiant qualities from great intelligence to "indescribable bliss." Yet it was not always so. Primitive Buddhism tended to deprecate the sensations that would logically give rise to the smile, and nothing short of complete sensual evacuation was the highest pinnacle of enlightenment. Early Gandhara imagery, for example—that is, the early Buddhist art of the region stretching from Afghanistan in the west to Pakistan and northwest India in the east—is largely solemn, not unlike Classical Greek sculpture, which exerted such a strong influence over it. But later traditions gradually admitted the possibility that the smile of the Buddha might not only relate to his great intelligence, shining like a beacon, but might also indicate his infinite compassion and endurance.

The idea that a face might radiate wisdom or "shine" is not confined to the Buddhist tradition. According to the ancient Hebrew text of Exodus (34: 29–30), after Moses received the Ten Commandments at the summit of Mt. Sinai and brought the stone tablets down to the people, the prophet's face "shone" or, literally, "sent forth beams." The compilers of the fourth-century A.D. Vulgate Latin text of the Bible, traditionally ascribed to St. Jerome, famously mistranslated the Hebrew phrase "sent forth beams" as "sent forth *horns.*" This error eventually found literal expression in Medieval and Renaissance art, of which the most famous example is Michelangelo's powerful, horned Moses carved for the tomb of Pope Julius II in the Church of S. Pietro in Vincoli in Rome. By the nineteenth century, when the source of confusion was well understood, the tradition of a "horned" Moses was so strong that even representations of the infant Moses, lifted from among the bulrushes by Pharaoh's daughter, still showed little clusters of beams of light protruding from his forehead in a decidedly horn-like manner.

If the faces of wise men could "shine," there was in Medieval culture a firm belief that radiating light or color could smile or even laugh. The association between "illuminated" manuscripts and their capacity to smile was noted in a number of texts, most famously in Canto XI of *Purgatorio* where Dante salutes a fine miniature painter called Oderisi of Gubbio, who in turn protests that the work of another man, Franco of Bologna, smiles or laughs more than his. This reference draws on a long tradition that extends back as far as St. Bernard. Poems decorated with gold or vermilion, it was thought, made the letters smile, while laughter was one of the motions of the mind which "shone" from the body.

The oriental art scholar Peter Fingesten has suggested that the enlightened smile of the Buddha originated as a conscious reference to the smile of the dead, a symbol of the Buddha's overcoming of life, dead to the world: "Buddha's smile could only have been inspired by the observation of the apparently blissful smile of corpses which was interpreted as a meaningful, almost intelligent reaction, that death was a wonderful, desirable and superior state of being, as the long tradition of Hindu and Buddhist thought infers. This smile, the so-called *risus sardonicus*, produced by the contraction of the facial muscles in rigor mortis, must have made a startling impression upon the pre-scientific minds of Hindus and Buddhists."

Today the *risus sardonicus* is not associated with death, but with alarming spasms of the facial muscles encountered most commonly in the early stages of tetanus, but also caused by some poisons, such as strychnine, and other conditions, such as rheumatic pericarditis. Modern medical dictionaries prefer to call this awful condition a grimace, not a smile, though in its conservative way the *Oxford English Dictionary* still calls it a "grin," even while noting that in the second quarter of the nineteenth century Robert Bentley Todd, in his *Cyclopædia of Anatomy and Physiology*, clearly felt the word grin was not quite right. He called it "a peculiar expression *or* grin." The related expression *trismus sardonicus* refers specifically to the contraction of the masticatory muscles that normally let us chew, a ghastly condition that makes it impossible to open the mouth. Again, tetanus is the celebrity culprit (hence the old name lockjaw), but there are many other causes as well, including abscesses in the neighborhood of the tonsils, a dental disease called pericoronitis, and plain hysteria.

The adjective *sardonicus* first appears in Homer, who, as we have seen, tells us Odysseus wore in his heart "a *sardonic* smile." The basic meaning of *sardonic* in this, and any other context, has always been *bitter*. The term was apparently derived from the sour taste of an herb that grows in Sardinia and, when eaten, caused an involuntary distension of the mouth muscles. (To observe it, watch yourself eating a lemon in front of the mirror.) According to a later, fifth-century source, Simonides, the expression originated with Talos, the brazen man of Crete, who traveled to Sardinia, slew many of the inhabitants, and watched them grinning horribly at him as they died. The saying also caught on in Rome, where, following a political defeat, Caius Gracchus gloomily recalled being greeted by his triumphant enemies' sardonic laughter.

So while the *risus sardonicus* is not something that doctors who have seen it will easily forget, it is not today normally associated with the peaceful smile that is sometimes observed on the face of the dead. An eerie example of the smiling corpse was apparently preserved early last century by an art student who was struck by the beauty of an unidentified young woman in the Paris morgue whose body had been recovered from the River Seine. She had apparently drowned herself. Somehow he obtained permission to cast her death mask, which evidently captures a smile of deceptive tranquility. It was photographed and published by the morbid German collector of death masks, Ernst Benkard, who described her as "a dainty butterfly fluttering without a care around the flame of life and so destroying and burning her wings before her time." The extent to which the casting process altered the expression we see in the photograph of the plaster head, not to mention the effect of any "improvements" made by the artist later, perhaps even unwittingly, in the course of cleaning and finishing the model, is hard to determine, but it would be foolish to take this ghoulish document at face value. She is remembered simply as *l'inconnue de la Seine* (*The Unknown Woman of the Seine*), and the original model has vanished without trace. Leonard and Virginia Woolf published an English translation of Benkard's book at the Hogarth Press, and it is tempting to ask whether, just possibly, Sylvia Plath was thinking of something rather similar years later when she wrote the first three lines of her bleak 1963 poem "Edge":

> *The woman is perfected*
> *Her dead*
> *Body wears the smile of accomplishment,*
>   [though an imaginary model of greater
>   antiquity better suits the lines that follow]
> *The illusion of a Greek necessity*
> *Flows in the scrolls of her toga,*
> *Her bare*
> *Feet seem to be saying:*
> *We have come so far, it is over.*

It was the mask of *l'inconnue de la Seine* in Benkard's book that reminded Fingesten of Buddhist imagery and led him to ask whether the smile of the Buddha was in fact the smile of death—not death as we understand it in the West, but the Eastern notion of death as the final stage of rising above, transcending or gaining release from life. It led Fingesten to distinguish between five distinct types of holy smile worn by the Buddha in different eras. The first, he thought, was the "hidden" smile, detectable in various examples of Gandhara sculpture. This reading of the graceful undulations of full cheeks and lips, perhaps a little more sensual than comparable Classical Greek heads, is, it seems to me, only to be comprehended as a smile with the benefit of hindsight, and I do not see it myself. The second, similar he thought to some Egyptian portrait sculptures in granite of Dynasty XVIII (1570–1293 B.C.), is the "implicit" smile, which is also difficult to detect unless you attach particular weight to the deeply gouged corners of the mouth, a quality it shares with the corners of some Gandhara mouths, which in every other respect appear relaxed. A third, "explicit" smile is to be found in sculptures from Mathura (India), which drew heavily on Hindu traditions, in which the smile was associated with the ideas of release and *nirvana*. This is clearly visible in surviving examples, such as a particularly red sandstone fragment of a statue from Mathura, dating from the Kushan Period (second century), which is in the collection of the Museum of Fine Arts in Boston.

The fourth kind of smile is the one we see on the face of Jayavarman VII, the "sublime" smile, whose mysterious allure is strengthened by his closed eyes, the tilt of his head, and the pious attitude of the pose. Finally, there is the "stereotype" smile, not unlike the archaic smile of Greek sculpture in the sense that it is modeled according to strict convention. This sort of smile may be found among many later phases of Buddhist art, in Thailand in about the fourteenth century, but hardly ever in Japan.

The representation of deities elsewhere in the Buddhist world was far more willing to accommodate the boisterous facial expressions caused by involuntary laughter than we find in the coolly sedate Khmer (Cambodian) tradition of Angkor. Big, laughing, fat-bellied monks, such as the famous fifteenth-century Chinese "*Budai*" in London (Fig. 5.2), an enduring and hugely popular symbol of good luck, throw into high relief the composed portraits and effigies of the Buddhist tradition. His open mouth, exposed teeth (both rows), and carefully delineated laughter lines in the cheeks are explicit indications of forthright jocularity. A slightly later, sixteenth-century Japanese ink painting in Nara, by the artist Sesson Shūkei (c. 1504–c. 1590), represents a big-bottomed deity, *Lu Dongbin* (*Lu Tung-pin*) *A Chinese Taoist Immortal* (Fig. 5.3). Here, *Lu* is shown stomping on the head of a wonderfully fierce dragon, whose fangs and popping eyes are clearly visible under his feet. He throws his arms wide apart, tosses his head back, and cackles gleefully at another dragon that writhes furiously above. Sesson shows us that *Lu* is drinking. He holds a bottle in his left hand, and the round stopper in his right, while his long beard and moustaches are swept upward in the swirling wind. Despite his comical shape and awkward posture, he is in complete control. The painting is on one level an exhilarating essay in sinuous, fluid brushwork, something with which we know

FIGURE 5.2   Unknown Chinese sculptor, Ming dynasty,
Stoneware figure of 'Budai,' the fat, smiling monk, 1486, stoneware
with green and ochre glazes. London, The British Museum.

Sesson transformed his more sedate Chinese exempla, but it is also
an uninhibited display of gleeful humor, even though the subject is
firmly grounded in the higher realm of divinity.

Lu Dongbin is not an isolated example of this phenomenon. Other
famous subjects concerning Taoist belief readily combined serious

FIGURE 5.3   Sesson Shūkei (*c.* 1504–*c.* 1590), *Lu Dongbin*
(*A Chinese Taoist Immortal*), hanging scroll, ink on paper,
46½ × 23½ in. Nara, Japan: Yamato Bunkakan.

philosophical points with unrestrained humor. The allegory known
as *The Three Laughters of Tiger Valley*, which in literature may be
traced to the late Tang period (ninth century A.D.), concerns three
celebrated men of antiquity, the poet Tao Yuanming (T'ao Yüan-
ming), the monk Hui Yuan (Hui-yüan), and the pioneer of Taoist

theology Lu Xiuching (Lu Hsiu-ching). Hui Yuan was famous for the austerity of his contemplative life, which for many years was conducted in a monastery on top of Mount Lu, close to the southern bank of the Yangtse River. He took a solemn vow never to pass beyond the Tiger ravine, a place that marked the boundary of his monastic sanctuary and the impure, outside world. The poet and the Taoist came to visit and, after a long and convivial evening, Hui Yuan accompanied them down the mountain path away from the monastery, crossing the Tiger ravine by mistake, thus violating his vow. In this awful moment, all three men realized what had happened and, instead of being dismayed or distraught, they all roared with laughter, realizing that the spiritual purity of a man is not contained by something as artificial or arbitrary as a mere geographical boundary. Thus, in the allegorical story, as well as in the poems and vividly engaging paintings later inspired by it, three wise men, dwarfed by precipitous mountains, pause in a ravine and laugh merrily. Here, humor, wisdom, and holiness achieve a kind of balance, which strikes me as very beautiful.

In the late 1960s, on television and in print, the art historian Kenneth Clark observed a similar conjunction, if not of holiness, then at least of wit and wisdom. He laid some emphasis in his remarks about Houdon's seated portrait statue of Voltaire in Montpellier, as well as other portraits of great French men and women of the Enlightenment, on the fact that they were shown smiling "the smile of reason." No doubt their reputation for ready wit and brilliant word play had something to do with the smile. Voltaire loved jokes. And certainly one is struck by the spry quick-wittedness of each smiling portrait head.

Perhaps this state of mind originated with the French philosopher Fontanelle who, by living to be nearly a hundred, bridged the seventeenth and eighteenth centuries—the world of Newton and the world of Voltaire. . . . He told someone that he had never run and never lost his temper. A friend of his asked him if he had ever laughed. He said: "No, I have never made *ha ha*." But he smiled, and so do all the other distinguished writers, philosophers, dramatists and hostesses of the French eighteenth century.

Although Fontanelle, like Lord Chesterfield, claimed not to laugh, *his* smile underlines the seriousness of Clark's point, which was that the wearers of this urbane expression were not shallow, but among the finest intellects of the age. "The smile of reason may seem to betray a certain incomprehension of the deeper human emotions," he continued, "but it didn't preclude some strongly held beliefs—belief in natural law, belief in justice, belief in toleration. Not bad." Not bad at all.

In the West we do not so readily associate the smile worn by presidents, prime ministers, and monarchs with the quality of wisdom. As we have seen, in the nineteenth century gravity was on the whole thought more likely to give that impression. Nor are we very accustomed to the idea of smiling monarchs. This was certainly true in England prior to the present reign. The late Queen Mary, for example, rarely smiled in public and on formal occasions never smiled at her husband, King George V. As well, perhaps owing to her erect posture, and to her taste for the tall, cylindrical style of hat called a *toque*, the queen occasionally seemed taller than the king. This gave rise to a widespread belief in Britain that Queen Mary was severe, and that the king was frightened of her—which was not true, as many sources attest. Yet in Germany, Queen Mary's appearance was not considered at all forbidding. There, she was admired and celebrated in Court circles as "stately" or "imposing," and capable of wearing large quantities of superb jewels, such as the enormous cleavings of the gorgeous Cullinan diamond, without seeming in any way overladen. She held in balance, it was thought, regal splendor, poise, grace, and *simplicity*. Today it is scarcely conceivable that the following costume worn by Queen Mary at Court on May 11, 1911, along with several of the largest diamonds in the world, would be described as the outward manifestation of simplicity: "White and gold *broché* silk gown. Train of white satin embroidered silver & gold. Jewels: diamond crown, rows of diamonds forming collar, with large necklace under, lesser South African stars [that is, diamonds], the Koh-i-Noor [diamond], Star of Africa [diamond] . . . " and so on.

In fact, British monarchs have tended not to be severe. There is no evidence that Queen Victoria ever uttered the stock phrase "We are not amused," and her private secretary Sir Henry Ponsonby remembered an occasion when the queen turned purple in the face trying not to laugh when at Crathie Church near Balmoral "wee" Dr. MacGregor prayed "that the Almighty would send down His wisdom on the Queen's Meenisters, who sorely needed it." Meanwhile, according to William Makepeace Thackeray, the queen's grandfather King George III used to laugh outrageously at the theater. And, when Prince of Wales, the future King Charles II was repeatedly punished for laughing in church. According to one account his mother, Queen Henrietta Maria, had terrible teeth which "poked out of her mouth like battlements," and upon entering London in state in 1604, Henry, Prince of Wales, the eldest son of King James I and Anne of Denmark, was observed "smiling and over-joyde to the people's eternall comfort."

But it is among smiling kings, queens, and princes of western Europe following the "Gothic moment" of the twelfth century and its aftermath that we discover one of the most remarkable clusters of smiling faces in art. Surviving accounts of the Holy Roman Emperor Frederick I "Barbarossa" (literally Red-Beard), who died suddenly on the Third Crusade, lay particular emphasis on the fact that his entire face was habitually "glad and hilarious" and that he took particular care always "to give the impression of smiling or laughing." In this case, the expression has been attributed to the emperor's desire to seem royally superior, but there is plenty of evidence in sculpture to suggest that it could mean other things as well.

A Romanesque statue of the Prophet Daniel, for example, on the Pórtico della Gloria of the Cathedral of Santiago de Compostella, wears an open smile and directs it toward the neighboring Prophet Jeremiah. On the facade of the Cathedral at Reims, the Angel Gabriel likewise communicates with the Virgin Mary by means of a subtly formulated smile of exquisite cheerfulness, the lower lids of the eyes carefully undercut to give the strongest impression of plasticity and animation, the corners of the mouth turned emphatically upward. Radiating from the sculptural program at Reims and other new cathedrals in France, this new "Gothic" smile spread to England and Germany, where in the Last Judgment Portal of Bamberg Cathedral the Elect wear vividly plastic smiles of utter satisfaction, while the damned are led away weeping. The Wise Virgins at Magdeburg Cathedral, meanwhile, are starkly differentiated from the Foolish by their broad smiles. Angels and saints smile sweetly at Lincoln, Regensburg, and elsewhere. In the manuscript called the *Douce Apocalypse* in the Bodleian Library in Oxford, the Great Angel of the Apocalypse wears a tooth-revealing smile of particular enthusiasm, framed between protruding, scroll-like ears. At the same time the Virgin Mary and the infant Jesus begin to display powerfully animating smiles, ranging from subtle expressions of tenderness between a mother and her baby to more schematic attempts to render the face of each more animated.

Occasionally there have been doubts about whether this Gothic smile worn by saints and angels is a smile at all. The Cambridge scholar Paul Binski wondered if these smiling faces did not carry "a special menace," while the smile worn by a queen on a statue-column from Saint-Thibaut, Provins, was for a time thought to have been the product of skillful restoration in the early twentieth century and not, in fact, an original feature of the work. This has now been refuted by the scholar Pamela Z. Blum, who nevertheless in 1990 made the following remarks about the statue of a queen in the right embrasure of the central portal of Chartres Cathedral: "Although *not* a true smile, a look of awareness enlivens her face. Her lips, parted, slightly pursed, and tucked in at the corners, complete the lifelike response suggested by her observant gaze from under partially lowered lids." If this is not a faint smile, it is difficult to imagine what facial expression worn by the anonymous queen would match this description. To me the queen smiles, and the more puzzling question is what, according to Blum, might count as a "true" smile.

Even so, as Binski remarked, "The phenomenon of smiling seems at odds with the expressive character of the Christian religion as charted in the Gospels, apocryphal and hagiographic literature, and indeed much Christian art: Jesus wept, but no one in the canon of 'authentic' early Christian literature smiles, though smiling does occur in later hagiography. How then is this mismatch between the fundamental letter of Christianity, whose central signs seem so mournful, and the Gothic smile to be negotiated?" The point is even more puzzling when one is confronted by something as bizarre as the smiling crucified Christ at the Benedictine Abbey of St. Walburg in Eichstätt, which seems entirely at odds with the tears He shed on the Cross.

The startling difference between these vividly human expressions and the far more solemn masterpieces of Romanesque sculpture of the preceding (eleventh and early twelfth) centuries relate mainly to the treatment of eyes and the shape of the head. In Romanesque sculpture the eyes are generally very large and almond-shaped, providing the strongest suggestion of silent animation in the head and face. Romanesque mouths, by contrast, are generally quite small. Christ the King reigns majestically from the tympanum above the west door of Sainte-Madeleine at Vezelay (1120–1132). The overwhelming impression he conveys is one of formality, grandeur, power, distance.

Two posthumous portraits, one from the thirteenth and the other from the fourteenth century, illustrate the deep gulf that separates the spare, lofty forms of the heads of Romanesque statues from the

Figure 5.4 Unknown German sculptor (mid-thirteenth century), *Reglindis (Posthumous portrait of one of the twelfth-century founders of Naumberg Cathedral)* (detail), *c.* 1250-1260, west chancel, Naumberg: Cathedral of SS. Peter and Paul. Photo: Bildarchiv Foto Marburg.

burgeoning naturalism of the Gothic face, with its life-like smile. In the west chancel of Naumberg Cathedral in Germany there are statues of the twelfth-century founders, including a noblewoman called Reglindis (Fig. 5.4). She stands alongside her long-haired husband, Hermann, and turns her head toward him. Both lived more than 100 years before their statues were carved, but, framed by a jeweled diadem and a wimple that passes under her chin, her face is especially lively. The eyes, cheeks, and mouth are modeled in unison, a bright smile plotted with unequivocal German verity.

The second portrait is also posthumous, and comes from Verona in the north of Italy. It is an equestrian portrait by an unknown sculptor of the great *signore* or military strongman Cangrande I della Scala, who died in 1329 (Fig. 5.5). Cangrande was shrewd and cultivated, providing hospitality to the exiled Dante, who gave him a glowing account in a few lines of his *Paradiso* (17:78–86). Boccaccio, meanwhile, cast him in the *Decameron* as a great and munificent lord. He was certainly a seasoned military campaigner. In 1314 he conquered the neighboring city of Vicenza, and a few years later (1318) he took Padua. By clever political and diplomatic maneuverings, Cangrande aligned himself with successive Holy Roman emperors and in return obtained the titles of imperial vicar and captain general of the Ghibelline League, making him a significant powerbroker in the complicated political melting-pot of northern Italy.

In his life-sized tomb statue, which was originally raised over the portal of the Church of S. Maria Antica, Cangrande is mounted on horseback, wears a full suit of armor, and holds in his right hand a drawn sword. Though his face is carefully framed by chain mail and a helmet, the elaborately crested vizor lifted back, all strong indicators of martial prowess, his plump cheeks are lifted and the corners of his mouth drawn into a merry grin made more alert and vibrant by the treatment of his uplifted eyes. His face seems to reflect the same

FIGURE 5.5 Unknown Veronese sculptor (mid-fourteenth century), *Equestrian Monument of Cangrande I della Scala* (detail), *c.* 1350. Verona: Museo di Castelvecchio. Photo © Alinari / Art Resource.

hilaritas that was observed on the face of Frederick Barbarossa 150 years earlier.

Reglindis helped raise a great cathedral; Cangrande consolidated and expanded the power of his family and of the city-state over which he ruled with considerable ability. Both were dead when their portrait statues were carved. Both were made to smile. Why? One explanation for the spread of Gothic smiles from the third quarter of the twelfth century onwards that has long intrigued scholars is that the phenomenon somehow reflects the rapid development and flowering in this period of the Romance and other European languages. The proliferation of vernacular modes of expression, it has been suggested, made possible an entirely different, increasingly secular approach to the nuances of facial expression, made them infinitely more digestible, created an appetite for them. The idea is attractive but, according to Binski, is not sufficient to explain the upsurge of smiling in the purely religious context. Beyond this general point that the Gothic smile was tied to language, there was also some kind of recognition that the smile functioned as a sophisticated metaphysical sign, a natural channel of holy wisdom.

Beards, whiskers, and moustaches have from time to time offered sovereigns and rulers a more concrete prop than the smile with which to convey the impression of wisdom. Certain ancient Roman emperors—Hadrian (76–138 A.D.), for example, and the Antonines—grew beards in an effort to associate themselves with the Greek philosophers Aristotle and Plato, and thus play the role of wise rulers. This is the more remarkable because the Romans were also accustomed to using the term "barbarian" to describe the bearded Germanic hordes beyond their jurisdiction in the north.

The idea that leonine beards served to demonstrate not only manly dignity but wisdom also was widespread and crosses many cultural boundaries in history, especially as it relates to priestly or royal office. Muslims swear the gravest oaths "by the beard of the Prophet." Moses and the high priest Aaron were famously bearded and, emulating them, Pope Julius II della Rovere (1503–1513) took a vow not to shave until he had taken possession of the besieged city of Bologna; Raphael's splendid portrait of the Pope from 1511–1512, in which he wears a very long white beard, is therefore to be understood in political terms—the portrait of a warrior-Pope, determined, patient, and not to be underestimated. Pope Julius II's is probably the best-documented beard in history, flourishing from October 1510 until he shaved it off in March 1512. By many accounts it was remarkably long and snowy white. No one had ever seen a pope wear anything like it.

Even within the last hundred years, King Edward VII, who for most of his adult life wore a neatly trimmed spade-shaped beard, cared a great deal about who around him should be permitted to wear one too. When in 1908 the prime minister, H. H. Asquith, nominated Cosmo Gordon Lang as archbishop of York (he went to Canterbury later on), the king received the prelate at Windsor. His only instructions to Lang were to "keep the parties in the Church together and to prevent the clergy from wearing moustaches." Even lately, in our time, the elderly Cuban revolutionary leader Fidel Castro has done his best to uphold the ancient tradition of "power beards." In many places he is known simply as *El barbudo*, the bearded one.

By contrast the smile is a far more potent emblem of wisdom than beards or moustaches, which can be grown or shaved off, combed, twirled, trained this way or that. Jayavarman VII's delicate moustache is hardly visible at all; the holy smile of divine radiance that enlivens his sandstone head seems to convey his full humanity, as well as a measure of his authority as a Buddhist king. No doubt Gothic kings and emperors conveyed by their cheerful *hilaritas* something similar. Many of us can think of wise people we know whose smile seems to reflect that wisdom. We will do our best not to think of it as something that is worn for our benefit. We will gladly see it as radiant.

For many people the most radiant smile of all is that of the infant. Is there anything so liable to reduce healthy adults to a state of incoherent rapture than the sight of an impromptu smile illuminating the face of a baby (Fig. 5.6)? More importantly, is there any more

Figure 5.6   Desiderio da Settignano (c. 1429–1464), *Cherub's Head* (detail), c. 1460–1464, marble, 12½ × 18½ in. Courtesy of Salander–O'Reilly Galleries, New York.

profound sign of the potential for intelligence than the smile of a baby, which in the first six months of human life offers us a glimpse of incipient cognition?

The spontaneous or endogenous smile that animates the face of a newborn baby, then through the first twenty-six weeks gradually and seamlessly develops into a sophisticated mechanism of affective interaction, has always fascinated parents, who are themselves naturally and deeply stimulated by their own infant's smile. The scientific literature surrounding the earliest stages of infant development is vast and is still growing exponentially, the product of numerous studies of the interaction of mothers and infants all over the world at various ages, anywhere from a few days, two, four, six, or eight weeks, three, four, or six months. In many cases, hours of film, sound, and videotape have yielded immense quantities of data by which a newborn baby's complex path of development may be plotted, studied, and interpreted. And we surely look for more in the smile of the newborn infant than signs of comfort or happiness.

Apart from the more wholly understandable and necessary behavioral phenomena of crying, sleeping, and feeding with which babies occupy most of their time in the earliest days—a time in which they must somehow come to terms with the bombardment of light and all the other stimuli of the outside world, a raucous whirlpool of colors and light, hot and cold, bumping and uproar—involuntary movements of the lips and mouth, some of which may approximate and, later, assume the obvious form of a smile, offer a parent the most eloquent signs of her baby's well-being. They also provide welcome evidence of the primitive stirrings of a future mind, a new personality.

In the absence of any observable prompt or stimulus, the earliest smiles were for a long time thought to be the product of wind or gas or some other gastric disturbance causing sensations of discomfort. The movements of the mouth that we recognize as smile-like were, in fact, a reflex making possible the rapid and effective expulsion of gas. Nowadays the phenomenon is less and less common, but one can still observe and hear it among old men in the public bars of certain metropolitan racecourses.

An alternative view is that the earliest smiles were somehow an expression of what one scientific study in the 1970s described as "the silent, bared-teeth submissive grimace of primates," and that the very mobile lip-curling and wide mouth movements of apes and monkeys were associated not necessarily with happiness or friendliness or good cheer but with some different kind of display. According to another school of thought, the primitive "animal" origins of smiling relate instead to rage, and in both situations (that is to say, discomfort and vexation), the delighted response of the mother to her baby's smile rapidly impresses itself upon the baby, teaching him how valuable the smile can be and how numerous intangible benefits may result from flashing it, and, in due course, deploying it strategically. The social function of the smile is thus gradually established by association or conditioning, rather than as a consequence of any innate sensations of satisfaction or well-being that one might be tempted to read into the spontaneous, endogenous, or reflex smile. Most parents find this view unsustainable and are extremely reluctant to interpret the smile of their own baby as anything other than the outward manifestation of contentment or happiness. This is entirely understandable, yet it is also a valuable reminder that the baby's perceptual hold over the parent is surprisingly strong and that the exchange of smiles between parent and baby is a complex transaction, or at the very least a two-way street.

In his *The Expression of the Emotions in Man and Animals* (1872), Charles Darwin considered the origins of smiling in infants. He made a firm distinction between what he called real smiling and the merely reflexive and (to him) essentially meaningless smiling activity of the newborn baby. Predictably, perhaps, Darwin thought that gentle smiling was "the last trace of a habit, firmly fixed during many generations, of laughing whenever we are joyful. . . ." The path of development that he observed in his own children enabled him to observe the gradual passage or development of smiling into laughter. His idea appears to have been that the infant's smile was some kind of vestigial remnant of an inherited, latent tendency towards joyful laughter. The smile, he rightly observed, comes to babies before laughter, but, as is well known, "to those who have the charge of young infants, it is difficult to feel sure when certain movements about their mouths are really expressive; that is, when they really smile." Darwin noted that when his son Doddy reached the age of forty-five days, and, appearing to be in an altogether happy frame of mind, he smiled for the first time. That is, the corners of his mouth were retracted, and simultaneously the eyes became decidedly bright. I observed the same thing the following day; but on the third day the child was not quite well and there was no trace of a smile, and this renders it probable that the previous smiles were real. Eight days subsequently and during the next succeeding week, it was remarkable how his eyes brightened whenever he smiled, and his nose became at the same time transversely wrinkled. This was now accompanied by a little bleating noise, which perhaps represented a laugh. At the age of 113 days these little noises, which were always made during expiration, assumed a slightly different character, and were more broken or interrupted, as in sobbing; and this was certainly incipient laughter. The change in tone seemed to me at the time to be connected with the greater lateral extension of the mouth as the smiles became broader.

Darwin observed what he called the "first real smile" on the face of another of his children at exactly the same age, day forty-five, though by sixty-five days this more cheerful infant was smiling a lot more than the first and tended to make more incipient laughter noises. A third child began to smile earlier than the other two. In his rather cold way, observing and describing his children in the disengaged manner of a propagator of rare ferns or some other kind of greenhouse curiosity, Darwin's effort to understand the genesis of the smile is also moving, because in many respects we are no further forward than he in arriving at any firm conclusions from the observation of infants and babies. When does the smile of the infant become meaningful, indicative, "real"?

Along with various vocal utterances apart from crying, babies' smiles and other open-mouthed expressions—ogling, blowing, noise-making, sucking, and so on—appear to occur pretty randomly up to the age of six weeks, that is, they do not appear to relate to any prompting of the mother or father. In controlled environments in which the interaction of mothers and babies under the age of six weeks has been closely observed, relatively little evidence has been found of anything other than the apparently spontaneous smile reflex, although in the second month babies become more and more fixated upon their mother's eyes, far more so than their mouth or nose. Even so, anecdotal evidence of responsive or social smiling is notoriously difficult to substantiate. Moreover, parents tend to read their baby's smile as a social phenomenon well before it is a genuine response to their presence, or the sight of their faces. Parents also tend to create in their mind an artificial sense of dialogue or conversation, again sooner than the time at around eight weeks when smiling may be described as more truly social. The sense that the baby is responding to the mother can be irresistible, just as the mother's sensitivity to the tiniest of behavioral phenomena has been amply demonstrated, for example her impulse to unclench the baby's fists, or unravel the fingers, at times of anxiety or distress, often without being aware that she is doing it. One remarkable study demonstrated the way in which the pupils of some women's eyes instantaneously dilated upon being shown the photograph of a baby.

At eight weeks, a baby is aware of the difference between the mother and somebody else. On the other hand, it has been observed that later on, at three months, a baby may still smile to the nodding head of a wooden model or a balloon with two circles painted on, as if these substitutes were the face of a real person. In these well-known cases, a good deal of perplexity arose when the wooden model and the living, breathing person were both turned away and presented to the baby in profile. Neither profile could be made to elicit a smile from the baby, who responded only to the sight of the whole face, front on.

At the same time as these responses are beginning to take place, the mother feels able to supply her baby with steadily increasing verbal and other stimuli with which to elicit the smile response. One perfectly understandable reason for this is that by now smiles can be elicited rather more easily than a month ago, and it is a matter of some considerable satisfaction to discover that one can successfully coax that precious smile from the baby much more effectively than before. The extent to which the mother's verbal stimuli begin to provide a framework within which the baby's further development takes place may be illustrated by this transcript of the mother of an infant boy at thirteen weeks:

> Are you going to give me a smile?
> Or are you going to be naughty?
> Come on Alan.
> Come on.
> You can give Mommy a smile . . .
> [*etc.*]

The manner and kind of social interaction with which Alan responds to his mother is bound to evolve according to the patterns by which the mother forms a mental picture of Alan. Is he going to give Mommy a smile, or will he be naughty?

The most obvious conclusion to be drawn from studies of these early phases of infant development is that the social smiling of two- to three-month old babies is closely related to the spontaneous or primitive smile of the neonatal period. Only at four months does it seem universally accepted that the stimuli with which a smile is prompted or elicited from the baby are, in fact, familiar, in other words that the baby smiles in response to a recognizable face, a known voice, or a familiar prompt or gesture—rather than as a hitherto less salient kind of reflex. Even then, it seems clear that the four-month smile cannot yet be described as a message or a gesture passing from baby to mother. At that date it remains a relatively passive, rather generalized response to her deeply comforting presence, although at seventeen weeks the eyes are a far more engaging feature of the mother's face than her mouth. It is presumably this greater responsiveness that leads many parents to act as if they expect infants to be able to imitate them before they are in fact capable of doing so. Likewise, to the evident frustration of many scientists seeking definite signs of earlier, more sophisticated cognition, there is not much evidence to suggest that babies younger than six months discriminate between more than a few different sorts of facial expression adopted by their mother. Nor can they make many distinctions between faces that clearly do not belong to their parents.

This four-month hurdle is in many respects a crucial point of no return for babies, the time when, in psychological terms, the process of separation–individuation commences. The meaning of that rather ugly term is quite straightforward. Having hitherto dwelt in an environment in which the mother largely *was* the environment, and having already made some tentative steps toward familiarizing himself with the mothering side of his symbiotic self—a self that is yet to distinguish between the outside world and the internal world of his own body—the baby is now ready to establish a sense of his own bodily separateness from the world of reality that surrounds him, a world in which his mother still occupies an immensely important place as the primary love object. At six to seven months, this process is driven along by a great deal of experimentation, the pulling of mother's hair, the yanking of mother's ears or her necklace, the dogged putting of food into mother's mouth, and a good deal of forthright manual exploration of every nook and cranny of mother's head. All of this can be rather inconvenient, not to say painful, for the mother.

The old actor W. C. Fields advised never to work with animals or children. Many artists, particularly portrait painters, would say amen to that, because a subject that is incessantly moving about is obviously far more difficult to draw with precision than a subject that sits still. With little children you must work quickly and keep them sufficiently amused or distracted to keep them in one spot. Tiny babies are different; they can be held. But as everybody knows, from twelve to eighteen months and beyond, children are simply unstoppable. It is pointless to try to get them not to move a muscle. You must not only work around their irresistible urge to fidget or squirm, but find a way to stop them from jumping down and running away. When their patience is at an end there is no possibility of going on. Time passes very slowly for children, but it races along for the artist. The difficulties multiply with the number of sittings, unless of course they go well. Perhaps it is the challenge of capturing a child's unselfconscious smile that has caused many great artists to overcome these obstacles and produce images of great beauty and spontaneity, such as the host of memorable infant Jesuses in Renaissance painting and sculpture, or Bartolomé Esteban Murillo's mischievous, game-playing urchins in the Dulwich Picture Gallery, or the charming 1742 portrait of *The Graham Children* by William Hogarth in London.

In each case the representation of each child's smiling face is to the adult observer the more appealing surely because we sense that it is in some fundamental way genuine, not staged or "put on." Many little children find it quite difficult to sustain a fake grin, as many snapshot photographs attest. Some are rather better at it, evidently having in store what, in his 1845 poem "Rules and Regulations," Lewis Carroll called "ready quick smiles." Yet still we think we can tell when children are trying too hard. Maybe we sense that the open smile of a child is not yet overshadowed by the emotional bluster of adolescence, the experience of which most of us shudder to recall. Nor do we feel it is wholly reined in by the moderating conventions of adult behavior. The powerful concept of innocence makes a tremendous difference to the way we read the smile on the face of a little child. No doubt we expect and hope that older children will be well behaved, but we also know that there are no guarantees about that.

Murillo's children in Dulwich are obviously naughty, the one luring the other away from his chores to play a game that is much more fun. The fact that the game-player grins enthusiastically from ear to ear demonstrates that this must be what is going on. Yet, though naughty, that same smile must also reassure us (especially those of us who recall being naughty once) that this little drama is unfolding in exactly the way one might reasonably expect it to, and that with this particular child nothing is too seriously wrong.

Eternal Smiles his Emptiness betray,
As shallow streams run dimpling all the way.

ALEXANDER POPE, from
"An Epistle to Dr. Arbuthnot," 1735

"Well! I've often seen a cat without a grin," thought Alice; "but a grin without a cat! It's the most curious thing I ever saw in my life!"

LEWIS CARROLL, from
Alice's Adventures in Wonderland, 1865

6

Deceit

Most people have from time to time found themselves having to pose for a photograph in which they are expected to smile. For the benefit of those who find it difficult to do so consciously, without strain or artifice, the photographer may assist by inviting them to say "cheese." For those who have no difficulty in smiling naturally for the camera, saying *cheese* will be redundant. Yet they respond, not wishing to seem uncooperative. For others, having to pose for this particular photograph may for various reasons seem amusing or ridiculous; they will break into an involuntary smile, suppress a laugh, or both, and will not need prompting. For the rest of us, however, speaking the word *cheese* will apparently reproduce the appearance and effect of a natural smile for the benefit of the camera and, at least in theory, will relieve us of any need to simulate or feign a happy mood that may for any number of reasons elude us. Such assisted or simulated smiles may vary in effectiveness. In the resulting photograph they might seem entirely natural or hesitant or boisterous or pretty or ugly or slightly deranged, as the case may be. Inevitably these impressions will vary from person to person.

The convention of saying *cheese*, which originated in British public schools in about 1920, now seems well established in the English language. Yet there have been alternatives to *cheese*. Cecil Beaton apparently preferred *lesbian* and, according to Nancy Mitford in her novel *Love in a Cold Climate*, Cedric Hampton, the exotic Canadian protegé of Lord and Lady Montdore, persuaded his patroness to say *brush* before entering a room because "it fixes at once this very gay smile on one's face." Some Australian households have begun to use *money*, while the less materialistic but equally forthright *sex* is rapidly gaining in popularity. There are, as well, numerous equivalents of *cheese* in other languages, most of which are also foodstuffs. Spaniards say *patata* (potato). The Danes use *appelsin* (orange); the Swedes *omelett* (sic); the Finns *muikku* (a kind of fish); the Koreans *kim chi* (cabbage); the Poles *dzem* (marmalade) and the Chinese *qiezi* or *ch'ieh tzu* (eggplant). The Japanese use the English word *whisky*. Some Persian Farsi speakers say *holu* (peach), but only when the subject of the photograph fails to smile when asked.

By coincidence, the Czechs used to say *sýr* (cheese) but have apparently now opted for *fax*, which they regard as less bucolic for a newly constituted republic with strong aspirations toward modernity. The Dutch and the Greeks do not say anything. Malays and some other Muslims, Gypsies, North American Indians, and certain tribes of Aboriginal Australians, among many other indigenous peoples, have traditionally avoided having their photograph taken, so they do not say anything either. Some other languages have merely co-opted the English word *cheese*, for example Russian, Norwegian, Hungarian, Maltese, Swahili, and modern Hebrew, while the letter *x*, pronounced *sheez*, much like *cheese*, though far softer, is used by Brazilian Portuguese-speakers. Most other languages adopt the most obvious, least complicated course; photographers simply ask their subjects to smile, and they get on with it as best they can.

Who has not been struck by the incongruity of television news? Having read bulletins rich in famine, war, or some other manmade catastrophe, news editors beguile us with some carefully chosen odd-ity or snippet, the purpose of which is to lighten the burden of bad tidings and prevent us from jumping out the window. Such stories are not necessarily trivial, although Elizabeth Taylor, a scientific dis-covery with potentially enjoyable applications, celebrity weddings, an exotic arrival at the zoo, and other topics considered to be of hu-man interest—as if for those affected, earthquake or flood were not—save the day at times when something is needed to lighten our impression of what is happening in the world.

At these moments, news anchors, those responsible for mediating all this information with varying degrees of formality, give the audi-ence a radiant, dentally flawless smile. It is part of the performance. The anchor in question may have a headache. She may be concen-trating on a stream of instructions sent through her invisible earplug by a producer sitting in the booth upstairs. Yet she will smile, and her smile will make a fundamental difference to the way we absorb what she has told us. This is especially interesting given the fact, now much studied, that as soon as we have heard it, bad or happy, the news recedes into a quiet backwater of the brain whence it mostly evaporates. Many of us have great difficulty remembering what we have seen and heard on the news. Others will confess that it goes in one ear and out the other. What was on last Thursday's news bulletin? The answer to that question is comforting to those who, rightly or wrongly, find themselves engulfed in scandal.

Although by its very nature journalism is ephemeral, to the relief of most experienced journalists, for as long as it has existed there have been plenty of people with a low opinion of it. "The man who never looks into a newspaper," wrote Thomas Jefferson, "is better informed than he who reads them; inasmuch as he who knows nothing is nearer to the truth than he whose mind is filled with falsehood and errors." The cynical mode obviously suited the third president. These days, however, you do not have to look far to find a similar degree of hostility directed toward the fourth estate by people who, paradoxically, tend to have an insatiable appetite for newspapers and television, apparently unaware that if you do not like it, you can ignore or switch it off. While people complain that the media have plumbed new depths, we can rest assured that nothing has changed.

Of course, news anchors were not always noted for smiling. Thirty years ago, television networks clung to the idea of authority, which naturally filtered down to a distinguished-looking, fatherly anchor who, in the words of the critic, media academic, and commentator Neil Postman, "summoned forth men, events, and images at will," speaking in tones of certainty, fulfilling the role of a great sybil "with whom all things begin and end." Walter Cronkite was for years the paragon, and he did not smile often. Nor would his audience have expected him to. The very term *anchor*, with its nautical air and pig-iron weight, suggests something of the old approach. Naturally, the electronic media may no longer depend on this type of omniscient authority, though despite widespread cynicism (and much better knowledge about how the system works), many people obviously still thirst for it. Today they may feast on the outrageous opinions that spill copiously from commercial radio.

Instead, as is well known, the suited gentleman has been replaced by younger, equally persuasive personalities, and alternative formats have transformed news into "news entertainment." Some of these were deliberately made to resemble a family, whose tedious banter putatively makes more plausible the information purveyed between coffee breaks. Elsewhere, in more conventional formats, it became fashionable for a man and a woman of roughly equal age to read the news together, looking (at least in theory) not unlike a married couple. This had the advantage of providing each with another person to cajole or smile at in lighter moments and, it was thought, engage the sympathies of suburban millions. Further latitude was given to the person reading the weather forecast, who is allowed to engage in Puckish drollery, even when warning of hail or blizzards.

We may be perfectly aware that the winning smile of the news anchor is part of a seamless performance, but we are also aware that it conforms to wider expectations in respect of public behavior. The person behind a desk whose smile flickers in the ghostly blue light of the television set would presumably look rather similar if we found ourselves sitting in the same room on opposite sides of a boardroom table, or being interviewed by her for a job. Not for one moment do we suppose that her posed smile is in any of these situations a sincere expression of fondness directed to us personally, but we have some difficulty locating the precise degree to which she depends upon its masking function. Is the smile of the newsreader a highly evolved version of the mask of comedy, primarily a piece of theater, or is it inherently deceitful? Does the truth lie somewhere in between?

Setting aside the important question "What is truth?" as Pontius Pilate did—and one has some sympathy for him—psychologists have for many years been intrigued by the subject of deceit. This term, which for most of us is laden with moral connotations, is in the psychological literature generally treated as neutrally as possible. In other words, issues of deceit and lying are often kept separate from the larger ethical questions of which we are aware in day-to-day life, although as everyone knows there can be morally defensible lies, just as there can be situations in which to tell someone the plain truth with all its consequences can be cruel. Moreover, the ability of a person to succeed in telling a lie, or of another to detect it, is in this context treated largely as an exercise in perception. Numerous studies and experiments have sought to pin down the various ways in which we try to find out whether somebody is lying, or at least disguising various degrees of insincerity, by observing in minute detail their behavior and their facial expressions: whether or not, for example, our interlocutor makes eye contact, moves his head, blinks, pats his thighs, touches himself in some other way, makes flourishing hand gestures, pauses mid-sentence, or smiles.

In the late 1980s, an experiment was conducted among nurses who were filmed on segments of video. Off camera they were shown an obviously horrifying picture and invited first to record a deliberately false statement, describing what they saw as if it were something blissful. As they did so, the whole of their body and behavior were clearly visible. Then they were asked to record a second piece of video, this time describing honestly an agreeable image, which, like the first, was shown to them off camera.

Another crop of nurses, students this time, were then asked to view the pairs of videotaped statements and assess whether they thought the nurse in each segment was uttering a true statement or a false one. This study established that we are much better at detecting lies if we are given an opportunity to observe the liar twice, once when she is lying and a second time when she is telling the truth, or vice versa. Moreover, we get it right more often if we are given the truth first.

The reason for this may simply be that most people approach a task of this kind with the underlying expectation that they will be told the truth, or ought to be, which is from the social point of view reassuring. However, it was also found that when we suspect that a statement is deceptive, we tend to concentrate on the quality and consistency of the information contained in it, rather than on the wealth of signals carried by behavior that might better alert us to the right answer. It seems we are rather better at telling lies than detecting them. Indeed, another aspect of the same study demonstrated that nurses who were exceedingly good liars knew very well that they were, and frankly acknowledged that they lie effectively in real life. For the benefit of people who are out of sympathy with the nursing profession, I should add that the purpose of the study was to enable nurses to detect and foil the strategem regularly employed by deeply depressed, chronically ill patients who feign rapid improvement or recovery in order to escape supervision for the purpose of committing suicide.

Another, slightly earlier study showed that "the typical liar fools 86 percent of would-be detectors" and that we on the receiving end tend to base our judgments as to whether we are being told the truth on whether the teller *looks* honest. Naturally it follows that people who look honest, particularly (it seems) those with fresh, youthful, cherubic faces, make better liars. Intriguingly, it was also found that people from radically different cultural backgrounds, for example separate cohorts of Jordanian Arabs in Amman and university students in Texas, are surprisingly consistent in their opinions about what an honest or a mendacious face should look like. It goes deeper still, because not only do many of us think we can tell if a person is dishonest by the appearance of his face, but it seems that honesty and attractiveness go hand-in-hand; statistically, the ugly man is far more likely than an Adonis to be a thief.

Which of us does not recoil from such a cold hypothesis? Surely a sound case against it would proceed from the fact that if the beautiful man is more readily believed, and makes a better liar, he is therefore more likely to get away with a crime than the bumbling thief with dirty hair and spots whom everybody distrusts. Western society has amply demonstrated that what begins as distrust may soon turn into cold rejection, thus propelling the ugly or disfigured person into the category of outsider. Obviously it suits us when thieves look the part.

More recently, an attempt was made to find out exactly how smiling modifies or alters our perception of attractiveness in faces. This built on earlier work that suggested that without being aware of it, we tend to rely more heavily on the disposition of the lips and mouth than any other facial feature for guidance when we assess the attractiveness of another person's face. And we tend to process and absorb this information about the mouth in isolation from the whole face. The point is easily demonstrated by means of a curious illusion concocted some time ago in the Department of Psychology at the University of York in England. Two identical studio photographs of a smiling Margaret Thatcher were obtained from an unsuspecting branch of the British Conservative Party. One photograph was untouched. The other was altered by carefully cutting out the mouth and eyes, and pasting them back in the same position but inverted, so that the upper lip took the place of the lower, and vice versa. The two photographs were then displayed upside down and side-by-side. In this orientation, the expression on Mrs. Thatcher's face in each photograph appeared rather similar. However, when seen the right way up, the doctored photograph looked hideously disfigured, the corners of the mouth dragged menacingly down, the mad eyes leering horribly. This illusion, which is easily reproduced using a photograph clipped from the newspaper, suggests that in making sense of *upside-down* faces we "forgive" the topsy-turvy orientation of individual facial features, and greet with subconscious relief the sight of a smiling mouth, right way up, in isolation. Despite its manifest wrongness, we seem far happier with this than the sight of an inverted mouth on an *upright* face, scowling where a soothing, prime-ministerial smile should be.

The Margaret Thatcher illusion, as it came to be known, is not about distinguishing between doctored and un-doctored versions of the same photograph. Instead, the effect demonstrates how the uprightness of individual features on a distorted head will disturb the mind far less than distorted features on an upright head. And it is consistent with what we know about the precise way our eyes provide a complex web of data to the brain, which in fact informs our conscious mind of what we "see," obviously not what is projected onto the rear wall of the interior of our eyeballs (which is, in any case, upside down). The eyes do not capture a focused image of the face of the person standing in front of us. Instead, the eye moves over the surface of that face, fixing upon numerous separate points in rapid succession. Each point is very small, and sharply focused, but the surroundings that extend to the outer boundary of our field of vision are a blur. The brain uses the information provided by each fixture to build a cogent image of the whole, fooling us into thinking that our eye has captured it all, seamlessly focused. Paradoxically, this clever form of deception is what enables us to see perfectly, or imperfectly for those of us who wear spectacles. We do not understand how, between them, the brain and the eye decide where to alight, nor how a sequence is determined. The mind with its vast store of knowledge, prejudices, and expectations obviously controls this process, and ensures that our eyes never scan a familiar face in exactly the same way. However, we do know that when we look at faces our eyes tend to make the mouth a first port of call and that they focus on the other person's eyes almost as soon. There may be whole areas of the face that our eyes completely ignore, although we are generally intrigued, it seems, by anything out of the ordinary, such as a scar. We know this because for many years we have been able to track and record the precise motions of the eyeball.

Common sense tells us that an ugly person who grins from ear to ear will strike us as more cheerful and possibly even less ugly than when his face is in repose. This was indeed found to be true of a co-hort of male college undergraduates, who in addition attributed to smiling faces, as distinct from solemn ones, a variety of positive traits such as sincerity, sociability, and competence. But the same students thought that those smiling faces they regarded as attractive struck them also as less masculine and less independent than those faces they judged to be attractive in repose. (Walter Cronkite would presumably be gratified by this!)

Students of natural selection in the animal kingdom have known for years that effective liars far outnumber successful lie-detectors. As the authors of one comparative study point out: "In struggles over scarce resources and conflicts between predator and prey, deception confers a selective advantage. For thousands of generations the more cunning have left behind more offspring; hence deception has come to dominate the gene pool." Hundreds of species of animal are capable of extraordinary techniques of camouflage, mimicry, and deception. Some insects are indistinguishable from twigs. The chameleon adopts the color of its surroundings. The polar bear would appear to embody the same principle, except that the icy surroundings rarely change color. One parasitic beetle cunningly exposes wood ants to attack by using the ants' own "intraspecific" signals to trick them into grooming or regurgitating their food, thereby adopting positions that make it comparatively easy for the beetle to pounce. The more effective the techniques of deception these creatures adopt for their own protection and competitive advantage, the stronger is their chance of survival and the likelihood that their genetic characteristics will be passed from generation to generation, gaining in effectiveness. Though rare, such techniques of deception are sometimes used on each other by members of a single species. Some territorial birds mimic the loud squawking of stronger species to deter their rivals. This is advantageous in the avian mating game, and evidently works for some humans as well.

So in the course of millions of years, survival has depended more on the ability to deceive than to detect deceit, since recognizing a camouflaged predator at the last moment is no guarantee that you can catch and eat it—nor indeed of survival should it come after you—whereas ingenious camouflage both protects the wearer from its own predators while making it a more effective hunter. These observations have led psychologists to ask whether good liars, among whom a large proportion look honest, owe their capacity to lie successfully to the genetic inheritance of which their looks are one important manifestation. Could it be that truly honest people whom we tend to think look dishonest and untrustworthy are not only afflicted (like the prophetess Cassandra whom the god Apollo cursed by causing her prophecies to be disbelieved), but threatened with extinction as well?

In his macabre way Charles Dickens gave almost literal, if unwitting, expression to this idea in an essay in *The Uncommercial Traveller* (1861). "Whenever I am at Paris I am dragged by invisible force into the Morgue," he wrote.

I never want to go there, but am always pulled there. One Christmas Day, when I would rather have been anywhere else, I was attracted in, to see an old grey man lying all alone on his cold bed, with a tap of water turned on over his grey hair, and running drip, drip, drip, down his wretched face until it got into the corner of his mouth, where it took a turn, and made him look sly.

Dickens evidently found it possible to conceive the trickle of water playing over the mouth of a sodden corpse as something inherently shifty, possibly even deceitful, the fascinating leer of death to which he regularly directed his readers' attention.

A memorable symbol of the posed smile is the Cheshire Cat, one of the most remarkable of Lewis Carroll's imaginary inventions for *Alice's Adventures in Wonderland* (1865) and the subject of several of

John Tenniel's most famous illustrations. The text provides no clue as to the origin or meaning of the cat or the grin:

> The only two creatures in the kitchen, that did *not* sneeze, were the cook, and a large cat, which was lying on the hearth and grinning from ear to ear.
>
> "Please would you tell me," said Alice, a little timidly, for she was not quite sure whether it was good manners for her to speak first, "why your cat grins like that?"
>
> "It's a Cheshire-Cat," said the Duchess, "and that's why. . . . "
>
> "I didn't know that Cheshire-Cats always grinned; in fact, I didn't know that cats *could* grin."
>
> "They all can," said the Duchess; "and most of 'em do."
>
> "I don't know of any that do," Alice said very politely, feeling quite pleased to have got into a conversation.
>
> "You don't know much," said the Duchess; "and that's a fact."

There has never been a breed of cat known as the Cheshire. Yet the idea of the cat, and the phrase *to grin like a Cheshire cat* (as well as the rare local variants *to grin like a Cheshire polecat* and *to grin like a Cheshire cat eating gravel*), were not invented by Lewis Carroll. Instead it was a fairly common expression in Regency and Victorian England. The earliest printed reference comes in 1792 in the concluding lines of Peter Pindar's *A Pair of Lyric Epistles to Lord Macartney and His Ship*:

> *Yet, if successful, thou wilt be ador'd—*
> *Lo, like a Cheshire cat our Court will grin!*
> *How glad to find as many gems on board,*
> *As will not leave thee room to stick a pin.*

Intriguing explanations of the origins of the Cheshire cat have been proposed from time to time, several of them relating to badly painted heraldic imagery that was easily mistaken for the rounded forms of a well-fed cat. Maybe it is a vestigial reference to the wolf's head on the escutcheon of Hugh Lupus, the first earl of Chester, or perhaps a corruption of the old Cheshire emblem of a man standing astride a lion. Meanwhile, according to local historians, Cheshire cheeses were molded in the form of a cat, sometimes with whiskers and other feline motifs added for effect.

But why does the Cheshire cat grin? Elsewhere in *Alice* it is made clear that while the cat grins *all the time*, some variation is possible, as, for example, when Alice asks it for directions and it "grinned a little wider." The forthright way in which the cat conducts itself through the rest of their interview further underlines the weirdness of the grin. For according to the Cheshire cat the world is mad.

"But I don't want to go among mad people," Alice remarked.

"Oh, you can't help that," said the Cat: "we're all mad here. I'm mad. You're mad."

"How do you know I'm mad?" said Alice.

"You must be," said the Cat, "or you wouldn't have come here."

Alice didn't think that proved it at all; however, she went on "And how do you know that you're mad?"

"To begin with," said the Cat, "a dog's not mad. You grant that?"

"I suppose so," said Alice.

"Well, then," the Cat went on, "you see, a dog growls when it's angry, and wags its tail when it's pleased. Now I growl when I'm pleased, and wag my tail when I'm angry. Therefore I'm mad."

"I call it purring, not growling," said Alice.

Alice is not fooled by the Cheshire cat's line on growling. She knows very well that purring is not only a manifestation of deep contentment, but a social one as well. Cats cannot fake purring; nor, it is claimed, do they purr when they are alone. Though playful, real cats are almost entirely free of deceit.

At the time Lewis Carroll devised his version of the Cheshire cat, western attitudes towards grinning, smiling, and, indeed, facial beauty were being transformed by two parallel technological and scientific developments: the rapid growth of modern dental science and the spread of photography. The possibility not only of retaining one's teeth in adulthood, but also improving their appearance, changing their position, shape, and color, disguising their loss, even replacing them with artificial teeth, altering the contours of the face, eliminating deformities through surgery—all of these astonishing developments brought about a fundamental change in the way people saw the human face, and how they expected it to look back at them (Fig. 6.1).

Up to a point, bad teeth had been simply irrelevant to an estimation of facial beauty. Lord Palmerston, for example, Queen Victoria's Whig prime minister, was universally regarded as unusually good-looking. In fact, as a young man he was considered dazzlingly beautiful, possessed of a "strikingly handsome face and figure." Later he matured into an almost archetypical model of Victorian manhood, attracting among others the epithets "tall, dark and handsome," possibly for the first time. Palmerston's complexion was clear, his hair was black, his nose was small, and he had piercing blue eyes. The fact that he was missing several prominent teeth owing to hunting accidents was merely regarded as an additional demonstration of his dash and vigor, and by no means inconsistent with his looks.

From its tentative beginnings toward the end of the seventeenth century and its rapid development into full professional status in the nineteenth, the modern scientific development and clinical practice of dentistry brought about a revolution in private life. The grim task of tooth extraction was for centuries undertaken by doctors and surgeons, but had also been the province of barbers, blacksmiths, itinerant quacks, and others. King James enjoyed extracting other people's

FIGURE 6.1 L. Pousthomis (active late nineteenth century), *L'Avenir Dentaire* (*Dentistry of the Future*), c. 1895, color lithograph (poster), 34¾ × 24 in. Philadelphia Museum of Art, The William H. Helfand Collection.

teeth as a pastime and, according to the historian of dentistry Elisabeth Bennion, paid eighteen shillings to anyone willing to give him access to their mouth for his private amusement. The enormously fat "tooth-breaker," *Le Grand Thomas*, who plied his grisly trade on the Pont-Neuf in Paris in the first half of the eighteenth century, was a relatively late practitioner of a carnivalesque rite that had for centuries been conducted in market places and at fairs.

Primitive tools such as the "pelican," so-called because its levering handle resembled the bird's beak, were, in the hands of the wrong person, easily capable of botching the job and fracturing the lower jaw. Most people were so terrified of the pain of having a tooth extracted by leverage that they chose to grapple instead with agonizing toothache. Queen Elizabeth, who had terrible teeth, would not consent to have a rotten tooth pulled until she observed the bishop of London have one of his own healthy ones extracted, to prove it was tolerable. The toothkey, invented in the early eighteenth century, improved matters by making it possible to secure a tooth and extract it in a more or less perpendicular direction, which is less painful than levering it out sideways.

The dentist's art was from the earliest times not just concerned with the draining of abscesses and the solution of potentially dangerous medical problems arising from the corruption of teeth; it was always to some extent concerned, as it is today, with appearance, disguise—smoke and mirrors. Teeth excavated from ancient graves around the Mediterranean offer remarkable evidence of quite advanced techniques of wiring, bridgework, and the use of substitute or replacement teeth made of bone, ivory, or wood. All three were used in Rome. Later Muslim doctors regularly made dental prostheses and created wire ligatures for loose teeth between solid ones. Pre-Columbian graves in America have brought to light a jaw bone of a person who appears to have had carved pieces of sea shell implanted where the natural lower incisors once were. Frightful decorative tooth mutilations were also practiced, forming either a serrated edge or, by carving or shaving, fang-like points. Other teeth have been found in Mesoamerican graves that were inlaid with jade.

In the West many substances were experimented with, both as suitable materials with which to manufacture false teeth and as sound and satisfactory bases in which to set them, which in fact turned out to be the knottier problem. From the eighteenth century much improved methods of taking impressions of the jaws in beeswax and plaster vastly improved the standard of previously ill-fitting dentures, but the ever-widening smorgasbord of materials from which to carve or mold the actual teeth included coral, pearls, whalebone, walrus ivory, hippopotamus ivory, elephant ivory, the sterilized teeth of animals (goats, baboons, dogs, and sheep), and the bones of oxen, as well as copper, gold, silver, and agate, the metals sometimes enameled, sometimes not. In Japan flint was used, and sometimes nails driven into wooden dentures for an improved surface for biting. Imagine grinding fish and rice between wooden false teeth studded with iron nails.

In Regency London the satirical artist Thomas Rowlandson lampooned the glamorous fashion for porcelain false teeth, introduced by the French *dentiste* Nicolas Dubois de Chémant, who in his 1797 treatise on artificial teeth advocated the use of mineral substances instead of animal (Fig. 6.2). Experiments with transplanting real human teeth plundered from graves and battlefields (the nineteenth-century term was "Waterloo teeth," for obvious reasons) were unsuccessful, as may be imagined, though there was a persistent effort to keep trying until the more practical solution of mounting them instead gained wide acceptance. Indeed as late as the 1860s, the battlefields of the American Civil War yielded a rich vein of good young teeth from which to construct dentures.

Dentists have long balanced comfort, practicality, and the ability to eat and speak without "stuttering"—meaning without being interrupted mid-sentence by loose dentures clacking in your mouth—with more firmly cosmetic considerations, which remain a powerful underpinning of the dental profession today. The muscular and labial superstructure of the smile depends to a very large extent upon the infrastructure of the teeth or what, through technical ingenuity,

FIGURE 6.2   Thomas Rowlandson (1756–1827), *A French Dentist Shewing a Specimen of His Artificial Teeth and False Palettes*, 1811, hand-colored etching, 9¾ × 13¾ in. Philadelphia Museum of Art, The William H. Helfand Collection.

we succeed in substituting for the ones to which we are from time to time obliged to bid farewell.

The second nineteenth-century development that began to transform and, like dental science, continues to revolutionize western attitudes towards smiling was the invention of photography in about 1840, simultaneously by Niépce, Daguerre, Fox Talbot, and others. The excitement aroused by the rapid development of photography stimulated an even more fundamental revolution in the processes of human perception than did the spread of adequate dental care. Photography made it possible for artists and viewers to shape their expectations of facial beauty, and of the smile, by means of an ever-expanding range of spontaneous images, among an ever-widening population of subjects that spread far beyond the conventional boundaries of portraiture.

The portrayal of the face had always been an immensely complex and ever-changing transaction between artists, their subjects, and a growing population of onlookers. In history such a transaction was frequently regulated by social and cultural beliefs, governed by now-forgotten standards of decorum, and handled according to strict workshop practices. At the mid-point of the nineteenth century, however, a variety of private gestures that had previously been secluded behind a curtain of domesticity, manners that by general agreement had been excluded from the western portrait, were increasingly passing into the public realm through the medium of photography. Before long, more sensitive emulsions and accelerating shutter speeds would make it possible for photographers to capture people, not necessarily against their will, engaged in the unselfconscious acts of walking, talking, and laughing.

Yet in the realm of portrait photography, smiling was relatively slow to assume its triumphant, twentieth-century status as the dominant facial expression adopted before the lens of the camera. In his poem called "Hiawatha's Photographing," a brilliant parody of the verses of Henry Wadsworth Longfellow, Lewis Carroll, himself a skilled amateur photographer, wrote about a Victorian family sitting individually for a series of photographs. The high comedy of this ghastly event, in which every member of the family contrives to spoil the exposure, demonstrates how contradictory expectations, overwhelming practical difficulties, and social embarrassment overshadowed the practice of portrait photography in the earliest decades, up to the 1860s.

Hiawatha, Carroll's alter ego, tries hard to do justice to his subjects, but is confounded by a succession of mishaps. The father is naturally the first to pose, and though clearly trying for something grand and heroic adopts instead "a look of pensive meaning,/ As of ducks that die in tempests." Also, the old gentleman cannot keep still, so the photograph fails utterly. Then the mother, his simpering wife, insists on sitting in profile and holding a nosegay as big as a cabbage. She never stops chattering "Like a monkey in the forest." Her photograph fails as well. Next comes the beautiful eldest son, "the stunning Cantab," whose dandified costume and "curves of beauty" Carroll mocks (and evidently admires). After him the eldest daughter begs Hiawatha to give her a "look of 'passive beauty',," which appears to mean a "squinting of the left eye," a "drooping of the right eye," and "a smile that went up sideways/ To the corner of the nostrils." And so on down to the scruffy youngest son with tousled hair and a dusty jacket, who fidgets. After the sitting is over and the photographs are developed, Hiawatha presents the fruit of his labors to each member of the family:

> Then they joined and all abused it—
> Unrestrainedly abused it—
> As "the worst and ugliest picture
> That could possibly be taken
> Giving one such strange expressions!
> Sulkiness, conceit and meanness!
> Really anyone would take us
> (Anyone who did not know us)
> For the most unpleasant people!"
> (Hiawatha seemed to think so—
> Seemed to think it not unlikely).

In the earliest decades of photography, portraiture such as Hiawatha's was severely constrained by the immense length of time required for an adequate exposure. Early calotypes produced up to the mid-1850s frequently required exposures of up to forty-five minutes, making it very difficult even to photograph trees in the landscape, and quite impossible to photograph animals, water, or people. Through constant experimentation with alternative chemicals and processes like collodion, rapid advances were made so that by the late 1850s "instantaneous" photographs were becoming both practical and effective methods of capturing portrait likenesses. Still, however, it was essential to keep absolutely still for as long as possible. To that end a variety of iron head braces, calipers, straps, and rods were employed to stabilize the sitter in the photographer's studio, while an ever-growing repertoire of props and accessories crowded in to provide visual interest, composition, and exotic backgrounds. The long average duration of these early exposures simply made it impossible to smile.

By contrast, an enormous number of European genre painters were in the same period serving up smiling adolescent girls to an appreciative, not to say prurient, adult male audience. Each season deshabillé milkmaids with cracked pitchers, minstrels plucking stringed instruments, barefoot gypsies and shepherdesses, sea-nymphs, pale little flower-sellers, even lost children and vagrants, cloyingly sanitized, tumbled in their thousands from the walls of the annual salons, exhibiting societies, and picture galleries of every European capital. A large proportion of these subjects begin to smile "sweetly," coquettishly, or suggestively well before the end of the nineteenth century. Yet portrait paintings and photographs, images of real people, particularly adults, are conspicuous in lagging behind this very widespread genre of young girls who smiled with their mouths open.

The so-called *grandes horizontales*, famous European courtesans such as Cléo de Mérode, La Belle Otero, Lillie Langtry, and Lina Cavalieri, many of whom became celebrities of the highest order during the 1890s, tended to be photographed without smiling, or else wearing the faintest of smiles. But their poses, décolletage, the tilt of the head, and the various accoutrements were unmistakably demi-monde—and no-one was under any illusion as to the question of their identity, source of income, and high professional standing. When therefore did smiling pass into the language of portrait photography? Why did respectable people, and everybody else for that matter, start saying "cheese"? The answer to that question must emerge not so much from static photographs, paintings, or engravings, but rather from motion pictures, which in so many respects revolutionized the way people looked at the world and at each other in the twentieth century, and today continue to dominate the way we perceive the world through the porthole of television.

The paradox contained in a static image of the smile is that it holds in isolation a single instant, borrowed with varying degrees of skill and subtlety from the unending sequence of motions that flicker restlessly across the human face. It is a crystallized fragment of that larger, living thing we perceive in real life. We do not see the path it steers from speech or repose to radiant energy and back again. The frozen image argues against the elasticity of the smile. It is, in its way, deceptive. The illusion of the living, breathing smile of the news anchor, the person advocating such-and-such a brand of toothpaste, the actor, the politician, and the used-car salesman, which we see in complex detail, close up, moving up and down, in all its stages over time, is powerful indeed. The moving image makes us think their smiles look exactly like the real thing.

The acceleration of shutter speeds and the introduction of better and more versatile lenses in our time has made it possible to freeze ever more exact moments of spontaneity that eluded artists in the past, and further transform the values associated with smiling. The open smile in this way emerged from the sphere of domestic privacy and adopted its present position as an apparently universal symbol of health and happiness. Look at the advertising campaign of any insurance company and you will see this kind of smile exploited with brio. In another sense, the open smile heralded the relaxation of western attitudes about erotic desire and human sexuality. These changes affected the way modern society observed the face of the public person, from the movie star to the president, from a face that sells lipstick to a face that feeds propaganda. In totalitarian art of the 1930s to 1960s (Hitler, Stalin, Mao), young heroes of the Revolution were inevitably portrayed with dazzling smiles. Indeed as the young Australian artist Tom Nicholson has pointed out, the fact that in Chinese revolutionary banner art every single person wears a laminated smile of equal resonance brings the strategy to its peak, and to a dead end. Mural-sized crowds of identical "Long March" smilers strike a dismally hollow chord.

Gnostic philosophers, who flourished in the eastern provinces of the late Roman Empire, thought that teeth were the battlements of the body. No less than the human skin, the lips, and the mouth, teeth still form a perceptual barrier between our self and what lies beyond. Although healthy teeth have obviously been embraced in our current iconography of glamour, it seems to me that they still retain some faint echoes of old attitudes. If the symmetry and whiteness of the teeth of the news anchor and the fashion model may be described as a modern phenomenon, we should also remember that, more than ever before, through the same mass media, teeth still have widespread associations with vampire myths, bizarre crime, the savage biting of hand-to-hand combat (even sport), unstoppable monsters of science fiction, and dozens of other manifestations of the horror esthetic. In fact, the dark irony with which many contemporary artists attack the meanings of the modern smile may reflect the unlikely persistence of that very ancient impulse to measure it against fluctuating standards of decorum, permissible boundaries of lewdness, and various conventions of concealment and display, to say nothing of how we might expect to observe in another person's face the outward signs of true happiness, or deceit.

The chief's eye flashed; but presently
    Softened itself, as sheathless
A film the mother-eagle's eye
    When her bruised eaglet breathes;
"You're wounded!" "Nay," the soldier's pride
    Touched to the quick, he said:
"I'm killed, Sire!" And his chief beside,
    Smiling the boy fell dead.

ROBERT BROWNING, from
"Incident of the French Camp," 1842

Dear Dawkins died very nicely in front of the college. He fell down in the street and was off to eternity. As he lay there he looked like a schoolboy, with all the wrinkles gone and a beatific smile on his face, the crutch flung aside. A nice end, and may I have one like it.

SIR MAURICE BOWRA, 1955

7

Conclusion: Happiness?

One of the greatest and enduring achievements of the Enlightenment in Europe was to uphold the right to what the historian Roy Porter calls "the pursuit of temporal happiness as the *summum bonum*." How fortunate we are to have inherited this noble idea; how few of us recognize its value and take advantage of it when in so many other places it is denied to so many.

Yet it seems our quest for happiness is fraught with difficulties. Many people who are healthy and relatively rich in material comforts find themselves inexplicably dissatisfied and unhappy; to those who suffer from it, the "black dog" of depression is a cruel and tenacious reality of modern life. Others find real happiness in simple pleasures such as sunshine and fresh fruit, or in the Eastern religions. We know that we cannot rely on the smile worn by another person as an infallible gauge of their happiness any more than we may conclude from the exhausted panting of the Olympic swimmer that she is disappointed with the record-breaking performance that won her the gold medal and not, in fact, deeply elated. Yet we will be reluctant to think that a person who positively beams with pleasure is deeply unhappy.

In our time we have made a concerted effort to exploit the powerful effects of the smile to make other people happy, with mixed success. We may deploy a sympathetic smile to alleviate the distress of a widowed relative, for example, or somebody in trouble or in need. It strikes us as strange that a nineteenth-century Scottish clergyman could knock on the door of a recently-bereft widow, enter, sit with her in the parlor for twenty or thirty minutes, head bowed, and then take his leave without at any stage speaking or smiling. For their part both widow and parson might have found anything else entirely inappropriate, trivializing, even disrespectful. By the fact of his visit alone, and his thoughtful, solemn silence, the clergyman fulfilled his Christian obligation to a member of his flock; she, in turn, weeping, drew comfort from that moving demonstration without the need to waste words or trade smiles.

Today we tend to find solemnity discomfiting, and at times do our best to fill leaden silences, alleviate gloom, ease tension. We seek smiles at times when once they were rarely deployed. One of the most macabre images in Evelyn Waugh's brief novel *The Loved One* is that of Mr. Joyboy the mortician putting the finishing touches to a corpse. His assistant "watched with never-failing admiration the deft flick of the thumbs" with which Mr. Joyboy applied a template made from his visiting card to the lifeless mouth, and "the caress of the rubber finger-tips with which he drew the dry and colorless lips into place. And behold! Where before had been a grim line of endurance, there was now a smile. It was masterly. It needed no other touch." How distant this cosmetic smile seems from the lurid sneer that Charles Dickens observed on the face of a wet corpse in the Paris morgue.

The modern funeral trade is still an easy target for satire, with its hushed formality and taste for illusion. Yet the tactful, professional smile of the modern undertaker is no more than a reflection of a widespread impulse to offer friendship or sympathy to someone in need; and the smile we apply to the lips of a corpse is a manifestation (admittedly extreme) of our modern disinclination to see death for what it is. Many of us in such moments will smile at the bereft widower, a silent acknowledgment that there is nothing much more we can do for him. We do not for a moment expect that it will make him happy, but we think it may in some small way ease the burden of grief that he carries for the time being, and we may be concerned (though hardly surprised) when that smile appears to do no good. Those of us, like the widower, who find ourselves on the receiving end will appreciate the gesture, even though we may find it impossible to respond. Do we expect too much from our smile? Is it a devalued currency?

As in every other aspect of modern life, living artists are mulling over these questions and weighing them up in their work. Responding to the unashamed glamour of the late twentieth-century smile as it is mediated by photography, cinema, advertising, and television, to say nothing of the size, symmetry, and whiteness of the contemporary tooth, many artists, such as Barbara Kruger, wonder what effect this visual language might have upon modern women's perception of themselves. In her wall-sized, silkscreen print on vinyl, Kruger beckons us to consider whether a dentally-flawless, laughing Marilyn Monroe is "not stupid enough" (Fig. 7.1).

The French performance artist Orlan approached a similar set of ideas from a more fundamental maxillofacial direction. In 1990, she embarked upon a project to transform her own face and body in seven stages of cosmetic surgery designed to yield particular facial features to be found in famous works of art, the nose of a School of Fontainebleau sculpture of Diana, the mouth of François Boucher's

Figure 7.1 Barbara Kruger (born 1945), *Untitled* (*Not stupid enough*) 1997, photographic silkscreen on vinyl, 109 × 109 in. Courtesy of the artist and Mary Boone Gallery, New York.

Europa, the forehead of the *Mona Lisa*, the chin of Sandro Botticelli's *Venus*, the eyes of Jean-Léon Gérôme's *Psyche*, and so on. Each stage was to be recorded on video and in various residues—photo documentation, vials of blood, and other "relics." The use of local anesthetic enabled Orlan to assume as far as possible the simultaneous roles of prone subject and detached onlooker, offering a surreal commentary, reading from texts, choreographing the people standing next to her. The operating table was decorated with bunches of grapes and other props "suitably sterilized in accordance with operating room standards," the surgeons and O.R. nurses were dressed in costumes designed by Paco Rabanne and joined by various other dancers and musicians. In the words of the critic Barbara Rose, "Orlan's brutal, blunt and sometimes gory imagery . . . transmits disquieting and alarming signals of profound psychological and social disorder that nobody in his or her right mind wants around the house. Her program also provides a devastating critique of the psychological and physical consequences of the distortion of nature implied in the advanced technology discovered by scientific research, from microsurgery to organ transplants to potential genetic engineering."

Although she is unique—but for certain echoes of late, camp Sarah Bernhardt—Orlan is not alone. A far more practical convergence of art and surgery occurred recently under the aegis of the Laboratory, a contemporary art project based at Oxford University's Ruskin School of Drawing, in association with the Cleft Palate Unit at Guy's Hospital in London. The project provided invaluable assistance to cleft palate patients undergoing a variety of maxillofacial surgery procedures by helping them to construct images that guided the surgeon within reasonable limits towards a preferred facial appearance. Previously, patients were confronted by the problem of how to describe in words how they wanted their face to look. The surgeon was similarly confronted with the problem of how to interpret what the patient said, and to make sure that it squared with what was practical or feasible in each case. The partnership of patients and artists, who together developed images that express in an immediate, visual form what previously had to be expressed in words alone—this partnership suddenly offered the patient access to a far more vivid means of communication with the surgeon, and offered the surgeon a solid diagram of the patient's wishes. The process unlocked desires that the patient, perhaps thinking them frivolous or unimportant, had not expressed. It might emerge, for example, that the shape of the patient's nose bothered him or her far more than a scar on the lip. This collaborative process made it possible to modify treatments accordingly and also offered the surgeon and the artist a way of developing alternative images with which to respond to the various issues raised by the patient.

Who knows what will happen to the smile in the future? If current trends in dental science develop as they have in the last thirty years, we may expect more and more effective cosmetic treatments to enhance and improve the function and appearance of our teeth. We will be able to make more subtle adjustments to our facial appearance, no doubt bearing in mind what can happen as a result of the "Michael Jackson" phenomenon. Cleft palate and harelip surgery will become ever more effective. Our teeth will get whiter, and possibly bigger. Their shape and disposition will become more regular, if we want them to. Gummy smiles, which have never bothered me, will gradually disappear, as will all sorts of other irregularities. No doubt this will benefit hundreds of thousands of people whose teeth and gums give them trouble. The smile, meanwhile, is getting broader, wider, fiercer, and seems certain to become more so. Faint smiles are increasingly thought of in scientific and psychological circles as something that falls short of a "true" smile. Gestures of modesty that rein in the smile in other parts of the world are today challenged as never before by the imagery that swims about in the western mass media. The old remark about somebody who smiles an awful lot, namely that "they are all eyes and teeth," is increasingly moribund. Varieties of smile that were observed in the past increasingly strike us as alien, such as "the pathetic forced smile of people who do not respect themselves," which jumps out of Anton Chekhov's *The Letter*, hits us on the head, and makes us wonder if we may still observe such a thing today or if it has, instead, receded into the world of vanished usage.

My own teeth are small and somewhat discolored. So I was told some years ago by my unselfconscious seven-year-old niece. I have a lot of fillings in the molars, and according to my dentist I grind my teeth at night without being aware of it. As I write this I am running my tongue over the rough upper edge of one of the canines, which I chipped a few weeks ago while I was speaking on the telephone. Yet I feel reluctant to exchange my teeth for something else. They are part of me, and I suppose I am aware that my smile will also change if they do. In the distant past we were encouraged to regard the loss of a rotting tooth as a bodily manifestation of moral corruption, and the pain of having the offending tooth extracted as a kind of penance with important moral consequences extending far beyond the relief of bodily discomfort. One seventeenth-century Dutch poet, Jacob Cats, summed up these considerations in verses he addressed to his own extracted tooth: "You were my own member, part of my own sick frame, now . . . you lie there rotten, hollow, worthless, lifeless bone. Part of me is dead—how can the rest last much longer?"

Yet there was a flip side to this outlook. The Renaissance historian Cynthia Troup has rediscovered the fascinating case of a nun of an order of oblates founded in Rome in the fifteenth century by St. Francesca Romana. Discovering a front tooth among the relics of the foundress, the nun secretly kept it for her own private devotional use. According to the eighteenth-century document in which this case was recorded, St. Francesca appeared to the unfortunate nun in a vision, instructing her to restore the missing tooth to its proper place in the jaw of her skeleton, thereby reuniting her mortal remains and strengthening their power to work miracles. Hurriedly, the nun returned tooth to socket, but an investigation of the incident led to an attempt to extract it once again from St. Francesca's jaw. The tooth could not be budged, a fact immediately attributed to the miraculous intervention of the saint. The sinner's tooth will fester and rot; the saintly tooth is immovable.

Like Jacob Cats, I had a little glimpse of mortality when I chipped my tooth, and I am aware that when I smile their imperfect state is clearly visible to others. Perhaps I am old-fashioned in feeling attached to my teeth, even if they do not seem quite so attached to me. Nowadays plenty of people willingly refurbish theirs, although the enormous cost of complicated dental procedures is a powerful incentive to preserve what remains of my own. The prospect of transforming one's smile by altering the teeth is much encouraged in the current literature of esthetic dentistry and yet that can only be one part of the whole story.

As we have seen, the motions and general disposition of the whole face make of our smile a fabulously versatile contortion, capable of many meanings, which we relish, weigh, and constantly build on. Only partly does it hinge upon the teeth, when indeed they are exposed. True, cosmetic surgery, botulinum toxin, and other methods of smoothing out creases, inflating saggy lips, and renovating tired faces are to some extent creating new canons of beauty, just as they have meandered about in the past, driven this way and that by fashion. But I doubt if the product of these more and more intrusive techniques will do more than straddle like so many bumps and troughs the muscles we use to marshal and display our smile, just as the arching mouse-skin eyebrows glued on some smooth eighteenth-century English foreheads tended to peel or droop when the glue dried up. We can be sure that no matter what we do to improve or alter the way we look, we will all continue to smile. Some of us will do it more than others; others will give the impression that they twinkle, smirk, grin, or beam, touching different nerves as the case may be. Babies will continue to delight us with their endogenous smile. Above all, we will not hesitate to "read" the smiling face, or its reflection in art, as we always have done, with profound interest in the progress and possibilities of the unique moment in which we watch it unfurl.

Appendix

The Spectator
no. 173
Tuesday, September 18, 1711.

Remove fera monstra, tuaeque
Saxificos vultus, quaecunque ea, tolle Medusae.

Ovid, *Met.*

In a late Paper I mentioned the Project of an Ingenious Author for the erect-ing of several Handicraft Prizes to be contended for by our *British* Artizans, and the tendency they might have to the Improvement of our several Manu-factures. I have since that been very much surpriz'd by the following Adver-tisement which I find in the *Post-Boy* of the 11th Instant, and again repeated in the *Post-Boy* of the 15th.

On the 9th of October next will be run for upon Coleshill-Heath in Warwickshire, a Plate of 6 Guineas Value, 3 Heats, by any Horse, Mare or Gelding that hath not won above the Value of 5*l*., the winning Horse to be sold for 10*l*. to carry 10 Stone weight, if 14 Hands high; if above or under, to carry or be allowed weight for Inches, and to be entered Friday the 5th at the Swan in Coleshill, before 6 in the Evening. Also a Plate of less value to be run for by Asses. The same Day a Gold Ring to be Grinn'd for by Men.

The first of these Diversions, that is to be exhibited by the 10£ Race-Horses, may probably have its use; but the two last, in which the Asses and Men are concerned, seem to me altogether extraordinary and unaccountable. Why they should keep Running Asses at *Coleshill,* or how making Mouths turns to account in *Warwickshire,* more than in any other parts of *England,* I cannot comprehend. I have look'd over all the Olympick Games, and do not find any thing in them like an Ass Race, or a Match at Grinning. However it be, I am inform'd that several Asses are now kept in Body-Cloaths, and sweated every Morning upon the Heath, and that all the Country Fellows within ten Miles of the *Swan,* grinn an Hour or two in their Glasses every Morning, in order to qualifie themselves for the 9th of *October.* The Prize which is proposed to be grinn'd for, has raised such an Ambition among the Common People of Out-grinning one another, that many very discerning Persons are afraid it should spoil most of the Faces in the Country; and that a *Warwickshire* Man will be known by his Grinn, as Roman Catholicks imagine a *Kentish* Man is by his Tail. The Gold Ring which is made the Prize of Deformity, is just the Reverse of the Golden Apple that was formerly made the Prize of Beauty, and should carry for its Posie the old Motto inverted.

Detur tetriori.

Or to accommodate it to the Capacity of the Combatants,

The frightfull'st grinner
Be the winner.

In the mean while I would advise a *Dutch* Painter to be present at this great Controversy of Faces, in order to make a Collection of the most remarkable Grinns that shall be there exhibited.

I must not here omit an Account which I lately received of one of these Grinning Matches from a Gentleman, who, upon reading the above-mention'd Advertisement, entertained a Coffee-house with the following Narrative. Upon the taking of *Namur,* amidst other publick Rejoicings made upon that Occasion, there was a Gold Ring given by a Whig Justice of Peace to be grinn'd for. The first Competitor that entred the Lists, was a black swarthy *French* Man, who accidentally passed that way, and being a Man naturally of a wither'd Look, and hard Features, promised himself good Success. He was placed upon a Table in the great Point of View, and looking upon the Company like *Milton's* Death,

Grinn'd horribly a ghastly smile.

His Muscles were so drawn together on each side of his Face, that he showed twenty Teeth at a Grinn, and put the County in some pain, least a

Foreigner should carry away the Honour of the Day; but upon a further Tryal they found he was Master only of the Merry Grinn.

The next that mounted the Table was a Malecontent in those Days, and a great Master in the whole Art of Grinning, but particularly excelled in the angry Grinn. He did his Part so well, that he is said to have made half a Dozen Women miscarry; but the Justice being apprised by one who stood near him, that the Fellow who Grinned in his Face was a *Jacobite*, and being unwilling that a Disaffected Person should win the Gold Ring, and be looked as the best Grinner in the Country, he ordered the Oaths to be tendered him upon his quitting the Table, which the Grinner refusing, he was set aside as an unqualified Person. There were several other Grotesque Figures that presented themselves, which it would be too tedious to describe. I must not however omit a Plowman who lived in the farther Part of the Country, and being very lucky in a Pair of long Lanthorn-Jaws, wrung his Face into such an hideous Grimace that every Feature of it appeared under a different Distortion. The whole Company stood astonished at such a complicated Grinn, and were ready to assign the Prize to him, had it not been proved by one of his Antagonists that he had practised with Verjuice for some Days before, and had a Crab found upon him at the very time of Grinning, upon which the best Judges of Grinning declared it, as their Opinion, that he was not to be looked upon as a fair Grinner, and therefore ordered him to be set aside as a Cheat.

The Prize, it seems, fell at length upon a Cobler, *Giles Gorgon* by Name, who produced several new Grinns of his own Invention, having been used to cut Faces for many Years together over his Last. At the very first Grinn he cast every Human Feature out of his Countenance; at the second he became the Face of a Spout; at the third a Baboon, at the fourth the Head of a Base-Viol, and at the fifth a Pair of Nut-Crackers. The whole Assembly wondered at his Accomplishments, and bestowed the Ring on him unanimously; but, what he esteemed more than all the rest, a Country Wench, that he had wooed in vain for above five Years before, was so charmed with his Grinns, and the Applauses which he received on all sides, that she Married him the Week following, and to this Day wears the Prize upon her Finger, the Cobler having made use of it as his Wedding Ring.

This Paper might perhaps seem very impertinent, if it grew serious in the Conclusion. I would nevertheless leave it to the Consideration of those who are the Patrons of this monstrous Tryal of Skill, whether or no they are not guilty, in some measure, of an Affront to their Species, in treating after this manner the *Human Face Divine*, and turning that Part of us, which has so great an Image impressed upon it, into the Image of a Monkey; whether the raising such silly Competitions among the Ignorant, proposing Prizes for such useless Accomplishments, filling the common Peoples Heads with such Senseless Ambitions, and inspiring them with such absurd Ideas of Superiority and Preheminence, has not in it something Immoral as well as Ridiculous.

Notes

Numbers preceding notes refer to pages on which corresponding passages of text appear.

EPIGRAPHS

vii "Shakespeare, *Twelfth Night*": The lines (78–80, Arden Shakespeare ed., p. 88) are spoken by Maria, the Countess Olivia's waiting gentlewoman, and refer to the Countess's pompous steward Malvolio, who has been tricked into thinking that his mistress is in love with him. (The map with "augmentation" has been identified as the chart prepared under the supervision of the geographer Richard Hakluyt [1552–1616] among others, and published in London in about 1600. Employing the principles of projection, it showed North America and the East Indies in greater detail than ever before. It was also notable for radiating rhumb lines, akin to "laughter lines," that indicated the meridians. See the Arden Shakespeare ed. [1975], London: Methuen, p. xxxii, citing Coote, C. [1877–79]. *New Shakespeare Society Transactions*, June 14, 1878, p. 88.)

vii "Shelley after Dante": Shelley, P. (1876). *The Poetical Works of Percy Bysshe Shelley*, edited by H. Buxton Forman. London: Reeves & Turner, vol. IV, p. 247; after Dante Alighieri (1290–94/1980). *Vita Nuova*, edited by D. De Robertis. Milan: Riccardo Ricciardi Editore, XXI, 2, pp. 138–141. Dante's sonnet, *Ne li occhi porta*, concludes thus (lines 9–14):

> *Ogne dolcezza, ogne pensero umile*
> *Nasce nel core a chi parlar la sente,*
> *Ond'è laudato chi prima la vide.*

Quel ch'ella par quando un poco sorride,
non si pò dicer né tenere a mente,
sì è novo miracolo e gentile.

Shelley is said to have scratched his translation of these lines on a window-pane of the house in London where he lodged.

vii *"Pack Up Your Troubles"*: Harrowven, J. (1977). *The Origins of Rhymes, Songs and Sayings.* London: Kaye and Ward, pp. 307–309. Felix Asaf (Felix Powell), who wrote the tune, and his brother George, who wrote and sang the lyrics, were Welsh show-business professionals who worked in various troupes in the north of England. *Pack Up Your Troubles* won a competition run by the British music publishers Francis and Day to find the best marching song of the year. A "Lucifer" was a brand of match and a "fag" was a cigarette.

PREFACE

xvi "Rex Butler": Butler, R. (1996). *An Uncertain Smile.* Sydney: Artspace Visual Arts Centre, p. 17 ff. Butler's title alludes to *Un Certain sourire*, the 1956 novel by Françoise Sagan (Paris: Julliard), in which a young woman has an affair with her boyfriend's uncle.

xvi "BBC": Bates, B., with Cleese, J. (2001). *The Human Face.* London: BBC Worldwide.

xvi Vaizey, M. (2002). *The British Museum: Smile.* London: The British Museum Press.

xvi "literature for children": See for example Levinson, R. (1989). "Why Do We Smile?" in his *Why Do Eskimos Rub Noses?* London: Arrow Books, pp. 23–24.

INTRODUCTION: "THE SERIOUS AND THE SMIRK"

xxi "two styles of portrait painting": The words are uttered by Miss La Creevy, "sinking her voice to a confidential whisper," while painting the portrait of Kate Nickleby.

xxi "Horace in his Odes . . . ": Hutchings, M. (1951). *The Special Smile.* London: Hodder and Stoughton, p. ii.

xxii "Golden Mean": also known as the *section d'or*, an irrational proportion traditionally ascribed to the circle of Pythagoras (*c.* mid–late sixth century B.C.), and long believed to reflect some larger aesthetic or proportional harmony to be found in nature. It may be defined as a line divided so that the smaller part is to the larger as the larger is to the whole (that is, the sum of the smaller and larger parts), which in practice yields a ratio of approximately 8:13. The concept may also be expressed as follows: The line $\propto\beta$ is cut at γ, such that $\gamma\beta:\propto\gamma=\propto\gamma:\propto\beta$. After the invention of algebra, this ratio was more precisely defined as ϕ, where $\phi = ([1 + \sqrt{5}]\div 2)$, i.e. approx. 1.618. See Huntley, H. (1970). *The Divine Proportion: A Study in Mathematical Beauty*. New York: Dover Publications, and most recently Snow, S. (1999). "Esthetic smile analysis of maxillary anterior tooth width: the golden percentage," *Journal of Esthetic Dentistry, 11:4*, pp. 177–184.

xxiii "St. Apollonia": (d. c. 249 A.D.), of Alexandria, an elderly deaconess and martyr. Her feast day is February 9. The earliest hagiographers make it clear that St. Apollonia's teeth were knocked out while she was being beaten, not extracted one by one—the more lurid torture imagined in later accounts. See Bruck, W. (1915). *Das Martyrium der heiligen Apollonia und seine Darstellung in der bildenden Kunst*. Berlin: Hermann Müsser, and Nux, H. (1947). "Saint Apolline, patronne de ceux qui souffrent des dents," *Revue d'odontologie, de stomachologie, 3*, pp. 113–153.

xxiii For the Habsburgs' mandibular prognathism, see Hart, G. (1971). "The Habsburg Jaw," *Canadian Medical Association Journal, 104*, April 3, pp. 601–603; Loevy, H., and Kowitz, A. (1982). "The Habsburgs and the 'Habsburg Jaw'," *Bulletin of the History of Dentistry, 30:1*, April, pp. 19–23, and Wolff, G. (1993). "On the Genetics of Mandibular Prognathism: Analysis of Large European Noble Families," *Journal of Medical Genetics, 30*, pp. 112–116.

xxiii "the worst teeth": The examples I have in mind occur regularly from the twelfth century onwards in northern European paintings of scenes of the passion, particularly the *Mocking of Christ* and the *Flagellation*. The same treatment is meted out to the Roman soldiers in the *Crucifixion*, particularly the sponge-bearer, and to Jews *en masse*. See Mellinkoff, R. (1993). *Outcasts: Signs of Otherness in Northern European Art of the Late Middle Ages*. Berkeley: University of California Press, pp. 121–122.

xxiv "an old sale catalogue": Sotheby's (1990). *European Works of Art, Tapestries and Furniture*. New York: Sotheby's, May 31, 1990.

xxv "Fuseli": Becker, C. (1997). *Johann Heinrich Füssli: Das Verlorene Paradies*. Stuttgart: Staatsgalerie, nos. 66, 68, 69, and 70.

xxv "Dolly Varden": Lambourne, L. (1982). *An Introduction to 'Victorian' Genre Painting from Wilkie to Frith*. London: Her Majesty's Stationery Office, p. 39.

xxv "Cruickshank's oyster": Sandback, A. (1993). "George Cruickshank: In Appreciation of a Knowing Smile," *Print Collectors' Newsletter, 24:3*, July–August, p. 98. The illustration appears in successive editions of Clarke's immensely popular 1830 *Three Courses and a Dessert: Comprising Three Sets of Tales*. London: Vizetelly, Branston & Co., Fleet Street.

xxv "boy cleaning fish": The painting is by Nicolaas Rijnenburg, who was active in Leiden, and is dated 1782. It was offered in Sotheby's sale *Old*

Master Paintings and Frames, including Property from the Südwestrundfunk Collection, Amsterdam, Tuesday, November 9, 1999, lot 98, p. 62.

xxv "buttons": Ertell, V. (1973). *The Colorful World of Buttons.* Princeton: The Pyne Press, plate 40, in particular certain cuff buttons: nos. 2 & 6 (both smiling), and 15 & 19 (one jolly, one weeping).

xxv "spoons": Emery, J. (1976). *European Spoons Before 1700.* Edinburgh: Donald, pp. 1, 83.

xxv "Machiavelli": Viroli, M. (1998/2000). *Niccolò's Smile: A Biography of Machiavelli,* translated by Antony Shugaar. New York: Farrar, Straus and Giroux, pp. 4–5. See also Nicholas Fearn's review "Not Half So Bad as Painted," *Spectator,* March 17, 2001, p. 68.

xxv "Kant": Butler, R. (1996). *An Uncertain Smile.* Sydney: Artspace Visual Arts Centre, p. 17 ff.

xxv "Coquelin": Margot Asquith (Countess of Oxford and Asquith), *The Times,* February 8, 1938, p. 15.

xxvi "a talk about smiling": Trumble, A. (1998). "Changing Concepts of Decorum and Allure in the Representation of Teeth in Art," *Annals of the Royal Australasian College of Dental Surgeons, 14,* pp. 35–40.

xxvii "Taine": Taine, H. (1872). *Notes sur l'Angleterre,* Paris: Hachette *et cie;* Christiansen, R. (2000). *The Visitors: Culture Shock in Nineteenth-Century Britain.* London: Chatto & Windus, p. 128. The phrase is Peter Vansittart's: *Spectator,* May 27, 2000, p. 39.

xxviii "Anthony Trollope": Glendinning, V. (1992). *Trollope.* London: Hutchinson, pp. xxi–xxii.

xxviii *"Dombey and Son"*: Gane, G. (1996). "The Hat, the Hook, the Eyes, the Teeth: Captain Cuttle, Mr. Carker, and Literacy," *Dickens Studies Annual, 25,* pp. 91–126.

xxix "Sarah Bernhardt": Winter, W. (1893). *Shadows of the Stage.* New York: Macmillan and Co., vol. 2, p. 319.

xxix "Tasmanian Aborigines": The reference is in the journal of Ferdinand-Alphonse Hamelin, captain of the ship *Naturaliste,* of which a transcription exists in the National Library of Australia, Canberra: Hélouis MSS, folder 10, p. 391: *"Il serait difficile de trouver à Paris 36 bouches aussi bien garnies de dents très blanches sur le même nombre de personnes."* I am most grateful to Jane Southwood for alerting me to the existence of this intriguing reference.

xxx "traveling salesmen": Strasser, S. (1993). "'The Smile that Pays': The Culture of Traveling Salesmen, 1880–1920," in Gilbert, J., et al., eds., *The Mythmaking Frame of Mind: Social Imagination and American Culture.* Belmont, Calif.: Wadsworth Publishing Company, p. 167.

xxx "testosterone": Dabbs, J. (1997). "Testosterone, Smiling, and Facial Appearance," *Journal of Nonverbal Behavior, 21,* pp. 45–55; also Dabbs, J., with

Dabbs, M. (2000). *Heroes, Rogues, and Lovers: Testosterone and Behavior*. New York: McGraw-Hill.

xxx "people in restaurants": Adams, R. and Kirkevold, B. (1978). "Looking, Smiling, Laughing, and Moving in Restaurants: Sex and Age Differences," *Environmental Psychology and Nonverbal Behavior*, 3:2, winter, pp. 117–121.

xxx "Olympic gold medal winners": Fernandez-Dols, J., and Ruiz-Belda, M. (1995). "Are Smiles a Sign of Happiness? Gold Medal Winners at the Olympic Games," *Journal of Personality and Social Psychology*, 69, pp. 1113–1119.

xxxi "French attitudes": Platt, P. (1995). *French or Foe? Getting the Most Out of Visiting, Living and Working in France*. Paris: Culture Crossings, pp. 24, 25; also French, M. (2000). "Grin and Bare It," *Boston Globe Magazine*, September 11, p. 25.

xxxi "the Amrozi incident": Heryanto, A. (2002). "Politically Incorrect Smiles in Bali," *UniNews* (University of Melbourne), vol. 11, no. 26, December 16–30, 2002, p. 5.

xxxii "O. G. Roeder": Roeder, O. (1972). *Smiles in Indonesia*. Jakarta: Gunung Agung, pp. 8–9.

xxxiv "*Sulwan al-Muta* of Ibn Zafar": Yaboubi, M. (1999). *Islamic Art and Patronage: Treasures from Kuwait. An Exhibition from the Collection of Dar al-Athar al-Islamiyyah*. Kuwait: British Press, pp. 62–63.

xxxiv "book about on sexual desire": Scruton, R. (1986). *Sexual Desire: A Philosophical Investigation*. London: Weidenfeld and Nicolson, pp. 64–66.

xxxvi "Washington": Pryor, W. (1933). "The Closed Bite Relation of the Jaws of George Washington, With Comments on his Tooth Troubles and General Health," *Journal of the American Dental Association*, 20, April, pp. 567–577; Hilkene, R. (1965). "The Dental Health of the Presidents," *Bulletin of the History of Dentistry*, 13:4, October, pp. 13–50; see also Darnton, R. (1997). *George Washington's False Teeth: An Unconventional Guide to the Eighteenth Century*. New York: W. W. Norton & Co., pp. ix, xiv–xv.

xxxvi "Madison": Hunt, G. (1902). *The Life of James Madison*. New York: Doubleday, p. 151.

xxxvi "Jefferson": Schouler, J. (1897). *Thomas Jefferson*. New York: Dodd, Mead, p. 207.

xxxvi "Adams": Adams, J. (1860). *Memoir of the Life of John Quincy Adams*. Boston: Crosby, Nichols, Lee, p. 175.

xxxvii "Lincoln": Tarbell, I. (1909). *The Life of Abraham Lincoln*. New York: Doubleday, McClure & Co., vol. 1, p. 49, and vol. 2, pp. 51–52.

xxxvii "Grant": Boyd, J. (1885). *Military and Civil Life of Gen. Ulysses S. Grant*. Philadelphia: McCurdy, p. 114.

xxxvii "Cleveland": Stevenson, R. (1962). "The Secret Operation on President Cleveland," in his *Famous Illnesses in History*. London: Eyre & Spottiswoode, pp. 44–51.

xxxviii "Theodore Roosevelt": Pringle, H. (1931). *Theodore Roosevelt: A Biography*. London: Jonathan Cape, Ltd., p. 519; see also King, O. (1919). "Did 'Theodore Roosevelt's Teeth Kill Him?'," *The Journal of the National Dental Association*, 6:6, June, pp. 561–565.

xxxix "proud, prelatical, and pompous": Lockhart, J. (1949). *Cosmo Gordon Lang*. London: Hodder & Stoughton, pp. 290–291; Chadwick, O. (1983). *Hensley Henson*. Oxford: Oxford University Press, p. 244, and Beeson, T. (2002). *The Bishops*. London: SCM, p. 23. The more common but erroneous variant of this famous anecdote has it as "proud, pompous and prelatical." Henson, it is said, "had startling eyebrows that pointed diagonally outwards."

xxxix "Sir William Erle": For this and other observations from the bench I am indebted to Sir John Young.

xl "A small sample from America in 1950s": Heiman, J., ed. (2001). *50s American Ads*. Cologne and New York: Taschen. "Cigarillo": p. 94; "Blatz": p. 43; "Jeris": p. 378; "Broil Quik": p. 394; "Nadinola": p. 383; "10 minutes of fun" (the Jowett Institute of Physical Training): p. 376; "*I Married a Communist*": p. 537; "boxing champions": p. 535; "seductresses": pp. 503, 519; "Edward G. Robinson": p. 73; "Winston Churchill": p. 360. This advertisement predated Churchill's victory at the general election of October 1951.

xli "Littell": Littell, R. (2002). *The Company*. London: Pan Macmillan, p. 60.

xli "P. G. Wodehouse": Wodehouse, P. (1962). *Service with a Smile*. London: Herbert Jenkins, p. 72. In every way, Lavender Briggs was the true successor of Lord Emsworth's better known secretary, the efficient Baxter. ("His going had relieved this Garden of Eden of its one resident snake.") See Wodehouse, P. [1937]. "The Crime Wave at Blandings," in *Lord Emsworth and Others*. London: Herbert Jenkins.

xlii "blind people": See, for example, "Anecdotes of the Life of Mademoiselle de Salignac, A Blind French Lady," in Wilson, J. (1821/1995). *Biography of the Blind* . . . , edited by K. Stuckey. Washington, D.C.: Library of Congress, pp. 457–462.

xlii "*The Laughing Cavalier*": Ingamells, J. (1992). *The Wallace Collection: Catalogue of Pictures, IV: Dutch and Flemish*. London: Trustees of the Wallace Collection, pp. 136–138. An earlier (1928) catalogue still referred to the sitter's "disdainful half-smile and provocative air".

Chapter 1: Decorum

1 "St. Jean-Baptiste de la Salle": La Salle, Jean-Baptiste de, Saint (1703/1990). *Les Règles de la Bien-Séance et de la Civilité Chrestienne (The Rules of Christian Decorum and Civility)*, translated by R. Arnandez and edited by G. Wright. Romeoville, Ill.: Lasallian Publications, p. 25.

1　"John Doran": Doran, J. (1855). *Habits and Men, with Remnants of Record Touching the Makers of Both, by Dr. Doran*. London: Richard Bentley, p. 204.

3　"cavemen": Moss, M. (1944). *The Origin of the Smile and Laughter*. Dayton, Ohio: Mortimer Moss, pp. 4–5. Note, however, that primitive scenarios such as this, in which the fighting caveman is "bound in fast knots of invisible embarrassment and resignation, with teeth bared and eyes shut," have also been considered in relation to the neuromuscular sequences that lead to yawning. See Provine, R. (1989a). "Contagious Yawning and Infant Imitation," *Bulletin of the Psychonomic Society*, 27, pp. 125–126, and Provine, R. (1989b). "Faces as Releasers of Contagious Yawning: An Approach to Face Detection Using Normal Human Subjects," *Bulletin of the Psychonomic Society*, 27, pp. 211–214. Some scholars of infant psychology concur with the idea that the smile came into being essentially as an appeasement signal. See, for example, Lewis, D. (1978). "How to Read a Smile," in *The Secret Language of Your Child: How Children Talk Before They Can Speak*. London: Souvenir Press, p. 85.

3　"etiquette and manners": Turner, E. (1962). *What the Butler Saw: Two Hundred and Fifty Years of the Servant Problem*. London: Michael Joseph, pp. 218–219 (special voice), pp. 109–110 (holidays, books, gratitude), 126 (lady's maids).

5　For St. Jean-Baptiste de la Salle, see La Salle, Jean-Baptiste de, Saint (1703/1990). *Les Règles de la Bien-Séance et de la Civilité Chrestienne (The Rules of Christian Decorum and Civility)*, translated by R. Arnandez and edited by G. Wright. Romeoville, Ill.: Lasallian Publications, particularly "The Mouth, Lips, Teeth, and Tongue," pp. 25–26, and "Amusements: Article 1: Conversation and Laughter," pp. 84–86.

7　"expectorating": See *The Times*, March 22, 1900, p. 6 ("A Sufferer") and March 24, p. 16 (Viscountess Harberton). See also *The Times*, January 16, 1903, p. 4 (Dr. Alfred Hillier, writing on behalf of the National Association for the Prevention of Consumption and Other Forms of Tuberculosis).

8　"Chinese dramatic art": Zhao, M., and Yan, J. (1996). *Peking Opera Painted Faces—With Notes on 200 Operas*. Beijing: Morning Glory Publications, p. 13.

8　"Noh": Noma, S. (1957). "Noh," in *Masks*, translated by M. Weatherby. Rutland, Vt., and Tokyo: Charles E. Tuttle Co., n.p.

8　"vizards": Doran, J. (1855). *Habits and Men, with Remnants of Record Touching the Makers of Both, by Dr. Doran*. London: Richard Bentley, pp. 204–207.

9　"ancient Greek masks": Webster, T. (1949–1950). "The Masks of Greek Comedy," *Bulletin of the John Rylands Library, Manchester*, 32, pp. 97–133.

10　"*Gorgoneion*": Napier, A. (1986). *Masks, Transformation, and Paradox*. Berkeley: University of California Press, pp. 91–108.

11　"archaic smile": Charbonneaux, J. (1938). *La Sculpture grecque archaïque*. Paris: Éditions de Cluny, p. 29; Taylor, F. (1958). "The Archaic Smile:

The Relation of Art and the Dignity of Man," *Daedalus: Proceedings of the American Academy of Arts and Sciences*, 86:4, pp. 286–287; Carpenter, R. (1959). *The Esthetic Basis of Greek Art of the Fifth and Fourth Centuries B.C.*. Bloomington, Ind.: Indiana University Press, pp. 64–67; Richter, G. (1960). *Kouroi: Archaic Greek Youths: A Study of the Development of the Kouros Type in Greek Sculpture*, London: Phaidon, pp. 1–6; Pollitt, J. (1972). *Art and Experience in Classical Greece*. Cambridge: Cambridge University Press, p. 9; Donohue, A. (1988). *Xoana and the Origins of Greek Sculpture*, Atlanta, Ga: Scholars Press, pp. 40–42; Stewart, A. (1990). *Greek Sculpture: An Exploration*. New Haven: Yale University Press, pp. 111–115; Ridgway, B. (1993). *The Archaic Style in Greek Sculpture*, second edition, Chicago: Ares, pp. 14–15. I am most grateful to Dr. Joan Mertens, Curator of Greek and Roman Antiquities at the Metropolitan Museum of Art in New York, for her help with this complex subject.

18   "Princesse de Broglie": The full details of the painting are as follows: Jean-Auguste-Dominique Ingres, French, 1780–1867, *Joséphine-Éléanore-Marie-Pauline de Galard de Brassac de Béarn (1825–1860), Princesse de Broglie*, 1853, oil on canvas, 47¾ × 35¾ in., Metropolitan Museum of Art, New York, Robert Lehman Collection, 1975.1.186. See Baetjer, K. (1995). *European Paintings in The Metropolitan Museum of Art by Artists Born Before 1865*. New York: Metropolitan Museum of Art, p. 400. See also Broglie, A., (1941). *Mémoires du Duc de Broglie*. Paris: Calmann-Lévy.

22   "Mona Lisa": The best diving board into the vast literature is now Sassoon, D. (2001). *Mona Lisa: The History of the World's Most Famous Painting*. London: HarperCollins. See also the convenient anthology of sources in Huyghe, R. (1974). *La Joconde*. Fribourg: Office du Livre, p. 45 ff. N.B. Boas, G. (1940). "The Mona Lisa in the History of Taste," *Journal of the History of Ideas*, 1:2, April, pp. 207–224, is still valuable.

29   "*giocondo*": I wish this were my own idea, but it comes from my colleague Dr. Malcolm Warner of the Kimbell Art Museum in Fort Worth, Texas, with subsequent help from Dr. Diana Glenn of the Flinders University of South Australia, Adelaide, and Professor Emeritus Antonio Comin, who paid me the compliment of not contradicting it. See also D'Anna, G. (1988). *Dizionario italiano ragionato*. Florence: Sintesi, p. 778.

Chapter 2: Lewdness

31   For this particular chicken groper, see Sotheby's sale, *Old Master Paintings, Part Two*. London, Thursday 13 December 2001, lot 126: Jan Tilius (active Hilvarenbeek–after 1694, London), *A Young Boy Holding a Hen*, c. 1680s, oil on canvas, 20½ × 15¼ in. The picture appeared not long before in Christie's sale, *Important Old Master Pictures*, London, Friday 7 July 2000, lot 135, as *A Youth in a Red Cap Holding a Hen*.

31   For chicken gropers in general and the curious proliferation of bird *double-entendre* in Dutch, see Jongh, C. de (1968–69). "Erotica in Vogelperspectief: De dubbelzinnigheid van een reeks 17de eeuwse genre voorstellingen," *Simiolus*, 3:1, pp. 22–74. See also the entries for Harmen Jansz. Muller in Kok, J., *et al.*, eds., *The New Hollstein Dutch and Flemish Etchings, Engravings and Woodcuts, 1450–1700: The Muller Dynasty, Part I*. Rotterdam: Sound & Vision Publishers, in co-operation with the Rijksprentenkabinet, Rijksmuseum, Amsterdam, no. 88 "A Peasant with a Hen in his Hand (The henpecked husband) [c. 1595]," pp. 180–181. Note, however, that cats, not birds, provided a similar range of lewd connotations in eighteenth-century France. See Darnton, R. (1984). *The Great Cat Massacre and Other Episodes in French Cultural History*. New York: Basic Books, p. 95.

32   For the rude symbolism of eggs, and Cornelis Massys's engraving, see Stewart, A. (1977). *Unequal Lovers: A Study of Unequal Couples in Northern Art*. New York: Abaris Books, p. 54, and Kratz, H. (1949). Über den Wortschatz der Erotik im Spätmittelhochdeutschen und Frühhochdeutschen. Columbus, Ohio: Unpublished Ohio State University dissertation, vol. 2, p. 91.

32   For the unequal couple, see Stewart, A. (1977). *Unequal Lovers: A Study of Unequal Couples in Northern Art*. New York: Abaris Books, *passim*.

33   For Brueghel the Elder's *The Netherlandish Proverbs*, see Dundes, A., and Stibbe, C. (1981). *The Art of Mixing Metaphors: A Folkloristic Interpretation of the Netherlandish Proverbs by Pieter Bruegel the Elder*. Helsinki: Suomalainen Tiedeakatemia (Academia Scientiarum Fennica), p. 45.

34   "dirty old men": A recent study demonstrates that this phenomenon is alive and well in modern Japan. From early childhood onwards, many Japanese women experience sexual harassment by old men of the most explicit, aggressively physical kind, while many young Japanese homosexual men tend to avoid gay neighborhoods for fear of being harassed, groped, and in some cases even raped by *henna ossan* (dirty, literally weird, old men). See Lunsing, W. (1999). "Love and Sex in Urban Japan," *Sex, Sexuality and the Anthropologist*, edited by F. Markowitz and M. Ashkenazi. Urbana and Chicago: University of Illinois Press, p. 181.

37   "Antonello": Pope-Hennessy, J. (1966). *The Portrait in the Renaissance*. Princeton: Princeton University Press, pp. 60, 62.

38   "pornography": For excursions into this penumbral zone I am indebted to my friend and former colleague Christopher Chapman, a man of the world, and to the staff of Beat Books in Melbourne, who have shared their considerable expertise in this field.

40   "obscenity": Scruton, R. (1986). *Sexual Desire: A Philosophical Investigation*. London: Weidenfeld and Nicolson, p. 139.

40   "Stubbes": cited by Sullivan, M. (1994). *Bruegel's Peasants: Art and Audience in the Northern Renaissance*. Cambridge: Cambridge University Press, p. 26.

40   "dancing": *Ibid.*, pp. 26–33. Sullivan argues that Bruegel's paintings reflect the ideas of the Christian Humanist circle to which he belonged and that his peasant feasts were, according to Erasmian ideals, devised with properness in mind.

41   "Steen": Westermann, M. (1997). "How Was Jan Steen Funny? Strategies and Functions of Comic Painting in the Seventeenth Century," in Bremmer, J., and Roodenburg, H., eds. *A Cultural History of Humour from Antiquity to the Present Day*. Cambridge, Mass.: Polity Press, pp. 134–178, passim. Steen's biographer was Arnold Houbraken.

43   "sheela-na-gig": Andersen, J. (1977). *The Witch on the Wall: Medieval Erotic Sculpture in the British Isles*. Copenhagen: Rosenkilde and Bagger. See also Weir, A., and Jerman, J. (1986). *Images of Lust: Sexual Carvings on Medieval Churches*. London: B. T. Batsford; and Hourihane, C. (2003). *Gothic Art in Ireland, 1169–1550: Enduring Vitality*. New Haven and London: Yale University Press, pp. 40–41.

44   "witches": Doherty, T. (1897). "Some Notes on the Physique, Customs and Superstitions of the Peasantry of Innishowen, Co. Donegal," *Folk-Lore: A Quarterly Review of Myth, Tradition, Institution and Custom*, 8:1, March, pp. 12–18.

44   "harelip": Anon. (1990). "Minerva Through the Decades," *British Medical Journal*, 301:6754, p. 769, citing the *Annals of Surgery*, 1, pp. 80–83 (1886).

46   "*vagina dentata*": Elwin, V. (1943). "The Vagina Dentata Legend," *British Journal of Medical Psychology*, 19, pp. 439–453; Lederer, W. (1968). *The Fear of Women*, New York: Grune and Stratton; Raitt, J. (1980). "The *Vagina Dentata* and the *Immaculatus, Uterus Divini Fontis*," *Journal of the American Academy of Religion*, 48:3, pp. 415–431. See also Sütterlin, C. (1989). "Universals in Apotropaic Symbolism: A Behavioral and Comparative Approach to Some Medieval Sculptures," *Leonardo*, 22:1, pp. 65–74.

47   "gestures": Bäuml, B., and Bäuml, F. (1975). *A Dictionary of Gestures*. Metuchen, N.J.: The Scarecrow Press, pp. 209–219 (lip); 220–224 (mouth); 228–230 (tongue, tooth).

CHAPTER 3: DESIRE

49   "What heavenly smiles!" Curtis, J., ed. (1999). *Last Poems, 1821–1850, by William Wordsworth*. Ithaca, N.Y.: Cornell University Press, p. 371.

49   "Auden": Mendelson, E. (1976). *W. H. Auden: Collected Poems*. London: Faber and Faber, 1976, p. 631.

50   For the neurological processes associated with smiling, as well as the relevant motor functions, I have been greatly assisted by my old friend Dr.

Adam Jenney of the Royal Melbourne Hospital and the University of Melbourne. See also Critchley, M. (1986). "The Land of Smiles," in his *The Citadel of the Senses*. New York: Raven, pp. 67–79, and Cole, J. (1998). "The Anatomy of a Smile," in his *About Face*. Cambridge, Mass.: MIT Press, pp. 46–48.

51 "Ozzy Ozbourne": I am grateful to Nick Trumble for bringing to my attention this person's distinctive manner of smiling, as well as his difficult relationship with Tipper Gore. This arose from the activities of the Parents' Music Resource Center (PMRC), which she and other influential Washington mothers co-founded in May 1985 for the purpose of lobbying the federal government and the music industry for the regulation and restriction of access to musical recordings with violent, sexually explicit, or otherwise objectionable lyrics. This, in turn, led to Congressional committee hearings and the adoption of "parental advisory warning" stickers by which such material has for gormless teenagers been deliciously glamorized ever since.

52 "children with encephaly": See Luyendijk, W., and Treffers, P. (1992). "The Smile in Anencephalic Infants," *Clinical Neurology and Neurosurgery*, 94 (suppl.), pp. 113–117.

52 For the anatomy of the muscles of the face see Fried, L. (1976). *Anatomy of the Head, Neck, Face, and Jaws*. Philadelphia: Lea & Febiger, pp. 58–73.

53 "flaring of the nostrils": Note, however, that the seventh-century Chinese physician Dong Xuan (Tung-hsüan) listed nostril-flaring as one of the ways in which to postpone orgasm. See Tannahill, R. (1980). *Sex in History*. New York: Stein and Day, p. 170.

55 "The nasolabial fold": See Rubin, L. (1999). "The Anatomy of the Nasolabial Fold: The Keystone of the Smiling Mechanism," *Plastic and Reconstructive Surgery*, 83:1, February, pp. 687–691; also the earlier Rubin, L. (1974). "The Anatomy of a Smile: Its Importance in the Treatment of Facial Paralysis," *Plastic and Reconstructive Surgery*, 53:4 (April), pp. 384–387.

55 "One study of 1,000 humans": Rubin, L. (1999). "The Anatomy of the Nasolabial Fold: The Keystone of the Smiling Mechanism," *Plastic and Reconstructive Surgery*, 83:1 February, p. 687.

56 "lipstick": Angeloglou, M. (1970). *A History of Make-Up*. London: Studio Vista, *passim*; Cohen Ragas, M., and Kozlowski, K. (1998). *Read My Lips: A Cultural History of Lipstick*. San Francisco: Chronicle Books, pp. 13–14. The style guru is Véronique Vienne, author of *The Art of Doing Nothing*, cited by Cohen & Kozlowski, *ibid.*, p. 11. For a grindingly serious account of modern cosmetics, see the 1976 article by A. F. Akhabadze in the *Great Soviet Encyclopedia*, third ed., New York: Macmillan, vol. 13, p. 172.

57 "sales of lipstick . . . Estée Lauder": These observations were reported in an unsigned article syndicated from Cox Newspapers, "Paying Lip Service to Hard Times," in the *Sydney Morning Herald*, Saturday, February 23, 2002, p.

23, along with numerous observations copied verbatim from Ragas & Ko-zlowski's *Read My Lips: A Cultural History of Lipstick.*

58 "cat fur": Masson, J. (2002). *The Nine Emotional Lives of Cats: A Journey Into the Feline Heart.* London: Jonathan Cape, p. 213. The phenomenon, wonderful to see, is known to the professionals as *horripilation* or, somewhat indelicately, as *piloerection.*

58 "Eskimos": Peyrère's *Relation du Groënland* was published in 1647. See Lobies, J.-P. (1999). "La Peyrère (Isaac de)," *Dictionnaire de biographie française,* fasc. 112. Paris: Librairie Letouzey et Ané, cols. 851–852.

59 "modern lipstick": DeNavarre, M. (1975). *The Chemistry and Manufacture of Cosmetics.* New York: Van Nostrand, 1941 (and later eds.), pp. 374–389; see also Winter, R. (1976). *A Consumer's Dictionary of Cosmetic Ingredients.* New York: Crown Publishers, pp. 149–150 (lipstick); 63–64 (cheilitis and other diseases).

59 "lips": Rogers, R., and Bekic, M. (1997). "Diseases of the lips," *Seminars in Cutaneous Medicine and Surgery,* 16:4, December, pp. 328–336; Constantinidis, J., Federspil, P., and Iro, H. (2000). "The functional and aesthetic reconstruction of lip defects," *HNO* (Organ der Deutschen Akademie für Hals-Nasen-Ohrenheilkunde), 48:7, July, pp. 517–526; Ferrario, V., Sforza, C., and Serrao, G. (2000). "A three-dimensional quantitative analysis of lips in normal young adults," *Cleft Palate–Craniofacial Journal,* 37:1, January, pp. 48–54; Ferrario, V., et al. (2000), "Normal growth and development of the lips: a 3-dimensional study from 6 years to adulthood using a geometric model," *Journal of Anatomy,* 196, April, pp. 415–423; Gur, E., and Zuker, R. (2000). "The diamond vermilion flap—A new technique for vermilion augmentation in cleft lip repair," *Cleft Palate–Craniofacial Journal,* 37:2, March, pp. 123–124. See also Margulis, A. *et al.* (1999). "Cross-lip vermilion 'tri-tailed' flap to correct the 'whistling lip' deformity," *Plastic and Reconstructive Surgery,* 103:3, March, pp. 1086–1087, and Howell, J., and Freeman, R. (2002). "The potential peril from caliber-persistent arteries of the lips," *Journal of the American Academy of Dermatology,* 46:2, February, pp. 256–259.

Nguyen, D., and Turley, P. (1998). "Changes in the Caucasian male facial profile as depicted in fashion magazines during the twentieth century," *American Journal of Orthodontics and Dentofacial Orthopedics,* 114:2, August, pp. 208–217, find that during the twentieth century fashion coaxed men's lips gradually forward and outwards, and that today we expect men to show far more vermilion than 100 years ago.

61 "Thomas Hall": The tribute to Hall was paid in 1675 by a Mr. Moore ("of Withal"). See Vernau, J. (1982). *British Library General Catalogue of Printed Books to 1975.* London: K. G. Saur, vol. 138, p. 52.

64 "*ohaguro*": Casal, U. (1966). "Japanese Cosmetics and Teeth Blackening," *Transactions of the Asiatic Society of Japan,* third series, supplement to vol. 9; Takahashi, M. (1983). "Cosmetics" and "Etiquette," *Kodansha Encyclo-*

pedia of Japan, vol. 2, p. 38, and pp. 232–234. See also Downer, L. (2000). *Geisha: The Secret Life of a Vanishing World*. London: Headline, and Jonathan Mirsky's remarks in the *Spectator*, November 25, 2000, p. 56; Turnbull, S. (1977). *The Samurai: A Military History*. London: Osprey Publishing, p. 69; Hickey, G. (1998). *Beauty & Desire in Edo Period Japan*. Canberra: National Gallery of Australia, *passim*. See also Nagashima, K., and Schellenberg, J. (1997). "Situational Differences in Intential Smiling: A Cross-Cultural Exploration," *Journal of Social Psychology*, 137, pp. 297–301.

70   "purdah": Wikan, U. (1982). *Behind the Veil in Arabia*. Chicago: University of Chicago Press; Papanek, H. (1982). "Purdah: Seprate Worlds and Symbolic Shelter," in *Separate Worlds: Studies of Purdah in South Asia*, edited by H. Papanek and G. Minault. Delhi: Chanakya Publications, pp. 3–53; Chatty, D. (1997). "The Burqa Face Cover: An Aspect of Dress in Southeastern Arabia," in *Languages of Dress in the Middle East*, edited by N. Lindisfarne-Tapper and B. Ingham. Richmond, Surrey: Curzon Press, pp. 127–148.

CHAPTER 4: MIRTH

73   "Esquiros": Esquiros, A. (1861). *The English at Home*, translated by L. Wraxall. London: Chapman and Hall, vol. 2, pp. 16–17.

74   "Johnson and Chesterfield": Brewer, J. (1997). *The Pleasures of the Imagination: English Culture in the Eighteenth Century*. London: HarperCollins, p. 164.

74   "Lavater/Le Brun": Brewer, G. (1815). *The Juvenile Lavater, or, A Familiar Explanation of the Passions of Le Brun: Calculated for the Instruction and Entertainment of Young Persons*. New York: R. M'Dermot & D. D. Arden, pp. 103–104 (fully-blown laughter), 94–95 (joy with tranquillity); cfr Montagu, J. (1994). *The Expression of the Passions: The Origin and Influence of Charles Le Brun's Conférence sur l'expression générale et particulière*. New Haven & London: Yale University Press, pp. 121, 137.

For Lavater, see Rivers, C. (1994). *Face Value: Physiognomical Thought and the Legible Body in Marivaux, Lavater, Balzac, Gautier, and Zola*. Madison, Wis: University of Wisconsin Press. See also Baudinet, M., and Schlatter, C. (1982). *Du Visage*. Lille: Presses Universitaires de Lille.

76   For Hogarth, see Hogarth, W. (1753/1955). *The Analysis of Beauty*, edited by J. Burke. Oxford: Clarendon Press, especially chapter XV, "Of the Face," pp. 134–145, and Uglow, J. (1997). *Hogarth: A Life and a World*. London: Faber & Faber, pp. 516–537.

78   "Duchenne": Duchenne de Boulogne, C. (1862). *The Mechanism of Human Facial Expression*, edited and translated by R. Andrew Cuthbertson. Cambridge: Cambridge University Press.

79   For the etymological links between smiling and laughter see (for Latin) Glare, P. (1980). *Oxford Latin Dictionary*. Oxford: Oxford University

Press, p. 1847; (Italian) Battaglia, S. (1998). *Grande dizionario della lingua italiana*. Torino: Editrice Torinese, vol. 19, pp. 504–505; (French) Institut National de la Langue Française (1992). *Trésor de la Langue Française*. Paris: Centre National de la Recherche Scientifique, vol. 15, pp. 782–786; Rey, A., ed. (1992). *Dictionnaire Historique de la Langue Française*. Paris: Robert, vol. 2, p. 1996; (German) Wahrig, G. *et al.*, eds. (1982). *Brockhaus Wahrig Deutsches Wörterbuch*. Stuttgart: Brockhaus, vol. 4, p. 374; Muret, E., and Sanders, D., eds. (1975). *Langenscheidts Enzyklopädisches Wörterbuch der Englischen und Deutschen Sprache*. Berlin and Munich: Langenscheidt, part 2, vol. 2, pp. 977–978. Note, however, the ancient Greek: *gelos*, laugh, and *meidian*, smile. Liddell, H., and Scott, R., eds. (1968). *A Greek–English Lexicon*, revised by Sir H. Jones and R. McKenzie. Oxford: Clarendon Press, pp. 341 and 1092.

79 For the etymology of smile words I am indebted to Simpson, J., and Weiner, E., eds. (1989). *The Oxford English Dictionary*, second edition. Oxford: Clarendon Press. See *smile* etc., vol. 15, pp. 789–791. See also Onians, C., Friedrichsen, G., and Burchfield, R. (1966). *The Oxford Dictionary of English Etymology*. Oxford: Clarendon Press, p. 838; Stevenson, B. (1948). *The Macmillan Book of Proverbs, Maxims, and Famous Phrases*. New York: Macmillan, pp. 2144–2146; Wright, T. (1857). *Dictionary of Obsolete and Provincial English*. London: Henry G. Bohn, vol. 2, p. 875; Lewis, R., *et al.*, eds. (1988). *Middle English Dictionary*. Ann Arbor, Mich.: University of Michigan Press, part S.9, pp. 26–27.

81 For "smirk": *OED*, vol. 15, pp. 791–792; Robinson, M. (1985). *The Concise Scots Dictionary*. Aberdeen: Aberdeen University Press, p. 635; Wright, J., ed. (1905). *The English Dialect Dictionary*. London: Henry Frowde, 1905, vol. 5, p. 554.

81 "leer": *OED*, vol. 8, p. 794.

82 For grin words, see also Smith, W., ed. (1970). *The Oxford Dictionary of English Proverbs*, third edition, revised by F. Wilson. Oxford: Clarendon Press, p. 339.

82 "Fatal grinning-match at Bridlington": *The Times*, 11 June 1804, p. 2, and mentioned in the relevant volume of *Palmer's Index* as "Bridlington, Fatal Grinning-Match at." It seems scarcely conceivable that facial contortions alone could have killed the Bridlington contestants in 1804, unless some accident, strangulation or even alcoholic poisoning had also occurred. It is possible that the horse's collar might have placed pressure on the carotid artery in the neck causing blackout, stroke, or even cardiac arrest. This misfortune is known as the Carotid Sinus Syndrome, in which pressure on the "carotid sinuses" at the branch of the carotid artery at either side of the neck can cause drastic reduction in blood pressure and fainting. A tight shirt collar is enough to do this, and, especially for older people with hardened arteries, death may result. It is impossible to die as a result of holding your breath. The brain is simply incapable of forcing the body to expire by this means. Choking is, of course, quite another matter, and cases of death by swallowing or choking on one's own tongue have been recorded. Carnival, sword-swallowing or Houdini-style accidental deaths have from time to time also been documented, in which an audience, coaxed into thinking that the frightful gurgling sound coming from the performer was all part of the act, duly responded with loud applause. Dying on stage with that sound ringing in one's ears would appear to be the Romantic actor's ultimate fantasy, but it has been given to few actually to fulfill it.

There is one further explanation for the report of the bizarre deaths at Bridlington. It is possible that *The Times* was simply mistaken, deceived by those far-fetched rumors which in the early to mid-nineteenth century still circulated widely and were quite often believed. Another item of news noted in the same column, for example, reported the recovery of a thirty-pound pike from the great pool at Packington Park, Warwickshire, the seat of the Earl of Aylesford, which had apparently been choked to death by a ten-pound carp swallowed whole.

The African nomadic people known as Peuhl or Peul or Fulani, who inhabit the Sahel and move back and forth between the Inland Delta region near Timbuktu in Mali across Niger and Chad to Sudan in the east, also conduct grinning and face-making contests.

83   For Addison's fascinating remarks, see *Spectator*, no. 173, Tuesday, September 18, 1711, and Appendix at pp. 167–169.

84   "as Roman Catholics imagine a Kentish Man is by his tail": According to Ebenezer Cobham Brewer "It was long a saying that the men of Kent were born with tails, as punishment for the murder of Thomas à Beckett." Brewer, E. (1870/1981). *Brewer's Dictionary of Phrase and Fable*, edited by I. Evans. London: Cassell, p. 1092. Hence Andrew Marvell's line (95) in "The Loyall Scot": "For Becketts sake Kent alwayes shall have tails." Margoliouth, H., ed. (1971). *The Poems and Letters of Andrew Marvell*, revised by P. Legouis, with E. Duncan-Jones. Oxford: Clarendon Press, p. 182. Two different explanations for the belief were offered by the editor of Book IV, Chapter X of Sir Thomas Browne's *Pseudodoxia Epidemica* (1646), namely that "Kentish men are said to have had long tails for some generations; by way of punishment, as some say, for the Kentish pagans abusing Austin the monk and his associates, by beating them, and opprobiously tying fish tails to their backsides, in revenge of which, such appendants grew to the hind parts of all that generation. But the scene of this wonder was not in Kent, but in Carne, Dorsetshire, many miles off. Others again say it was for cutting off the tail of St. Thomas [à Beckett] of Canterbury's horse, who, being out of favour with King Henry II riding towards Canterbury upon a poor, sorry horse, was so served by the common people." See Browne, T. (1646/1835–36). *The Works of the Learned Sir Thomas Browne*, edited by Simon Wilkin. London: William Pickering, Vol. 2, p. 154. According to eighteenth-century satirist John Wolcot, who wrote under the pseudonym of Peter Pindar, this last atrocity, the lopping of the tail of Beckett's poor old horse, was committed by the townsfolk of Strood (today absorbed into the conurbation of Rochester) whom Thomas à Beckett cursed by causing future offspring to be born with tails. See Pindar, P. (1793). *A Poetical, Serious and Possibly Impertinent Epistle to the Pope.* London: T. Evans, p. 41. According to Jasmin Johnson (personal communication), "to this day, asking to see the tail of a Strood native is considered fighting talk." As well there existed a more ancient belief that *all* Englishmen had tails. Before the Battle of Roslin (1303) Scottish soldiers mocked their English enemies by shouting "Cam here an' we'll cut yer tails aff!" This richly impressionistic translation has been provided by Brian Ditcham; the incident was, in fact, recounted in Middle French by Walter of Gisborough in his *Chronicle.* For Englishmen's tails see Duchet-Suchaux, G. (1998). *"Les Anglais ont-ils une queue?"* *L'Histoire,* 219, March, p. 20, and Randall, L. (1960). "A Mediaeval Slander," *Art Bulletin,* 42:1, pp. 25–38. According to Duchet-Suchaux, the myth was well enough established to lead to fights at the University of Paris in the 1220s. There was some attempt to link the legend to an episode in Wace's twelfth-century *Roman de Brut,* in which hostile pagans from Dorset mocked St. Augustine of Canterbury by hanging the tail of a skate on his vestments. As a result, the natives of that region were supposed to have grown tails. Even Boccaccio mentioned "some" Englishmen born with tails. There is presumably no connection between this ancient slander, and the view taken by that great Scottish Enlightenment eccentric James Burnett, Lord Monboddo (1714–1799), namely that all humans were born with tails but that there was a conspiracy of midwives to chop them off at birth. I am most grateful to Brian Ditcham and Jasmin Johnson for guiding me through this difficult field.

84 "old motto inverted": The Latin *detur tetriori* literally means "let it be given to the more horrible." By "old motto inverted" Addison presumably meant the inscription on the golden apple, which read "to the most beautiful."

85 "Mr. Cave": "Police," *The Times,* September 20, 1833, p. 4. Not having any money, Mr. Cave was locked up. He gave his coat to a strange man to pawn, in order to pay the fine, but the man made off with the coat. Reappearing before Sir Frederick, the defendant, "who appeared anything now but a votary of the laughing god, begged hard that the magistrate would remit the fine, in consideration of the loss he had sustained," to no avail.

86 "Rousseau": Launay, L., and Launay, M. (1979) *Le Vocabulaire Littéraire de Jean-Jacques Rousseau.* Geneva: Librairie Slatkine, pp. 681–682.

86 For the alcoholic associations of *smile* words, see Partridge, E. (1949). *A Dictionary of the Underworld.* London: Routledge & Kegan Paul, p. 645; Partridge, E. (1977). *A Dictionary of Catch Phrases.* London: Routledge & Kegan Paul, p. 194; Partridge, E. (1973). *The Routledge Dictionary of Historical Slang,* abridged by J. Simpson. London: Routledge & Kegan Paul, p. 865; Partridge, E. (1984). *A Dictionary of Slang and Unconventional English,* edited by P. Beal. London: Routledge, p. 1096. See also Hackwood, F. (1987). *Inns, Ales and Drinking Customs of Old England.* London: Bracken.

87 "electrophoresis": Simpson, J., and Weiner, E., eds. (1993). *Oxford English Dictionary Additions Series.* Oxford: Oxford University Press, Vol. 1, pp. 301–302, citing R. Davies in Rickwood, D., and Hames, B. (1982). *Gel Electrophoresis Nucleic Acids,* Oxford: IRL Press, Vol. 4, p. 144.

87 "finance": The smile or smirk is a reference here to the shape of the line of a graph which is revealed when the implied volatility of call options—which give the holder the right to purchase a specified quantity of stocks, bonds, currencies, or commodities, etc., depending on the type of option, at a specified strike price by a specified expiry date—is plotted against the strike price. The calculation is made according to a formula devised in 1973 by Fischer Black and Myron Scholes (the Black–Scholes formula, to wit), which was the first successful model for pricing financial options, specifically simple put and call options.

87 "souris": Robuchon, J., et al. (2001). *Larousse Gastronomique.* London: Hamlyn, p. 1120.

88 "I should smile": Partridge, E. (1977). *A Dictionary of Catch Phrases.* London: Routledge & Kegan Paul, p. 106. See also Mencken, H. (1921). *The American Language: An Inquiry into the Development of English in the United States.* New York: Alfred A. Knopf, p. 217; Harduf, D. (1990). *Transliterated English–Yiddish Dictionary.* Willowdale, Ontario: Harduf Books, vol. 2, p. 168.

88 "no worries": Ransom, W., ed. (1988). *The Australian National Dictionary.* Melbourne: Oxford University Press, p. 436.

89 "different phyletic origins": Lockard, J., et al. (1977). "Smiling and Laughter: Different Phyletic Origins?" *Bulletin of the Psychonomic Society,* 10, p. 183.

89 "rough and tumble": Pinker, S. (1997). *How the Mind Works.* New York: W. W. Norton & Co., pp. 546.

89 "laughter as noise": Mowrer, D., LaPointe, L., and Case, J. (1987). "Analysis of Five Acoustic Correlates of Laughter," *Journal of Nonverbal Behavior,* 11:3, Fall, pp. 191–199.

90 "components of laughter": Berlyne, D. (1972). "Humor and Its Kin: IV. Laughter," in J. Goldstein, and P. McGhee, eds., *The Psychology of Humor: Theoretical Perspectives and Empirical Issues.* New York: Academic Press, pp. 50–53; see also Pinker, S. (1997), pp. 545–549.

91 "traveler to Africa": Turnbull, C. (1961). *The Forest People.* London: Chatto & Windus, p. 4.

91 "Papuan hilarity/Melanesian dourness": LaBarre, W. (1947). "The Cultural Basis of Emotions and Gestures," *Journal of Personality,* 16, pp. 49–68; Firth, R. (1970). "Postures and Gestures of Respect," *Échanges et Communications: Mélanges offerts à Claude Lévi-Strauss à l'occasion de son 60ème anniversaire,* edited by J. Pouillon and P. Maranda. The Hague: Mouton, pp. 188–209;

Polhemus, T., ed. (1978). *Social Aspects of the Human Body*. Harmondsworth: Penguin, pp. 53, 99.

91   "Charles Darwin": Darwin, C. (1872/1998). *The Expression of the Emotions in Man and Animals*, edited by P. Ekman. London: HarperCollins, pp. 196–197.

92   "BBC": Antony Beevor, writing in the *Spectator*, April 5, 2003, p. 8.

92   "humor/laughter": Shammi, P., and Studd, D. (1999). "Humor Appreciation: A Role of the Right Frontal Lobe," *Brain*, *122*, pp. 657–666. See also Lefcourt, H., Davidson-Katz, K., and Kueneman, K. (1990). "Humor and Immune-System Functioning," *Humor*, *3*, pp. 305–321, and Fry, W. (1992), "The Physiologic Effects of Humor, Mirth, and Laughter," *Journal of the American Medical Association*, *267*, pp. 1857–1858.

93   "Tanganyika": Provine, R. (2000). *Laughter: A Scientific Investigation*. New York: Viking Penguin; I have relied on Provine's account of the Tanganyika episode, which was originally reported by Rankin, A., and Philip. P. (1963). "An Epidemic of Laughing in the Bukoba District of Tanganyika," *The Central African Journal of Medicine*, *9*, pp. 167–170.

95   "laughing gas": Porter, R. (1997). *The Greatest Benefit to Mankind: A Medical History of Humanity from Antiquity to the Present*. London: HarperCollins, pp. 254, 366.

96   "Stendhal": Bishop, M. (1975). "Laughter and the Smile in Stendhal," *The Modern Language Review*, *70*, January, pp. 50–55.

97   "Lorenz": Lorenz, K. (1954). *Man Meets Dog*. Translated by Marjorie Kerr Wilson. London: Methuen.

97   "Mann": Mann, T. (1961). *Stories of a Lifetime*. London: Secker and Warburg, Vol. 2, pp. 72–138.

100   "quickly drawn pictograph": Regard, M., and Landis, T. (1994). "The Smiley: A Graphical Expression of Mood in Right Anterior Cerebral Lesions," *Neuropsychiatry, Neurophysiology and Behavioral Neurology*, *7*:4, pp. 303–307.

100   "Trademarks": For this information which relates purely to trademarks registered in Australia I am indebted to Dr. Mark Williams of the firm of Logie-Smith Lanyon.

101   "Carson Roberts": Kerry, L. (1989). "The End of an Era: The West Mourns the Passing of Legendary Jack Roberts," *Adweek*, January 16. Roberts' partner was Ralph Carson. I am most grateful to Hugh Spencer and his American colleagues for this information. Tobie Cameron, Gerald Curtin, Martin Griffin, Steve Hurley, Jamie Lovick, Slavica Peters, and Hugh Spencer of the firm of Clemenger BBDO in Melbourne and Sydney, all provided through Nick Trumble exceedingly useful information about 'smileyana'. Dean Manderson remembers wearing a row of smiley buttons lovingly stitched onto an outfit he wore in 1973, by which time he suspects it was considered "old hat."

101   "Harvey R. Ball": Mr. Ball died in Worcester in April 2001. See Honan, W. (2001). "H. R. Ball, 79, ad executive credited with smiley face," *New York Times*, April 14, p. A13. Partly nodding to Mr. Ball's creative role, in Fall 1999 the U.S. Postal Service launched a new smiley postage stamp in Worcester. (Just under half a million people voted for the smiley image to represent the decade of the 1970s in a series of stamps called *Celebrate the Century*.)

101   "University Federal Savings & Loan": Lumpkin, L. (1993). "Not So Enigmatic: A History of the Smile," *Art Issues*, 30, November–December, pp. 24–30; also Lumpkin, L. (1999). "The Smiley Face," in her *Deep Design: Nine Little Art Histories*, Los Angeles: Art issues. Press, pp. 15–27.

101   "Bye, Bye, Birdie": Strouse, C. (1988). *Bye, Bye, Birdie: A Musical Comedy*. New York: Columbia Pictures Publications. The original book was by Mike Stewart.

Chapter 5: Wisdom

103   "Jesus wept; Voltaire smiled": Hugo, V. (1878). *Œuvres completes: Actes et paroles*. Paris: Hetzel-Quantin, vol. IV, p. 79: *L'œuvre évangelique a pour complement l'œuvre philosophique; l'esprit de mansuétude a commence, l'esprit de tolerance a continue; disons-le avec un sentiment de respect profound, Jésus a pleuré, Voltaire a souri; c'est de cette larme divine et de ce sourire humain qu'est faite la douceur de la civilisation actuelle* (Applaudissements prolongés).

103   "ancient Cambodian sculpture": The exhibition was called *Sculpture of Angkor and Ancient Cambodia: Millennium of Glory* and toured to the Galeries nationals du Grand Palais, Paris, January 31–May 26, 1997; the National Gallery of Art, Washington, D.C., June 29–September 28; the Tokyo Metropolitan Art Museum, October 28–December 21; and the Osaka Municipal Museum of Art, January 15–March 22, 1998. See Jessup, H., and Zephir, T. (1997). *Sculpture of Angkor and Ancient Cambodia: Millennium of Glory*. Washington, D.C.: National Gallery of Art.

105   "big feet": I am grateful to Ron Radford for bringing this point to my attention.

106   "holy king": See Anon. (1973). "The Mask and the Smile," *Marg: A Magazine of the Arts*, 27.1, December, n.p., and Fingesten, P. (1968). "The Smile of the Buddha," *Oriental Arts*, n.s., *14.3*, Autumn, pp. 176–183.

107   "horned Moses": Mellinkoff, R. (1970). *The Horned Moses in Medieval Art and Thought*. Berkeley: University of California Press.

107   "color and smiling/laughter": Gage, J. (1993). *Colour and Culture: Practice and Meaning from Antiquity to Abstraction*. London: Thames and Hudson, pp. 77–78; Eco, U. (1988). *Art and Beauty in the Middle Ages*, p. 10.

108 *"risus sardonicus"*: See the entry in Becker, E., *et al.*, eds. (1989). *Churchill's Illustrated Medical Dictionary*, Churchill Livingstone Inc., pp. 1657, 1992; *Odyssey*, Book XX, line 301; Simonides, *Fragments*, 204, cited by Edmonds, J. (1927). *Lyra Graeca: being the remains of all the Greek lyric poets from Eumelus to Timotheus, excepting Pindar*. London: Heinemann, vol. 2, pp. 406–407; Plutarch's *Life of Caius Gracchus*, 12.5; Todd, R. (1835–1859). *The Cyclopædia of Anatomy and Physiology*. London: Longmans, Brown, Green, Longmans & Roberts.

109 *"l'inconnue de la Seine"*: Benkard, E. (1929). *Undying Faces: A Collection of Death masks*, with a note by Georg Kolbe, translated from the German by Margaret M. Green. London: The Hogarth Press, no. 112, p. 118.

109 *"Sylvia Plath"*: Plath, S. (1981). *Collected Poems*, edited by Ted Hughes. Boston: Faber & Faber, p. 272.

111 *"Sesson"*: Shimizu, Y., and Wheelwright, C. (1976). *Japanese Ink Paintings from American Collections: The Muromachi Period: An Exhibition in Honor of Shūjirō Shimada*. Princeton: Princeton University Press, p. 40.

113 *"The Three Laughters"*: *Ibid.*, no. 7, pp. 78–79.

114 *"Kenneth Clark"*: Clark, K. (1969). "The Smile of Reason," *The Listener*, 81:2092, May 1, pp. 607–612, and Clark, K. (1969). *Civilisation: A Personal View*. London: BBC and John Murray, pp. 245–268.

115 For Queen Mary, see Pope-Hennessy, J. (1959). *Queen Mary, 1867–1953*. London: George Allen & Unwin, pp. 429–430. The German opinion comes from Daisy, Princess of Pless [Mary Theresa Olivia von Hochberg] (1936). *What I Left Unsaid*, edited by D. Chapman-Huston. London: Cassell & Co., p. 35. The description of her costume is Queen Mary's own: Dress Book, entry for May 10, 1911. Royal Archives, Windsor Castle.

116 *"We are not amused"*: The saying was attributed to Queen Victoria in 1919 by Caroline Holland (*Notebooks of a Spinster Lady*, Ch. 21, under January 2, 1900). But see Longford, E. (1989). *The Oxford Book of Royal Anecdotes*. Oxford: Oxford University Press, p. 399.

116 *"wee Dr MacGregor"*: Ponsonby, A. (1942). *Henry Ponsonby: Queen Victoria's Private Secretary: His Life and Letters*. London: Macmillan, p. 118.

116 *"Thackeray"*: Thackeray, W. (1861). *The Four Georges: Sketches of Manners, Morals, Court, and Town Life*. London: Smith, Elder & Co., p. 141.

116 *"the young Charles II"*: Ashley, M. (1972). *Charles II: The Man and the Statesman*. London: Weidenfeld & Nicolson, p. 5.

116 *"Queen Henrietta Maria"*: This was the opinion of Princess Sophia, Electress of Hanover, who met the queen in The Hague in 1641, and had previously known her only through Van Dyck's portraits. Verney, F. (1892). *Memoirs of the Verney Family During the Civil War*. London, vol. 1, p. 257.

116 *"Henry, Prince of Wales"*: Nichols, J. (1828). *The Progresses, Processions, and Magnificent Festivities of King James I, his Royal Consort and Family*. London: J. B. Nichols, Vol. 1, p. 193.

116 "Barbarossa and 'Gothic' smiling": Svanberg, J. (1993). "The gothic smile," in *Künstlerischer Austausch. Artistic Exchange*, edited by T. Gaehtgens. Berlin: Akademie Verlag, Vol. 2, p. 358 ff.

116 "The 'Gothic' smile": Kidson, P. (1987). "A Note on Naumburg," in Stratford, N., ed., *Romanesque and Gothic: Essays for George Zarnecki.* Wolfeboro, N.H.: Boydell Press, Vol. 1, p. 143. Binski, P. (1997). "The Angel Choir at Lincoln and the Poetics of the Gothic Smile," *Art History*, 20, pp. 350–374.

117 "Virgin and Child": See for example the superb later Gothic or Renaissance example by Veit Stoss in the Victoria and Albert Museum in London (646–1893): Baxandall, M. (1980). *The Limewood Sculptors of Renaissance Germany.* New Haven and London: Yale University Press, p. 271, pls. 43–45.

117 "statue-column from Saint-Thibaut": Blum, P. (1990). "The Statue-Column of a Queen from Saint-Thibaut, Provins, in the Glencairn Museum," *Gesta*, 29:2, pp. 214–233.

120 "Cangrande I della Scala": Seiler, P. (1999). "Das Lächeln des Cangrande della Scala," *Zeitschrift für Kunstgeschichte*, 63:1, pp. 136–143.

122 "Pope Julius II": Partridge, L., and Starn, R. (1980). *A Renaissance Likeness: Art and Culture in Raphael's Julius II.* Berkeley: University of California Press, pp. 43–47.

123 "prevent the clergy from wearing moustaches": Beeson, T. (2002). *The Bishops.* London: SCM, p. 22.

127 "up to the age of six weeks": Kaye, K. (1982). *The Mental and Social Life of Babies: How Parents Create Persons.* Chicago: Chicago University Press, pp. 90–91.

130 "separation–individuation": Mahler, M., Pine, F., and Bergman, A. (1975). *The Psychological Birth of the Human Infant: Symbiosis and Individuation.* New York: Basic Books, p. 52.

CHAPTER 6: DECEIT

133 "An Epistle to Dr Arbuthnot": Butt, J., ed. (1939). *The Poems of Alexander Pope, Volume IV: Imitations of Horace.* London, Methuen, p. 118. These lines (315–316) refer to "Sporus" or Lord Hervey of Ickworth (1696–1743), a former friend of Pope's, who was a cabinet minister and confidant of Queen Caroline, the consort of King George II.

133 "saying *cheese*": According to several sources quoted in the OED the word cheese, "notionally or actually pronounced to form the lips into a smiling expression," was in common use at Rugby School in England by the second decade of the twentieth century. Note, however, that Morris Marples credited this expression to the boys of Oundle: Marples, M. (1940). *Public School Slang.* London: Constable and Co., p. 40. It had nothing to do with *performing a cheese*, the very deep, ceremonial curtsey practiced by ladies at Court in the mid-nineteenth century, so called because the swelling of the petticoats resembled the rounded form of a cheese. Nor does it relate to the *Cheeses*, so-called, the First Life Guards Regiment of the British Army, whose nickname was coined in the late nineteenth century by retired officers who thought there were too many "cheesemongers" in the regiment, and not enough gentlemen. It seems more likely to bear some indirect relationship to the slang phrase "quite the cheese," which had for decades meant the same as "quite the thing" (that is, fashionable). Presumably *howling cheeses* (as dandies were called behind their backs) evolved from that usage. *Ibid.* The data about foreign words and phrases used instead of *cheese* were kindly supplied by numerous correspondents who answered my request for information, "Bad Teeth Day," *Spectator*, June 5, 1999, p. 27. I am particularly grateful to my teacher Professor R. T. Ridley for supplying the Japanese term *whisky*. Where possible these foreign expressions were checked with staff—the rather perplexed staff—of the relevant consulates, legations, high commissions, and embassies closest to Adelaide. Under the present, stubborn regime in Burma (Myanmar) photography is usually forbidden, and the question therefore rarely arises.

134   For Cecil Beaton and *lesbian* I am indebted to David Ekserdjian. Letter to the author, June 23, 1999.

134   For Lady Montdore and *brush* see Mitford, N. (1949), *Love in a Cold Climate*. London: Hamish Hamilton, p. 221. Cedric Hampton claimed to have got the idea from "an old book on deportment," presumably Edwardian or earlier. *Ibid.*

135   "photographers simply ask their subjects to smile": The French saying *"le petit oiseau va sortir!"* and variants were apparently coined in 1843 by the early daguerrotypist Marc-Antoine Gaudin (1804–1880). See Gernsheim, H., and Gernsheim, A. (1965). *A Concise History of Photography*. London: Thames & Hudson, p. 75. Interestingly, according to the *Trésor de la langue française*, the phrase is not necessarily intended to provide the subject with an opportunity to smile, but rather to keep still. It is a *"formule plaisante par laquelle le photographe demande à ceux qu'il photographie, de ne plus bouger et de fixer l'objectif."* See Institut National de la Langue Française (1992). *Trésor de la langue française*. Paris: Centre national de la recherche scientifique, vol. 12, p. 464, citing Sartre, J.-P. (1964). *Les Mots*. Paris: Gallimard, p. 16: *"Du plus loin qu'il nous voyait, il se «plaçait», pour obéir aux injonctions d'un photographe invisible la barbe au vent, le corps droit, les pieds en équerre, la poitrine bombée, les bras largement ouverts. À ce signal je m'immobilisais, je me penchais en avant, j'étais le coureur qui prend le départ, le petit oiseau qui va sortir de l'appareil . . . "* Meanwhile, *Birdie* and *dicky-bird* originated as affectionate diminutives probably prior to the eighteenth century, when the *OED* noted *birdie* in Robbie Burns (*viz* "The Braes o' Ballochmyle," 1783). Both expressions were co-opted by nineteenth-century English-speaking photographers in the phrase "watch the birdie." *Birdie* was taken up by American golfers in the 1910s. Their English opponents were in that period still describing as *birds* those holes that were played one shot under par, and regarded *birdie* as a colloquialism.

135 "television news": Postman, N. (1992). *How To Watch TV News*. New York: Viking Penguin, pp. 30–35. See also Iyengar, S. and Kinder, D. (1987). *News That Matters: Television and American Opinion*. Chicago: Chicago University Press, p. 126.

137 "What is truth?" (jesting Pilate): Gospel of John, 18: 38.

138 "numerous experiments and studies": For all of this I am indebted to Bond, C., et al. (1990). "Lie Detection Across Cultures," *Journal of Nonverbal Behavior*, *14.3*, Fall, pp. 189–204, and Ekman, P. (1985). *Telling Lies: Clues to Deceit in the Marketplace, Politics, and Marriage*. New York: W. W. Norton & Co., passim.

138 "nurses": O'Sullivan, M., et al. (1988). "The Effect of Comparisons on Detecting Deceit," *Journal of Nonverbal Behavior*, *12:3*, Fall, pp. 203–215.

140 "honesty and attractiveness": Bull, R., and Rumsey, N. (1988). *The Social Psychology of Facial Appearance*. New York: Springer-Verlag, pp. 91–94.

140 "Margaret Thatcher": Thompson, P. (1980). "Margaret Thatcher: A New Illusion," *Perception*, 9, pp. 483–484; see also Parks, T., Coss, R., and Coss, C. (1985). "Thatcher and the Cheshire Cat: Context and the Processing of Facial Features," *Perception*, *14:6*, pp. 747–754.

141 "what we 'see'": Sturgis, A. (2000). *Telling Time*. London: National Gallery Company, pp. 64–65.

141 "ugly person who grins": Reis, H., *et al.* (1990). "What is Smiling is Beautiful and Good," *European Journal of Social Psychology*, *20:3*, May–June, pp. 259–267.

142 "Students of natural selection": Dawkins, R. and Krebs, J. (1978). "Animal Signals: Information or Manipulation?" in *Behavioural Ecology: An Evolutionary Approach*, edited by J. Krebs and N. Davies. Oxford: Blackwell Scientific Publications, pp. 302–304.

142 "In struggles over scarce resources": Bond, C., *et al.* (1990), p. 190.

143 "Dickens": See Busch, F. (1976). "Dickens: The Smile on the Face of the Dead," *Mosaic*, *9:4*, pp. 149–156.

143 "The Cheshire cat": Oultram, K. (1973). "The Cheshire Cat and Its Origins," *Jabberwocky: The Journal of the Lewis Carroll Society*, *3.1*, Winter, pp. 8–12. See also Smith, W., ed. (1970). *The Oxford Dictionary of English Proverbs*, third edition, revised by F. Wilson. Oxford: Clarendon Press, p. 339. See also Martin Gardner's notes to Carroll, L. (1960). *The Annotated Alice*. New York: Clarkson N. Potter, Inc., pp. 88–91.

144 "Pindar": Pindar, P. (1792). *A Pair of Lyric Epistles to Lord Macartney and His Ship*. London: H. D. Symonds, No. 20, Paternoster-Row, pp. 21–22.

145   "cats cannot fake purring": Masson, J. (2002). *The Nine Emotional Lives of Cats: A Journey into the Feline Heart*. London: Jonathan Cape, pp. 45–46, 65–70.

146   For Lord Palmerston's physical appearance, see Lorne [John Douglas Sutherland Campbell], Marquis of (later ninth Duke of Argyll) (1892). *Viscount Palmerston, K.G.* London: Sampson Low & Co., p. 218. See also Bourne, K. (1982). *Palmerston: The Early Years, 1784–1841*. London: Allen Lane, *passim*.

146   "King James": Bennion, E. (1986). *Antique Dental Instruments*. London: Sotheby's Publications, p. 29.

147   "*Le grand Thomas*": Jones, C. (2000). "Pulling Teeth in Eighteenth-Century Paris," *Past and Present*, 166, February, pp. 100–145; see also King, R. (1998). *The Making of the* Dentiste, *1650–1761*, Aldershot: Ashgate Publishing, especially ch. 1, "Pretending to Draw Teeth: The Mountebank Drug-Seller of the Fairs and Markets," pp. 11–33.

148   "False teeth": Woodforde, J. (1968). *The Strange Story of False Teeth*. London: Routledge & Kegan Paul; Hoffman-Axtheim, W. (1981). *History of Dentistry*, translated by H. Koehler. Chicago: Quintessence Publishing Co. Ring, M. (1985). *Dentistry: An Illustrated History*. New York: Harry N. Abrams, *passim*.

149   "Rowlandson": Helfand, W. (1999). *Crowning Achievements: Dentistry in the Ars Medica Collection of the Philadelphia Museum of Art*. Philadelphia: Philadelphia Museum of Art, no. 47, p. 38.

151   "Hiawatha": Carroll, L. (1933). *The Collected Verse of Lewis Carroll (the Rev. Charles Lutwidge Dodgson)*. New York: Macmillan, p. 768–772.

Conclusion: Happiness?

157   "Smiling the boy fell dead": From *Bells and Pomegranates*, No. III, *Dramatic Lyrics*, London: Edward Moxon, King R., *et al.*, eds. (1971). *The Complete Works of Robert Browning*. Athens, Ohio: Ohio University Press, vol. 3, pp. 209–210. Browning's poem is about the storming of Ratisbon (Regensburg in Bavaria) by the forces of Napoleon in 1809.

157   "Sir Maurice Bowra": referring to Richard McGillivray Dawkins, Bywater and Sotheby Professor of Byzantine and Modern Greek at Oxford. The college is Wadham, and Bowra's wish was eventually granted in 1971. This anecdote comes from Annan, N. (1974). "A Man I Loved," in H. Lloyd-Jones, ed. *Maurice Bowra: A Celebration*. London: Duckworth, p. 85. See also slightly different version given by Bowra himself: Bowra, [C.] M. (1966). *Memories, 1898–1939*. London: Weidenfeld and Nicolson, p. 252.

Appendix

167 "Ovid, *Met*.": Ovid (Publius Ovidius Naso), *Metamorphoses*, Book V: lines 216–217: [*"Perseu!*] *Remove fera monstra tuaequae/ Saxificos vultus, quaecunque ea, tolle Medusae/ [tolle, precor! . . . "*]. ["O Perseus!] Take away that monstrous thing of yours: Remove your head of the Medusa, whoever she may be, that turns men to stone. [Take it away, I beg you! . . . "]. The lines are spoken by the cowardly Phineus, who begs for his life (in vain) after losing a vicious fight he picked at the wedding of Perseus and Andromeda.

167 "Post-Boy": *The Post Boy*, no. 2548, September 8–11, 1711, verso r. col., and no. 2550, September 13–15, 1711, verso r. col. The second advertisement was to announce a change in date, from October 9 to 12.

168 "Coleshill": Nine miles northeast of Birmingham.

168 "Golden Apple": One of the golden apples of the Garden of the Hesperides was the prize in a contest to determine which of the three goddesses Hera, Athena, and Aphrodite was the most beautiful. The handsome youth Paris was the judge, and declared Aphrodite, the goddess of love, the winner. In return, she assisted him in the abduction of Helen—the *casus belli* of the Trojan War.

168 "*Detur tetriori*": see note on p. 186, above.

168 "the taking of *Namur*": the fortified city on the Meuse in Alsace, taken against all odds, by William of Orange (after 1688 King William III of England, consort of Queen Mary II), August 30–September 1, 1695.

168 "Milton's Death": *i.e.*, in *Paradise Lost*, Book II, 1.864.

169 "the Conclusion": In due course Addison received a letter from Coleshill, informing him that "in deference to his opinion, and chiefly through the mediation of some neighbouring ladies, the Grinning Match had been abandoned." His advice was sought as to how to dispose of the prize. Lillie, C. (1725). *Original and Genuine Letters Sent to the Tatler and Spectator During the Time Those Works Were Publishing, None of Which Have Been Before Printed*. London: Printed by R. Harbin for C. Lillie, vol. 1, p. 86. See also the letter on grinners from "T. Bashfull," writing from "Eman. Coll. Camb.," October 14, 1712, vol. 1, pp. 174–176.

Bibliography

i. General

Barrow, R. (1980). *Happiness*. Oxford: Martin Robertson.

Bartillat, C. de (1995). *Le Livre du sourire: sourire des dieux, sourire des hommes*. Monaco: Éditions du Rocher.

Bates, B., with Cleese, J. (2001). *The Human Face*. London: BBC Worldwide.

Berlyne, D. (1972). "Humor and Its Kin: V. The Smile," in J. Goldstein, and P. McGhee, eds., *The Psychology of Humor: Theoretical Perspectives and Empirical Issues*. New York: Academic Press, pp. 50–53.

Brophy, J. (1945). *The Human Face*. London: George G. Harrap & Co.

———. (1963). *The Face in Western Art*. London: George G. Harrap & Co.

Bruce, V. (1988). *Recognizing Faces*. Hillsdale, N.J.: Erlbaum.

———, and Young, A. (1998). *In the Eye of the Beholder: The Science of Face Perception*. Oxford: Oxford University Press.

Cole, J. (1998). "The Anatomy of a Smile," in his *About Face*. Cambridge, Mass., and London: MIT Press, pp. 46–48.

De Saint-Denis, E. (1965). *Essais sur le rire et le sourire des latins*. Paris: Belles-Lettres.

Dong, J. et al. (1999). "The Esthetics of the Smile: A Review of Some Recent Studies," *International Journal of Prosthodontics*, 12:1, January–February, pp. 9–19.

Ekman, P. (1992). *Telling Lies: Clues to Deceit in the Marketplace, Marriage, and Politics*. New York: W. W. Norton.

Emery, A. (1996). "Genetic Disorders in Portraits," *American Journal of Medical Genetics*, 66:3, December 18, pp. 334–339.

Fagiolo, M. (1994). "Medardo Rosso tra Darwin e Bergson: il riso, il sorriso e il problema della raffigurazione fisionomica nella scultura dell'ottocento," *Bollettino della Accademia degli Euteleti della città di San Miniato*, 61, pp. 131–164.

Frey, M., et al. (1999). "Three-Dimensional Video Analysis of Facial Movements: A New Method to Assess the Quantity and Quality of the Smile," *Plastic and Reconstructive Surgery*, 104:7, December, pp. 2032–2039.

Fried, L. (1976). *Anatomy of the Head, Neck, Face, and Jaws*. Philadelphia: Lea & Febiger.

Gilman, S. (1999). *Making the Body Beautiful: A Cultural History of Cosmetic Surgery*. Princeton: Princeton University Press.

Goldstein, R. (1997). *Change Your Smile*. Carol Stream, Ill.: Quintessence Books.

Gombrich, E. (1960). *Art and Illusion: A Study in the Psychology of Pictorial Representation*. Princeton: Princeton University Press.

Haesaerts, P. (1971). "Joie rare, trop rare dans l'art," *Connaissance des Arts*, 233, July, pp. 80–87.

Haiken, E. (1997). *Venus Envy: A History of Cosmetic Surgery*. Baltimore: Johns Hopkins University Press.

Hatfield, E., and Sprecher, S. (1986). *Mirror, Mirror: The Importance of Looks in Everyday Life*. Albany, N.Y.: State University of New York Press.

Hoexter D. (1995). "The Background of a Smile," *Alpha Omegan*, 88:4, pp. 16–19.

Hogarth, W. (1753/1955). *The Analysis of Beauty*, edited by J. Burke. Oxford: Clarendon Press.

Hunt, K. (1995). "The Impact of Bioesthetics on the Face, Smile and Teeth," *Dental Economics*, 85:3, March, pp. 81–82.

Hunt, M. (1994). *The Natural History of Love*. New York: Anchor Books.

Izard, C. (1971). *The Face of Emotion*. New York: Appleton-Century-Crofts.

Landau, T. (1989). *About Faces: The Evolution of the Human Face*. New York: Anchor.

Lip, E. (1989). *The Chinese Art of Face Reading*. Singapore: Times Books International.

Lumpkin, L. (1993). "Not So Enigmatic: A History of the Smile," *Art Issues*, 30, November–December.

Lutz, T. (1999). *Crying: The Natural and Cultural History of Tears*. New York: W. W. Norton & Co.

Mabrito C. (1996). "Elements of a Beautiful Smile," *New Mexico Dental Journal*, 47:2, July, pp. 20–21.

McNeill, D. (1998). *The Face*. Boston: Little, Brown.

Marwick, A. (1988). *Beauty in History*. London: Thames & Hudson.

Matthews T. (1978). "The Anatomy of a Smile," *Journal of Prosthetic Dentistry*, 39:2, February, pp. 128–134.

Moore, B. (1984). *Privacy*. Princeton: Princeton University Press.

Morley, J., and Eubank, J. (2001). "Macroesthetic Elements of Smile Design," *Journal of the American Dental Association, 132:1*, January, pp. 39–45.

Nguyen, D., and Turley, P. (1998). "Changes in the Caucasian Male Facial Profile as Depicted in Fashion Magazines During the Twentieth Century," *American Journal of Orthodontics and Dentofacial Orthopedics, 114:2*, August, pp. 208–217.

Philips E. (1999). "The Classification of Smile Patterns," *Journal of the Canadian Dental Association, 65:5*, May, pp. 252–254.

Polhemus, T. (1988). *Body Styles*. Luton: Lennard, in association with Channel Four Television Co.

Porter, R. (1997). *The Greatest Benefit to Mankind: A Medical History of Humanity from Antiquity to the Present*. London: HarperCollins.

Powys, J. (1935). *Art of Happiness*. New York: Simon & Schuster.

Price, D. (2000). "My, what crooked teeth we have," *Independent*, November 30, Review p. 8.

Rivers, C. (1994). *Face Value: Physiognomical Thought and the Legible Body in Marivaux, Lavater, Balzac, Gautier, and Zola*. Madison, Wis.: University of Wisconsin Press.

Roeder, O. (1972). *Smiles in Indonesia*. Jakarta: Gunung Agung.

Rosenthal, A. (1968). "Weighing the Effect of a Smile," *New Society, 319*, pp. 667–670.

Rossi, S., ed. (1998). *Scienza e miracoli nell'arte del '600: Alle origini della medicina moderna*. Milan: Electa.

Schroeder, F. (1998). "Say Cheese! The Revolution in the Aesthetics of Smiles," *Journal of Popular Culture, 32*, pp. 103–145.

Sharpe, R. (1825). *Smiles for all Seasons: or, Mirth for Midsummer . . . Forming a Collection of Parlour Poetry . . .* London: Baldwin, Cradock & Joy.

Shorter, E. (1983). *A History of Women's Bodies*. London: Allen Lane.

———. (1992). *A History of Psychiatry*. New York: Free Press.

Spivey, N. (2001). *Enduring Creation: Art, Pain and Fortitude*. London: Thames & Hudson.

Sternberg, R., ed. (1990). *Wisdom: Its Nature, Origins, and Development*. Cambridge: Cambridge University Press.

———. (1998). *Cupid's Arrow: The Course of Love Through Time.* Cambridge: Cambridge University Press.

Tjan A., Miller G., and The, J. (1984). "Some Esthetic Factors in a Smile," *Journal of Prosthetic Dentistry, 51:1*, January, 24–28.

Tolmach Lakoff, R., and Scherr, R. (1984). *Face Value: The Politics of Beauty.* Boston: Routledge & Kegan Paul.

Vaizey, M. (2002). *The British Museum: Smile.* London: The British Museum Press.

Walton, J., Barondess, J., and Lock, S., eds. (1994). *The Oxford Medical Companion.* Oxford: Oxford University Press.

Wong, D., and Baker, C. (1989) "Smiling Face as Anchor for Pain Intensity Scales," *Pain*, 89:2–3, January, pp. 295–297.

Zeldin, T. (1994). *An Intimate History of Humanity.* London: Sinclair-Stevenson.

2. The Smile and Infant Development

Babad, Y., *et al.* (1983). *Returning the Smile of the Stranger: Developmental Patterns and Socialisation Factors.* Chicago: University of Chicago Press.

Blass, E. (2001). "The Ontogeny of Face Recognition: Eye Contact and Sweet Taste Induce Face Preference in 9 and 12 week-old human infants," *Developmental Psychology, 37:6*, November, pp. 762–774.

Dickson, K., Walter, H., and Fogel, A. (1997). "The Relationship Between Smile Type and Play Type During Parent–Infant Play," *Developmental Psychology, 33:6*, November, pp. 925–933.

Farris, M. (2000). "Smiling of Male and Female Infants to Mother vs. Stranger at 2 and 3 Months of Age," *Psychological Reports, 87:3*, December, pp. 723–728.

Field, T., *et al.* (1982). "Discrimination and Imitation of Facial Expressions by Neonates," *Science, 218*, pp. 179–181.

Freedman, D. (1964). "Smiling in Blind Infants and the Issue of Innate vs. Acquired," *Journal of Child Psychology and Psychiatry*, 5, pp. 171–184.

Hsu, H., Fogel, A., and Messinger, D. (2001). "Infant Non-Distress Vocalization During Mother–Infant Face-to-Face Interaction: Factors Associated With Quantitative and Qualitative Differences," *Infant Behavior and Development, 24:1*, January, pp. 107–128.

Jones, S., and Raag, T. (1989). "Smile Production in Older Infants: The Importance of a Social Recipient for the Facial Signal," *Child Development*, 60, pp. 811–818.

Kaye, K. (1982). *The Mental and Social Life of Babies: How Parents Create Persons.* Chicago: Chicago University Press.

Langlois, J., *et al.* (1987). "Infant Preferences for Attractive Faces: Rudiments of a Stereotype?" *Developmental Psychology, 23*, pp. 363–369.

Legerstee, M., and Varghese, J. (2001). "The Role of Maternal Affect Mirroring on Social Expectancies in Three Month-Old Infants," *Child Development*, 72:5, September–October, pp. 1301–1313.

Lewis, D. (1978). "How to Read a Smile," in *The Secret Language of Your Child: How Children Talk Before They Can Speak*. London: Souvenir Press, pp. 80–107.

Luyendijk, W., and Treffers, P. (1992). "The Smile in Anencephalic Infants," *Clinical Neurology and Neurosurgery*, 94 (suppl.), pp. 113–117.

Messinger, D., Fogel, A., and Dickson, K. (2001). "All Smiles Are Positive, But Some Smiles Are More Positive Than Others," *Developmental Psychology*, 37:5, September, pp. 642–653.

Moore, G., Cohn, J., and Campbell, S. (2001). "Infant Affective Responses to Mother's Still Face at 6 Months Differentially Predict Externalising and Internalizing Behaviors at 18 Months," *Developmental Psychology*, 37:5, September, pp. 706–714.

Stein, M., et al. (2001). "Selective Affective Response to a Parent in a 6 month-old Infant," *Journal of Developmental and Behavioral Pediatrics*, 22:5, October, pp. 316–322.

Washburn, R. (1929). "A Study of the Smiling and Laughing of Infants in the First Year of Life," *Genetic Psychology Monographs*, 6, pp. 397–535.

3. THE SMILE AND PERCEPTION

Averill, J. (1969). "Autonomic Response Patterns During Sadness and Mirth," *Psychophysiology*, 5, pp. 399–414.

Bond, C. et al. (1990). "Lie Detection Across Cultures," *Journal of Nonverbal Behavior*, 14:3, pp. 189–204.

Briton, N., and Hall, J. (1995). "Gender-Based Expectancies and Observer Judgments of Smiling," *Journal of Nonverbal Behavior*, 19, pp. 49–65.

Bull, R., and Rumsey, N. (1988). *The Social Psychology of Facial Appearance*. New York: Springer Verlag.

Corballis, M. (1988). "Recognition of Disoriented Shapes," *Psychological Review*, 95, pp. 115–123.

Craver-Lemley, C., and Reeves, A. (1992). "How Visual Imagery Interferes with Vision," *Psychological Review*, 98, pp. 633–649.

Duensing, S., and Miller, B. (1979). "The Cheshire Cat Effect," *Perception*, 8:3, pp. 269–273.

Ekman, P. (1992). *Telling Lies: Clues to Deceit in the Marketplace, Marriage, and Politics*. New York: W. W. Norton.

———, (1993). "Facial expression of emotion," *American Psychologist*, 48, 384–392.

Ekman, P., and Davidson, R. (1993). "Voluntary smiling changes regional brain activity," *Psychological Science, 4*, 342–345.

Ekman, P., and Friesen, W. (1982), "Felt, False, and Miserable Smiles," *Journal of Nonverbal Behavior, 6:4*, pp. 238–252.

Ekman, P., Freisen, W., and O'Sullivan, M. (1988). "Smiles When Lying," *Journal of Personality and Social Psychology, 54*, pp. 414–420.

Ekman, P., Sorenson, R., and Friesen, W. (1969). "Pan-Cultural Elements in Facial Displays of Emotion," *Science, 164*, pp. 86–88.

Etcoff, N. (1986). "The Neurophysiology of Emotional Expression," in Goldstein, G., and Tarter, R., eds. *Advances in Clinical Neuropsychology*. New York: Plenum, pp. 127–179.

———, Freeman, R., and Cave, K. (1991). "Can We Lose Memories of Faces? Content Specificity and Awareness in a Prosopagnosic," *Journal of Cognitive Neuroscience, 3*, pp. 25–41.

Feinman, S., and Gill, G. (1978). "Sex Differences in Physical Attractiveness Preferences," *Journal of Social Psychology, 105*, pp. 43–52.

Gosain, A. (2001). "Localization of the Cortical Response to Smiling Using New Imaging Paradigms with Functional Magnetic Resonance Imaging," *Plastic and Reconstructive Surgery, 108:5*, October, pp. 1136–1144.

Kraut, R., and Johnston, R. (1979). "Social and Emotional Messages of Smiling: An Ethological Approach," *Journal of Personality and Social Psychology, 37*, pp. 1539–1553.

Langlois, J., and Roggman, L. (1990). "Attractive Faces Are Only Average," *Psychological Science, 1*, pp. 115–121.

Moscovitch, M., Winocur, G., and Behrmann, M. (1997). "What is Special About Face Recognition? Nineteen Experiments on a Person with Visual Object Agnosia and Dyslexia but Normal Face Recognition," *Journal of Cognitive Neuroscience, 9:5*, September, p. 500.

Otta, E., Abrosio, F., and Hoshino, R. (1996). "Reading a Smiling Face: Messages Conveyed by Various Forms of Smiling," *Perceptual and Motor Skills, 82*, pp. 1111–1121.

Parks, T., Coss, R., and Coss, C. (1985). "Thatcher and the Cheshire Cat: Context and the Processing of Facial Features," *Perception, 14:6*, p. 747.

Perrett, D., May, K., and Yoshikawa, S. (1994). "Facial Shape and Judgments of Female Attractiveness: Preferences for Non-Average," *Nature, 368*, pp. 239–242.

Pinker, S. (1997). *How the Mind Works*. New York: W. W. Norton & Co.

Pugh, S. (2001). "Service With a Smile: Emotional Contagion in the Service Encounter," *Academy of Management Journal, 44:5*, pp. 1018–1027.

Sayette, M., *et al.* (2001). "A Psychometric Evaluation of the Facial Action Coding System for Assessing Spontaneous Expression," *Journal of Nonverbal Behavior, 25:3*, Fall, pp. 167–185.

Scharlemann, J., et al. (2001). "The Value of a Smile: Game Theory with a Human Face," *Journal of Economic Psychology*, 22:5, October, pp. 617–640.

Soldat, A., and Sinclair, R. (2001). "Colors, Smiles and Frowns: External Affective Cues Can Affect Responses to Persuasive Communications in a Mood-like Manner without Affecting Mood," *Social Cognition*, 19:4, August, pp. 469–490.

Soussignan, R., and Schaat, B. (1996). "Forms and Social Signal Value of Smiles Associated with Pleasant and Unpleasant Senory Experience," *Ethology*, 102, pp. 1020–1041.

Stevenson, K., and Welch, W. (2001). "Smiling Odontoid," *Journal of Neurology, Neurosurgery and Psychiatry*, 71:5, November, p. 706.

Vrana, S., and Rolock, D. (2002). "The Role of Ethnicity, Gender, Emotional Content, and Contextual Differences in Physiological, Expressive and Self-Reported Emotional Responses to Imagery," *Cognition and Emotion*, 16:1, January, pp. 165–192.

Winkielman, P., and Cacioppo, J. (2001). "Mind at Ease Puts a Smile on the Face: Psychophysiological Evidence that Processing Facilitation Elicits Positive Affect," *Journal of Personality and Social Psychology*, 81:6, December, pp. 989–1000.

Zuckerman, M., et al. (1976). "Encoding and Decoding of Spontaneous and Posed Facial Expressions," *Journal of Personality and Social Psychology*, 34, pp. 966–977.

4. THE SMILE AND ADULT BEHAVIOR

Adams, R., and Kirkevold, B. (1978). "Looking, Smiling, Laughing, and Moving in Restaurants: Sex and Age Differences," *Environmental Psychology and Nonverbal Behavior*, 3:2, winter, pp. 117–121.

Altmann, S. (1981). "Dominance Relationships: The Cheshire Cat's Grin," *Behavioral and Brain Sciences*, 4:3, September, p. 430.

Anon. (1999). "Smiley Face: Centuries of stoicism aside, Yoshihiko Kadokawa says the Japanese can profit by going from grimace to grin," *People Weekly*, 51:16, May 10, p. 255.

Argyle, M. (1975). *Bodily Communication*. London: Methuen.

———. (1987). *The Psychology of Happiness*. London: Methuen.

Bäuml, B., and Bäuml, F. (1975). *A Dictionary of Gestures*. Metuchen, N.J.: The Scarecrow Press.

Bremmer, J., and Roodenburg, H., eds. (1992). *A Cultural History of Gesture*. Ithaca, N.Y.: Cornell University Press.

Chambers, C., and Craig, K. (1989). "Smiling Face as Anchor for Pain Intensity Scales—Reply," *Pain*, 89:2–3, January, pp. 297–300. (See also Wong, D., and Baker, C. [1989].)

Eibl-Eibesfeldt, I. (1970). *Ethology: The Biology of Behavior*. New York: Holt, Rinehart & Winston.

———. (1972). "Similarities and Differences Between Cultures in Expressive Movements," in Hinde, R., ed. *Non-Verbal Communication*. Cambridge: Cambridge University Press, pp. 297–314.

Ekman, P. (1980). *The Face of Man*. New York: Garland STPM Press.

Fernandez-Dols, J., and Ruiz-Belda, M. (1995). "Are Smiles a Sign of Happiness? Gold Medal Winners at the Olympic Games," *Journal of Personality and Social Psychology*, 69, pp. 1113–1119.

Fisher, H. (1992). *Anatomy of Love: The Natural History of Monogamy, Adultery, and Divorce*. New York: W. W. Norton & Co.

Fridlund, A. (1991). "Evolution and Facial Action in Reflex, Social Motive, and Paralanguage," *Biological Psychology*, 32, pp. 3–100.

———. (1995). *Human Facial Expression: An Evolutionary View*. New York: Academic Press.

Frijhoff, W. (1992). "The Kiss Sacred and Profane: Reflections on a Cross-Cultural Confrontation," in Bremmer, J., and Roodenburg, H., eds. *A Cultural History of Gesture*. Ithaca, N.Y.: Cornell University Press, pp. 210–236.

Givens, D. (1986). "The Big and the Small: Toward a Paleontology of Gesture," *Sign Language Studies*, 51, pp. 145–170.

Goffman, E. (1959). *The Presentation of Self in Everyday Life*. Garden City, N.Y.: Anchor Books.

———. (1967). *Interaction Ritual: Essays on Face-to-Face Behavior*. Garden City, N.Y.: Anchor Books.

Goldstein, A. (1983). "Behavioral Scientists' Fascination with Faces," *Journal of Nonverbal Behavior*, 7:4, Summer, p. 223.

Gould, J. (1982). *Ethology*. New York: W. W. Norton & Co.

Gould, S. (1985). *The Flamingo's Smile: Reflections in Natural History*. New York: W. W. Norton.

Hall, J., *et al.* (2001). "Status, Gender, and Nonverbal Behavior in Candid and Posed Photographs: A Study in Conversations Between University Employees," *Sex Roles*, 44:11–12, June, pp. 677–692.

Hecht, M., and LaFrance, M. (1998). "License or Obligation to Smile: The Effect of Power and Sex on Amount and Type of Smiling," *Personality and Social Psychology Bulletin*, 62.

Kim, J. (2001). "Smile-Wink Phenomenon: Aggravated Narrowing of Palpebral Fissure by Smiling after Lenticulocapsular Stroke," *Journal of Neurology*, 248:5, May, pp. 389–393.

Morris, B. (1997). "Grin and Bear It: The Smile Attempts a Comeback in Society Circles," *New York Times Magazine*, 2 March, p. 47.

Morris, D., *et al.* (1979). *Gestures: Their Origin and Distribution*. London: Cape.

Niedenthal, P., *et al.* (2001). "When Did Her Smile Drop? Facial Mimicry and the Influences of Emotional State on the Detection of Change in Emotional Expression," *Cognition and Emotion*, 15:6, November, pp. 853–864.

Nyrop, C. [K.] (1901). *The Kiss and its History*, translated by W. Harvey. London: Sands & Co.

Ozerkan, K. (2001). "The Effects of Smiling or Crying Facial Expressions on Grip Strength, Measured with a Hand Dynamometer and the Bi-Digital O-Ring Test," *Acupuncture and Electro-Therapeutics Research*, 26:3, pp. 171–186.

Parlett, D. (1991). "Bluffing and Poking," in his *A History of Card Games*. Oxford: Oxford University Press, pp. 105–115.

Perella, N. (1969). *The Kiss Sacred and Profane: An Interpretative History of Kiss Symbolism and Related Religio-Erotic Themes*. Berkeley, CA: University of California Press.

Reis, H., *et al.* (1990). "What is Smiling is Beautiful and Good," *European Journal of Social Psychology*, 20:3, May–June, pp. 259–267.

Strasser, S. (1993). "'The Smile that Pays': The Culture of Traveling Salesmen, 1880–1920," in Gilbert, J., et al., eds., *The Mythmaking Frame of Mind: Social Imagination and American Culture*. Belmont, Calif.: Wadsworth Publishing Company, pp. 155–177.

Turner, E. (1962). *What the Butler Saw: Two Hundred and Fifty Years of the Servant Problem*, London: Michael Joseph.

Watts, A. (1974). *The Meaning of Happiness: The Quest for Freedom of the Spirit in Modern Psychology and the Wisdom of the East*. London: Village Press.

Williams, L., *et al.*, "In Search of the 'Duchenne Smile': Evidence from Eye Movements," *Journal of Psychophysiology*, 15:2, pp. 122–127.

Wünsche, A. (1911). *Der Kuss in Bibel, Talmud und Midrasch*. Breslau: M. & H. Marcus.

5. The Smile and Manners

Annett, J., and Collins, R. (1975). "A Short History of Deference and Demeanour," in Collins, R., ed. *Conflict Sociology*. New York: Academic Press, pp. 161–224.

Baldwin, F. (1926). *Sumptuary Legislation and Personal Regulation in England*. Baltimore: Johns Hopkins University Press.

Baudrillart, H. (1880). *Histoire du luxe public et privé de l'antiquité jusqu'à nos jours*. Paris: Hachette et Cie.

Caldwell, M. (1999). *A Short History of Rudeness: Manners, Morals, and Misbehavior in Modern America*. New York: Picador USA.

Cooper, E. (1986). "Chinese Table Manners: You Are How You Eat," *Human Organisation*, 45, pp. 179–184.

Curtin, M. (1985). "A Question of Manners: Status and Gender in Etiquette and Courtesy," *Journal of Modern History*, 57, pp. 395–423.

Doherty, T. (1897). "Some Notes on the Physique, Customs and Superstitions of the Peasantry of Innishowen, Co. Donegal," *Folk-lore*, 8, pp. 12–18.

Elias, N. (1978). *The History of Manners*, translated by Edmund Jephcott. New York: Pantheon Books.

Goody, J. (1988). *Food and Love: A Cultural History of East and West*. London: Verso.

La Fontaine-Verwey, H. (1971). "The First 'Book of Etiquette' for Children: Erasmus' *De civilitate morum puerilium*," *Quaerendo*, 1, pp. 19–30.

Langford, P. (2000). *Englishness Identified: Manners and Character, 1650–1850*. Oxford: Oxford University Press.

La Salle, Jean-Baptiste de, Saint (1703/1990). *Les Règles de la bien-séance et de la civilité Chrestienne* (*The Rules of Christian Decorum and Civility*), translated by R. Arnandez and edited by G. Wright. Romeoville, Ill: Lasallian Publications.

Lévi -Strauss, C. (1968/1978). *The Origin of Table Manners*, translated by J. and D. Weightman. New York: Harper & Row.

Quinlan, M. (1965). *Victorian Prelude: A History of English Manners, 1700–1830*. London: Cass.

Visser, M. (1991). *The Rituals of Dinner: The Origins, Evolution, Eccentricities, and Meaning of Table Manners*. New York: Grove Weidenfeld.

6. THE SMILE AND LAUGHTER

Adkin, N. (1985). "The Fathers on Laughter," *Orpheus*, n.s., 6, pp. 149–152.

Billington, S. (1984). *A Social History of the Fool*. New York: St. Martin's Press.

Bishop, M. (1975). "Laughter and the Smile in Stendhal," *The Modern Language Review*, 70, January, pp. 50–70.

Bremmer, J., and Roodenburg, H., eds. (1997). *A Cultural History of Humour from Antiquity to the Present Day*. Cambridge, Mass.: Polity Press.

Cameron, K., ed. (1993). *Humour and History*. Oxford: Intellect.

Ding, G., and Jersild, A. (1932). "The Study of Laughing and Smiling of Preschool Children," *Journal of Genetic Psychology*, 40, pp. 452–472.

Douglas, M. (1978). "Do Dogs Laugh? A Cross-Cultural Approach to Body Symbolism," in Polhemus, T., ed. *Social Aspects of the Human Body: A Reader of Key Texts*. Harmondsworth: Penguin, pp. 295–301.

Flory, S. (1978). "Laughter, Tears, and Wisdom in Herodotus," *American Journal of Philology*, 99, pp. 145–153.

Gifford, D. (1974). "Iconographical Notes Toward a Definition of the Medieval Fool," *Journal of the Warburg and Courtauld Institutes*, 37, pp. 336–342.

Grammar, K. (1990). "Strangers Meet: Laughter and Non-Verbal Signs of Interest in Opposite-Sex Encounters," *Journal of Nonverbal Behavior*, 14, pp. 209–236.

Hamamoto, D. (1989). *Nervous Laughter: Television Situation Comedy and Liberal Democratic Ideology*. New York: Praeger.

Heltzel, V. (1928). "Chesterfield and the Anti-Laughter Tradition," *Modern Philology*, 26, pp. 73–90.

Hoof, J. van (1972). "A Comparative Approach to the Phylogeny of Laughter and Smiling," in Hinde, R., ed., *Non-Verbal Communication*. Cambridge: Cambridge University Press, pp. 209–241.

Kayser, W. (1963). *The Grotesque in Art and Literature*, translated by Ulrich Weisstein. Bloomington, Ind.: Indiana University Press.

Kehl, D. (2000). "Varieties of Risible Experience: Grades of Laughter and Their Function in Modern American Literature," *Humor: International Journal of Humor Research*, 13:4, p. 379.

LaFrance, M. (1983). "Felt Versus Feigned Funniness: Issues in Coding Smiling and Laughing," in P. McGhee and J. Goldstein, eds. *Handbook of Humor Research*. New York: Springer-Verlag, vol. 1, pp. 1–12.

Le Goff, J. (1992). "Jésus a-t-il ri?" *L'Histoire*, 158, pp. 72–74.

Lockard, J., *et al.* (1977). "Smiling and Laughter: Different Phyletic Origins?" *Bulletin of the Psychonomic Society*, 10, pp. 183–186.

McGhee, P. (1979). *Humor: Its Origins and Development*. San Francisco: W. H. Freeman.

Ménard, P. (1969). *Le Rire et le sourire dans le roman courtois en France au moyen âge (1150–1250)*. Geneva: Droz.

Ménard, P. (1983). *Les Fabliaux: Contes à rire du moyen age*. Paris: Presses Universitaires de France.

Meredith, G. (1956). "An Essay on Comedy," in Sypher, W., ed., *Comedy*. Garden City, N.Y.: Doubleday Anchor.

Miedema, H. (1977). "Realism and the Comic Mode: The Peasant," *Simiolus*, 9, pp. 205–219.

Moss, M. (1944). *The Origin of the Smile and Laughter*. Dayton, Ohio: Mortimer Moss.

Moxey, K. (1981–82). "Sebald Beham's Church Anniversary Holidays: Festive Peasants as Instruments of Repressive Humor," *Simiolus*, 12, pp. 107–130.

Piddington, R. (1963). *The Psychology of Laughter: A Study in Social Adaptation*. New York: Gamut Press.

Provine, R. (1993). "Laughter Punctuates Speech: Linguistic, Social, and Gender Contexts of Laughter," *Ethology*, 95, pp. 291–298.

————. (1997). "Yawns, Laughs, Smiles, Tickles, and Talking: Naturalistic and Laboratory Studies of Facial Action and Social Communication," in Russell, J., and Fernandez-Dols, J., eds., *The Psychology of Facial Expression*. Cambridge: Cambridge University Press, pp. 158–175.

————. (2000). *Laughter: A Scientific Investigation*. New York: Viking Penguin.

Provine, R., and Fisher, K. (1989). "Laughing, Smiling, and Talking: Relation to Sleeping and Social Context in Humans," *Ethology*, 83, pp. 295–305.

Resnick, I. (1987). "'Risus Monasticus': Laughter and Medieval Monastic Culture," *Révue bénédictine*, 97, pp. 90–100.

Rosenthal, F. (1976). *Humor in Early Islam*. Westport, Conn.: Greenwood Press.

Rothbart, M. (1977). "Psychological Approaches to the Study of Humor," in Chapman, A., and Foot, H., eds. *It's a Funny Thing, Humor*. New York: Pergamon Press, pp. 87–100.

Screech, M., and Calder, R. (1970). "Some Renaissance Attitudes to Laughter," in Levi, A., ed. *Humanism in France at the End of the Middle Ages and in the Early Renaissance*. New York: Barnes and Noble, pp. 216–228.

Shammi, P., and Stuss, D. (1999). "Humour Appreciation: A Role of the Right Frontal Lobe," *Brain*, 122, pp. 657–666.

Stroufe, L., and Waters, E. (1976). "The Ontogenesis of Smiling and Laughter: A Perspective on the Organization of Development in Infancy," *Psychological Review*, 83, pp. 173–189.

Tatlock, J. (1946). "Medieval Laughter," *Speculum*, 21, pp. 289–291.

Thomas, K. (1977). "The Place of Laughter in Tudor and Stuart England," *Times Literary Supplement*, 21 January, pp. 77–81.

Weisfeld, G. (1993). "The Adaptive Value of Humor and Laughter," *Ethology and Sociobiology*, 14, pp. 141–169.

Willeford, W. (1969). *The Fool and his Scepter: A Study in Clowns and Jesters and their Audience*. Evanston, Ill.: Northwestern University Press.

7. Particular Smiles

Adour, K. (1989). "Mona Lisa Syndrome: Solving the Enigma of the Gioconda Smile," *Annals of Otology, Rhinology and Laryngology*, 98:3, pp. 196–199.

Andersen, J. (1977). *The Witch on the Wall: Medieval Erotic Sculptures in the British Isles*. Copenhagen: Rosenkilde and Bagger.

Anon. (1922). "Museum Gets an Archaic Smile," *International Studio*, 75:304, September, p. 503.

Anon. (1954–55). "The Archaic Smile," *Journal of Aesthetics and Art Criticism*, 13, p. 265.

Arduini, F. (1992–93). "Il sogno oscuro della morte e della vita nelle Arche degli Scaligeri," *Labyrinthos*, 11–12:21–4, pp. 139–189.

Battistoni, G. (1988–89). "Simboli e mitografie intorno a Can Grande della Scala," *Labyrinthos*, 7–8:13–16, pp. 35–62.

Béguin, S. (1988). "Un illustre sourire," in *Vraiment faux*. Jouy-en-Josas: Fondation Cartier pour l'art contemporain.

Binski, P. (1997). "The Angel Choir at Lincoln and the Poetics of the Gothic Smile," *Art History*, 20, pp. 350–374.

Blum, P. (1990). "The Statue-Column of a Queen from Saint-Thibaut, Provins, in the Glencairn Museum," *Gesta*, 29:2, pp. 214–233.

Borkowski, J. (1992). "Mona Lisa: The Enigma of the Smile," *Journal of Forensic Sciences*, 37:6, November, pp. 1706–1711.

Ceppa, L. (1989). "Freud e il sorriso della Gioconda," *Belfagor*, 44:5, September 30, pp. 589–593.

Cowling, M. (1989). *The Artist as Anthropologist: The Representation of Type and Character in Victorian Art*. Cambridge: Cambridge University Press.

Curry, W. (1916). *The Middle English Ideal of Personal Beauty*. Baltimore: J. H. Furst & Co.

Curtis, L. (1997). *Apes and Angels: The Irishman in Victorian Caricature*. Washington, D.C.: Smithsonian Institution Press.

Daston, L. (1999). "How to make a Greek god smile," *London Review of Books*, 21:12, June 10, pp. 11–12.

Evans, E. (1969). *Physiognomics in the Ancient World*, Philadelphia: American Philosophical Society.

Fau, G. (1961). *Le Sourire de la Joconde*. Paris: Librairie des Champs-Elysées.

Flory, S. (1987). *The Archaic Smile of Herodotus*. Detroit: Wayne State University Press.

Gilooly, E. (1999). *Smile of Discontent: Humor, Gender and Nineteenth-Century British Fiction*, Chicago: University of Chicago Press.

Howe, T. (1954). "The Origin and Function of the Gorgon-Head," *American Journal of Archaeology*, 58, pp. 209–221.

Kidson, P. (1987). "A Note on Naumburg," in Stratford, N., ed. *Romanesque and Gothic: Essays for George Zarnecki*. Wolfeboro, N.H.: Boydell Press, Vol. 1, p. 143.

Lartigue, J. (1980). *Les Femmes aux cigarettes*. New York: Viking.

Latimer, D. (1995). *Sardonic Smile: Nonverbal Behavior in Homeric Epic*. Ann Arbor, Mich.: University of Michigan Press.

Lumpkin, L. (1999). *Deep Design: Nine Little Art Histories*. Los Angeles: Art issues. Press.

Mellinkoff, R. (1993). *Outcasts: Signs of Otherness in Northern European Art of the Late Middle Ages*. Berkeley: University of California Press.

Percival, M. (2000). *The Appearance of Character: Physiognomy and Facial Expression in Eighteenth-Century France*. Leeds: W. S. Maney & Sons.

Perdrield-Vaissière, J. (1902). *Le Sourire de la Joconde*. Paris: Librairie de la Plume.

Raven, A. (1992). "Arts: The Archaic Smile," Ms Magazine, 3:1, July–August, pp. 68–72.

Sandback, A. (1993). "George Cruickshank, in Appreciation of a Knowing Smile," *Print Collector's Newsletter*, 24:3, July–August, pp. 96–98.

Sassoon, D. (2001). *Mona Lisa: The History of the World's Most Famous Painting*. London: HarperCollins, with exhaustive bibliography.

Seiler, P. (1999). "Das Lächeln des Cangrande della Scala," *Zeitschrift für Kunstgeschichte*, 63:1, pp. 136–143.

Stern, E. (1976). "Phoenician Masks and Pendants," *Palestine Exploration Quarterly*, 108, pp. 109–118.

Svanberg, J. (1993). "The gothic smile," in *Künstlerischer Austausch. Artistic Exchange*, edited by T. Gaehtgens. Berlin: Akademie Verlag, Vol. 2, pp. 357–370.

Taylor, F. (1958). "The Archaic Smile: The Relation of Art and the Dignity of Man," *Daedalus: Proceedings of the American Academy of Arts and Sciences*, 86:4, pp. 286–287.

Wallace-Hadrill, J. (1962). *The Long-Haired Kings, and Other Studies in Frankish History*. London: Methuen & Co.

Wechsler, J. (1982). *A Human Comedy: Physiognomy and Caricature in 19th Century Paris*. London: Thames & Hudson.

8. Lips

Benson, K., and Laskin, D. (2001). "Upper Lip Asymmetry in Adults During Smiling," *Journal of Oral and Maxillofacial Surgery*, 59:4, April, pp. 396–398.

Constantinidis, J., Federspil, P., and Iro, H. (2000). "The functional and aesthetic reconstruction of lip defects," *HNO* (Organ der Deutschen Akademie für Hals-Nasen-Ohrenheilkunde), 48:7, July, pp. 517–526.

Ferrario, V., et al. (2000). "Normal Growth and Development of the Lips: A 3-Dimensional Study from 6 Years to Adulthood Using a Geometric Model," *Journal of Anatomy*, 196, April, pp. 415–423.

Ferrario, V., Sforza, C., and Serrao, G. (2000). "A Three-Dimensional Quantitative Analysis of Lips in Normal Young Adults," *Cleft Palate–Craniofacial Journal*, 37:1, January, pp. 48–54.

Gur, E., and Zuker, R. (2000). "The diamond vermilion flap—A new technique for vermilion augmentation in cleft lip repair," *Cleft Palate–Craniofacial Journal*, 37:2, March, pp. 123–124.

Howell, J., and Freeman, R. (2002). "The potential peril from caliber-persistent arteries of the lips," *Journal of the American Academy of Dermatology*, 46:2, February, pp. 256–259.

McAlister, R., Harkness, E., and Nicoll, J. (1998). "An Ultrasound Investigation of the Lip Levator Musculature," *European Journal of Orthodontics*, 20:6, pp. 713–720.

Margulis, A. *et al.* (1999). "Cross-lip vermilion 'tri-tailed' flap to correct the 'whistling lip' deformity," *Plastic and Reconstructive Surgery*, 103:3, March, pp. 1086–1087.

Montagu, A. (1971). *Touching: The Human Significance of the Skin*. New York: Columbia University Press.

Rogers, R., and Bekic, M. (1997). "Diseases of the lips," *Seminars in Cutaneous Medicine and Surgery*, 16:4, December, pp. 328–336.

Trelles, M., *et al.* (2000). "The Search for a Youthful Upper Lip via Laser Resurfacing," *Plastic and Reconstructive Surgery*, 105:3, March, pp. 1162–1169.

Wohlert, A. (1996a). "Reflex Responses of Lip Muscles in Young and Older Women," *Journal of Speech and Hearing Research*, 39:3, June, pp. 578–589.

———. (1996b). "Tactile Perception of Spatial Stimuli on the Lip Surface by Young and Older Adults," *Journal of Speech and Hearing Research*, 39:6, December, pp. 1191–1198.

9. Teeth

Addis, R. (1939). "History of the Toothbrush," *British Dental Journal*, 66, May 1, pp. 532–533.

André-Bonnet, J. (1910). *Histoire générale de la chirurgie dentaire*. Paris: Société des Auteurs Modernes.

Baron, P., and Deltombe, X. (1997). "Dental Products in France in the Eighteenth Century: Their Production, Distribution, Commercialisation," *Dental Historian*, 32, pp. 66–82.

Bennion, E. (1986). *Antique Dental Instruments*. London: Sotheby's Publications.

Bird, E. (1987). "Dental Esthetics: A Bridge Too Far?" *Psychology Today*, 21:9, September, p. 16.

Campbell, J. (1963). *Dentistry Then and Now*. Edinburgh: Privately printed for J. Menzies Campbell.

Casotti, L. (1935). *Dentisti ed empirici nel settecento torinese*. Turin: C. Accame.

De Vecchis, B. (1929). "Dentisti, artisti, pazienti," *La cultura stomatologica*, 10, n.p.

Fastlicht, S. (1976). *Tooth Mutilations and Dentistry in Pre-Columbian Mexico*. Chicago: Quintessence Publishing Co.

Fauchard, P. (1946). *The Surgeon Dentist*, translated by L. Lindsay. London: Butterworth & Co.

Fox, J. (1803). *Natural History of the Human Teeth*. London: Thomas Cox.

Gariot, J. (1843). *Treatise on the Diseases of the Mouth*, translated by J. Savier. Baltimore: American Society of Dental Surgeons.

Glasstone, S. (1965). "The Concept of Tooth Development During the Seventeenth, Eighteenth and Nineteenth Centuries," *Bulletin of the History of Dentistry, 13:1–3,* January–July, pp. 15–54.

Gorman, J. (1980). "Sweet Toothlessness," *Discover, 1,* p. 52.

Gysel, C. (1990). "Toothache in the Seventeenth Century: Classical Remedies and New Medicines," *Bulletin of the History of Dentistry, 38,* pp. 3–7.

Helfand, W. (1999). *Crowning Achievements: Dentistry in the Ars Medica Collection of the Philadelphia Museum of Art.* Philadelphia: Philadelphia Museum of Art.

Hilkene, R. (1965). "The Dental Health of the Presidents," *Bulletin of the History of Dentistry, 13:4,* October, pp. 13–50.

Hillam, C. (1991). *Brass Plate and Brazen Impudence: Dental Practice in the Provinces, 1755–1855.* Liverpool: Liverpool University Press.

Hoffman-Axtheim, W. (1981). *History of Dentistry,* translated by H. Koehler. Chicago: Quintessence Publishing Co.

Hunter, J. (1778). *The Natural History of the Human Teeth.* London: J. Johnson.

Jones, C. (2000). "Pulling Teeth in Eighteenth-Century Paris," *Past and Present, 166,* February, pp. 100–145.

Kanner, L. (1928). *Folklore of the Teeth.* New York: Macmillan.

King, R. (1998). *The Making of the* Dentiste, *1650–1761.* Aldershot: Ashgate Publishing.

Kunzle, D. (1989). "The Art of Pulling Teeth in the Seventeenth and Nineteenth Centuries: From Public Martyrdom to Private Nightmare and Political Struggle? Fragments for a History of the Human Body," *Zone, 5,* pp. 29–89.

Kvaal, S., and Derry, T. (1996). "Tell-tale teeth: abrasion from the traditional clay pipe," *Endeavour, 20:1,* pp. 28–30.

Latronico, N. (1941). "Dentisti e cavadenti nel settecento Milanese," *Atti e memorie dell'Accademia di Storia dell'Arte Sanataria, 19,* second series, July–August, pp. 277–282.

Loux, F. (1981). *L'Ogre et la dent: Pratiques et savoirs populaires relatifs aux dents.* Paris: Berger-Levrault.

Mack, P. (1985). "Hairy Dentures: A Monosymptomatic Hypochondriacal Psychosis," *British Dental Journal, 158:2,* January 19, pp. 50–51.

Miles, A. (1973). "The Senile Mandible," *British Dental Journal, 134:10,* May 15, pp. 443–447.

Moskow, B. (1982). *Art and the Dentist.* Tokyo: Shorin.

Moskowitz M., and Nayyar A. (1995). "Determinants of Dental Esthetics: A Rationale for Smile Analysis and Treatment," *Compendium of Continuing Education in Dentistry, 16:12,* December, pp. 1164, 1166.

Nakahara, K., Shindo, Y., and Homma, K. (1980). *Manners and Customs of Dentistry in Ukiyoe.* Tokyo: Ishiyaku.

Nettleton, S. (1991). "Inventing Mouths: Disciplinary Power and Dentistry," in Jones, C., and Porter, R., eds., *Reassessing Foucault: Power, Medicine and the Body.* London: Routledge, pp. 73–90.

Niamtu, J. (2000). "The Use of Botulinum Toxin in Cosmetic Facial Surgery," *Oral and Maxillofacial Surgery Clinics of North America, 12:4,* November, pp. 595–612.

Petrich, G. (1969). "North American Indians and Dentistry," *Bulletin of the History of Dentistry, 17:2,* December, pp. 1–16.

Proskauer, C. (1961). "Catalogo degli oggetti pertinenti all'arte dentaria conservati nel Museo Storico Nazionale dell'Arte Sanataria di Roma," *Atti e memorie dell'Accademia di Storia dell'Arte Sanataria, 27,* second series, October–December, pp. 194–206.

Pryor, W. (1933). "The Closed Bite Relation of the Jaws of George Washington, With Comments on his Tooth Troubles and General Health," *Journal of the American Dental Association, 20,* April, pp. 567–577.

Ring, M. (1985). *Dentistry: An Illustrated History.* New York: Harry N. Abrams.

Sarver, D. (2001). "The Importance of Incisor Positioning in the Esthetic Smile: The Smile Arc," *American Journal of Orthodontics and Dentofacial Orthopedics, 120:2,* August, pp. 98–111.

Shklar, G. (1969). "Stomatology and Dentistry in the Golden Age of Arab Medicine," *Bulletin of the History of Dentistry, 17:2,* December, pp. 17–24.

Steinberg, L. (2001). "Your Teeth Are Showing," *New York Review of Books, 48:5,* March 29, p. 53, together with a reply by S. Schwartz.

Stevenson, R. (1962). "The Secret Operation on President Cleveland," in his *Famous Illnesses in History.* London: Eyre & Spottiswoode, pp. 44–51.

Trumble, A. (1998). "Changing Concepts of Decorum and Allure in the Representation of Teeth in Art," *Annals of the Royal Australasian College of Dental Surgeons, 14,* pp. 35–40.

Woodforde, J. (1968). *The Strange Story of False Teeth.* London: Routledge and Kegan Paul.

10. Masks and Concealment

Antoun, R. (1968). "On the Modesty of Women in Arab Muslim Villages: A Study in the Accommodation of Traditions," *American Anthropologist, 70,* pp. 671–697.

Bastian, A. (1883). "Masken und Maskieren," *Zeitschrift für Völkerpsychologie und Sprachwissenschaft, 14,* pp. 335–358.

Campbell, J. (1960). *Masks of God.* London: Secker & Warburg.

Cole, H. (1985). *I Am Not Myself: The Art of African Masquerade.* Los Angeles: Museum of Cultural History.

Croon, J. (1955). *"The Mask of the Underworld Daemon*—Some Remarks on the Perseus–Gorgon Story," *Journal of Hellenic Studies*, 75, pp. 9–16.

Dickins, G. (1929). "Terracotta Masks," in Dawkins, R., ed. *The Sanctuary of Artemis Orthia at Sparta*. London: Council of the British School at Athens, pp. 163–186.

Drewal, M. (1992). *Yoruba Ritual: Performers, Play, Agency*. Bloomington, Ind.: Indiana University Press.

Flower, H. (1996). *Ancestor Masks and Aristocratic Power in Roman Culture*. Oxford: Clarendon Press.

Gombrich, E. (1972). "The Mask and the Face: The Perception of Physiognomic Likeness in Life and Art," in E. Gombrich, J. Hochberg, and M. Black, eds., *Art, Perception and Reality*. Baltimore: Johns Hopkins University Press, pp. 1–46.

Goonatilleka, M. (1978). *Masks and Mask Systems of Sri Lanka*. Colombo: Tamarind Books.

Harrison, M. (1960). *The History of the Hat*. London: Herbert Jenkins.

Hawley, D., ed. (1984). *Debrett's Manners and Correct Form in the Middle East*. London: Debrett's Peerage.

Jevons, F. (1916a). *Masks and Acting*. Cambridge: Cambridge University Press.

———. (1916b). "Masks and the Origin of Greek Drama," *Folk-Lore*, 27, pp. 171–192.

Lindisfarne-Tapper, N., and Ingham, B., eds. (1997). *Languages of Dress in the Middle East*. Richmond, Surrey: Curzon.

Murphy, R. (1964). "Social Distance and the Veil," *American Anthropologist*, 66:6, pp. 1263–1274.

Mylius, N. (1961). *Antlitz und Geheimnis der uberseeischen Maske: Eine Einführung in das Maskenwesen der Ubersee*. Vienna: Verlag Notring der Wissenschaftlichen Verbände Österreichs.

Napier, A. (1986). *Masks, Transformation, and Paradox*. Berkeley: University of California Press.

Papanek, H., and Minault, G., eds. (1982). *Separate Worlds: Studies of Purdah in South Asia*. Delhi: Chanakya Publications.

Sharma, U. (1978). "Women and their Affines: The Veil as a Symbol of Separation," *Man*, n.s., 13:2, pp. 218–233.

Sorell, W. (1973). *The Other Face: The Mask in the Arts*. Indianapolis: Bobbs–Merrill.

Webster, T. (1949). "The Masks of Greek Comedy," *Bulletin of the John Rylands Library*, 32, pp. 97–133.

———. (1951). "Masks on Gnathia Vases," *Journal of Hellenic Studies*, 71, pp. 222–232.

———. (1952). "Notes on Pollux' List of Tragic Masks," in Dohrn, T., ed. *Festschrift Andreas Rumpf zum 60. Geburtstag dargebracht von Freunden und Schülern*. Krefeld: Scherpe, pp. 141–150.

Wiles, D. (1991). *The Masks of Menander: Sign and Meaning in Greek and Roman Performance*. Cambridge: Cambridge University Press.

11. Cosmetics and Adornment

Angeloglou, M. (1970). *A History of Make-Up*. London: Studio Vista.

Brdar, I., Tkalcic, M., and Bezinovic, P. (1996). "Women's Cosmetics Use and Self-Concept," *Studia Psychologica*, 38:1–2, pp. 45–54.

Chandra, M. (1940). "Cosmetics and Coiffure in Ancient India," *Journal of the Indian Society of Oriental Art*, 8, pp. 62–145.

Cohen Ragas, M., and Kozlowski, K. (1998). *Read My Lips: A Cultural History of Lipstick*. San Francisco: Chronicle Books.

DeNavarre, M. (1975). *The Chemistry and Manufacture of Cosmetics*. Orlando, Fla.: Continental Press.

Dixon, J. (1885). "Japanese Etiquette," *Transactions of the Asiatic Society of Japan*, 13, pp. 1–21.

Erickson, K. (2002). *Drop Dead Gorgeous: Protecting Yourself from the Hidden Dangers of Cosmetics*. New York: McGraw-Hill.

Etcoff, N. (1998). *Beauty*. New York: Doubleday.

Johnson, R. (1999). "Lipstick," *Chemical and Engineering News*, 77:28, July 12, p. 31.

Laba, D. (1993). *Rheological Properties of Cosmetics and Toiletries*. New York: Marcel Dekker, Inc.

Masao, T. (1983). "Cosmetics," in *Kodansha Encyclopedia of Japan*. Tokyo: Kodansha, Vol. 2, p. 38.

Monga, Y. (2000). "Dollars and Lipstick: The United States Through the Eyes of African Women," *Africa*, 70:2, pp. 192–208.

Rubinstein, H. (1963). *My Life for Beauty*. New York: Simon & Schuster.

Weyers, D. (1997). "The Lipstick: A Cultural Historical Overview," *Zeitschrift für Volkskunde*, 93:2, pp. 301–302.

Wolf, N. (1990). *The Beauty Myth: How Images of Beauty Are Used Against Women*. London: Chatto & Windus.

Wykes Joyce, M. (1961). *Cosmetics and Adornment*. New York: Philosophical Society.

12. The Smile and Animals

Bolwig, N. (1963–64). "Facial Expression in Primates with Remarks on a Parallel Development in Certain Carnivores," *Behaviour*, 22, pp. 167–192.

Darwin, C. (1872/1998). *The Expression of the Emotions in Man and Animals*, edited by P. Ekman. London: HarperCollins.

Hill, S. (2001). "The Smile of a Dolphin: Remarkable Accounts of Animal Emotions," *Anthrozoos*, *14:2*, pp. 120–121.

Kavanagh, A. (1986). "Parrots with a Smile," *Country Life*, *179:4617*, February 13, pp. 412–414.

Morel, P. (1997). *Grotesques: Les Figures de l'imaginaire dans la peinture italienne de la fin de la Renaissance*. Paris: Flammarion.

Oultram, K. (1973). "The Cheshire Cat and Its Origins," *Jabberwocky: The Journal of the Lewis Carroll Society*, *3.1*, Winter, pp. 8–12.

Preuschoft, S. (1995). *"Laughter" and "Smiling" in Macaques: An Evolutionary Perspective*. Utrecht: Universiteit Utrecht.

Sheridan, R., and Ross, A. (1975). *Gargoyles and Grotesques: Paganism in the Medieval Church*. Boston: New York Graphic Society.

Tanaka, J. (1965). "Social Structure of Nilgiri Langurs," *Primates*, *6:1*, pp. 107–122.

Index

(Numbers in italics refer to pages with illustrations.)

217